From Science to Subjectivity

Recent Titles in
Contributions in Philosophy

FROM SCIENCE TO SUBJECTIVITY

An Interpretation of Descartes' *Meditations*

Walter Soffer

Contributions in Philosophy, Number 33

Greenwood Press
New York • Westport, Connecticut • London

Library of Congress Cataloging-in-Publication Data

Soffer, Walter, 1941-
   From science to subjectivity.

   (Contributions in philosophy, ISSN 0084-926X ; no. 33)
   Bibliography: p.
   Includes index.
   1. Descartes, René, 1596-1650.   Meditationes de prima
philosophia.   2. First philosophy.   I. Title.
II. Series.
B1854.S64   1987   194   86-27117
ISBN 0-313-25571-7 (lib. bdg. : alk. paper)

British Library Cataloguing in Publication Data is available.

Library of Congress Catalog Card Number: 86-27117
ISBN: 0-313-25571-7
ISSN: 0084-926X

First published in 1987

Greenwood Press, Inc.
88 Post Road West, Westport, Connecticut 06881

Printed in the United States of America

The paper used in this book complies with the
Permanent Paper Standard issued by the National
Information Standards Organization (Z39.48-1984).

10   9   8   7   6   5   4   3   2   1

Copyright Acknowledgements

The author and publisher gratefully acknowledge permission to reprint material from the following sources.

J. L. Beck, *The Metaphysics of Descartes* (London: Oxford University Press, 1965). Portions reprinted with the permission of Oxford University Press.

Hiram Caton, *The Origin of Subjectivity* (New Haven: Yale University Press, 1973). Portions reprinted with the permission of Yale University Press.

Harry G. Frankfurt, *Demons, Dreamers, and Madmen* (Indianapolis: Bobbs-Merrill, 1970). Portions reprinted with the permission of Harry G. Frankfrut.

E. S. Haldane and G. R. T. Ross (trans.), *The Philosophical Works of Descartes* (New York: Cambridge University Press, 1969). Copyrighted by and reprinted with the permission of Cambridge University Press.

Anthony Kenny, *Descartes: A Study of His Philosophy* (New York: Random House, 1968). Portions reprinted with the permission of Random House, Inc.

Anthony Kenny (trans. and ed.), *Descartes' Philosophical Letters* (London: Oxford University Press, 1970). Portions reprinted with the permission of Oxford University Press.

Leon Pearl, *Descartes* (Boston: G. K. Hall & Company, 1977). Copyright 1977 and reprinted with the permission of Twayne Publishers, a division of G. K. Hall & Co., Boston.

Walter Soffer, "The Methodological Achievement of Cartesian Doubt," *The Southern Journal of Philosophy*, Vol. XVI, No. 1 (Spring 1978), 661-674. Portions reprinted with the permission of *The Southern Journal of Philosophy*.

Walter Soffer, "Descartes, Rationality, and God," *The Thomist*, Vol. 42, No. 4 (October 1978), 666-691. Portions reprinted with the permission of *The Thomist*.

Walter Soffer, "Descartes' Rejection of the Aristotelian Soul," *International Studies in Philosophy*, Vol. XVI, No. 1 (1984), 57-68. Portions reprinted with the permission of *International Studies in Philosophy*.

Walter Soffer, "Dreaming, Hyperbole, and Dogmatism," *Idealistic Studies* (forthcoming). Portions reprinted with the permission of *Idealistic Studies*.

Bernard Williams, *Descartes: The Project of Pure Enquiry* (New York: Penguin, 1978). Reproduced by permission of Penguin Books Ltd.

Margaret Dauler Wilson, *Descartes* (London: Routledge & Kegan Paul, 1978). Portions reprinted with the permission of Routledge & Kegan Paul, Inc.

TO MY PARENTS

CONTENTS

PREFACE

The past two decades have witnessed a flourishing of studies on Descartes by English language commentators. The focus of attention has been the Meditations, which continues to be regarded as the Archimedian point of Cartesian philosophy. The schism that has characterized the history of Cartesian scholarship persists throughout this most recent revival of interest in Descartes. The fundamental issue continues to be the question concerning the sincerity or insincerity of Descartes' theological metaphysics.

The majority view states that the doctrines of the Meditations and their place within Cartesian philosophy must be understood by a hermeneutics of sincerity. The Meditations is to be read as a self-reliant work in which Descartes is to be taken at his word. Accordingly the major thrust of Cartesian philosophy is claimed to be epistemological and metaphysical--the quest for certainty in the form of secure scientific foundations. The assumption that Descartes sincerely argues for the necessity of metaphysical foundations for science pushes the following problems and doctrines onto center stage: The origin of Cartesian philosophizing is taken as the movement from a brush with seriously entertained skepticism to the cogito as the lone refuge of certainty. The cogito is interpreted as a potentially solipsistic first principle, thereby posing the problem of external existence as a genuine aporia. Descartes' anthropology is read as a mind-body dualism facilitating an argument for the immortality of the soul. And, most significantly, the validation of Cartesian science as the hallmark of human reason requires God as the guarantor of the reliability of clear and distinct ideas. Such is the picture of the Meditations offered by the majority, or sincerity, approach.

To cite two recent examples of the sincerity hermeneutic, Margaret Dauler Wilson writes concerning the intentions of the Meditations:

> There is . . . not good reason to suppose that Descartes' sole concern in the Meditations is the introduction of a certain scientific perspective. With all due acknowledgment of Descartes'

powers as an ironist, it would be extreme
to doubt the sincerity of his repeated
self-congratulation for having proved,
in the Meditations, the immateriality
of the soul and the existence of God--and
that both are 'better known' than either
the truths of geometry or the existence
of matter.[1]

Concerning the order of the argument of the Meditations,
E. M. Curley writes:

The constructive portions of the
Meditations begin with the existence
of the human mind . . . from the
existence of the mind to the existence
of God, and only then go on to establish
the existence of material things.[2]

According to Curley the "whole machinery of proofs of God's
existence" must be taken as sincere since "no pupil of
the Jesuits wholly escapes their influence."[3]
     To these doctrines are applied the canons of
contemporary analytic philosophy, resulting in the judgment
that the Meditations and thereby the Cartesian enterprise
is a valiant but flawed attempt at metaphysics. Ironically,
one of the major reasons offered for the failure of the
Meditations is Descartes' inability to extricate himself
from scholastic metaphysics and theology, that is, his
sincerity.
     The most outspoken defense of the insincerity view
has been advanced by Hiram Caton, who argues that "the
Meditations must be evaluated from the perspective of
Descartes' attempts to secure the reception of his innovating
philosophy from a hostile audience and, in particular,
that the requirement of order demands that the Meditations
be approached directly from Cartesian physics."[4] Caton
argues not only that the self-sufficiency of Cartesian
science makes any metaphysical justification redundant
for Descartes, but that Descartes has done such a service
for all those who came after him. To Caton the Meditations
signals the once-and-for-all transition from philosophy
as metaphysics to the autonomy of science by presenting
a "metaphysics to end metaphysics":

To grasp the maxim that clear and
distinct ideas are true is to understand
that metaphysics is useless. For it
says, as Spinoza put it, that truth
is known by its own sign; hence, it
requires no 'justification' or
'validation'. The Meditations is a
satiric reductio of metaphysics showing
the delinquency of the idea that
conceptual analysis can remedy any
shortage of certainty from which science
might suffer. The lesson of the
Meditations is therefore contemporary.
Although positivists wished to eliminate

metaphysics, they unawares embraced
the hydra when they set out to 'justify'
science. They failed, of course, but
they did convince many that science
needed justification. The resulting
void of 'meaning' was filled by nocturnal
Teutonic and Gallic yearnings for
salvation in the Marxist church.
Meanwhile scientists, unaware that
philosophers had allowed their
certificate of rectitude to lapse whilst
handing them over to Cardinal Bellarmine,
moved as usual from one splendid
discovery to another. As a matter
of fact, progress in the biological
sciences during the past two decades
has brought to fruition the most splendid
discovery of all: the first stage
of an experimental science of man.
We are now in the midst of an
intellectual revolution as far-reaching
as the revolution of the spirit
inaugurated in the Seventeenth Century.
. . . 'The deus deceptor is slain;
long live clarite.' And so it will
be in the future.[5]

The aim of the present essay is a resolution of the
sincerity question concerning the Meditations as part of
an interpretation of its function within the Cartesian
enterprise and its metaphysical legacy. On the one hand,
I hope to show that the insincerity view of the Meditations
is faithful to Descartes' intentions. I argue, therefore,
that the Meditations cannot be read in isolation, but can
serve as a guide to the meaning of Cartesian philosophy
only when read in the light of what I term the Cartesian
"architectonic"--the properly philosophical (as opposed
to historical-sociological) context specifying the relation
between the parts of Cartesian philosophy. On the other
hand, however, I challenge Caton's futurology concerning
the demise of metaphysics. In this sense I support the
contention of the sincerity view concerning metaphysics
as a serious and enduring philosophical enterprise.

Since it is the Discourse on Method rather than the
Meditations which provides Descartes' architectonic, the
starting point for the reading of the Meditations is
the Discourse. To begin with the Discourse is to follow
the order prescribed by Descartes in the Preface to the
Principles of Philosophy. Commenting on his order of
publication, Descartes explains that "By this means I believe
myself to have commenced to expound the whole of philosophy
in its order without having omitted anything which ought
to precede the last of which I have written."[6]

The way in which the Meditations accomplishes the
subordination of theology and metaphysics to scientific
ontology and epistemology is argued as follows. Chapter
1 of the present study gives the following account of the
Cartesian architectonic. The Discourse teaches that
Descartes' theoretical philosophy (method, physics,
metaphysics) mediates between the practical origin of

philosophizing in the desire for mastery on the part of
prephilosophical egoism and the completion of philosophy
in technological control over nature. The hermeneutic
dilemma of the Meditations thus concerns the relation between
the theoretical parts of the architectonic. In the Discourse
order of presentation the account of physics follows the
account of metaphysics. However, I argue that in the
architectonic order their relation is the reverse, such
that in both the Discourse and Meditations the ground of
Descartes' theoretical philosophy is a prior identity between
method and science, rendering theology superfluous as a
metaphysical foundation.

     Chapter 2 shows how Cartesian science is responsible
for the critique of prescientific experience in Meditation
I. The doubt argument develops what I shall refer to as
an "epistemic-ontic regression" from sensation through
imagination to intellect, as the ways through which body
as res extensa is experienced by the mind-body complex.
The exemption of mathematics from doubt via the finitude
of the evil genius exposes the presuppositionality of
reason-science in Meditation I and the circularity involved
in science serving as both the cause and resolution of
the critique of prescientific experience.

     In Chapter 3 the influence of Cartesian science on
the arguments in Meditation II for the soul as res cogitans
and body as res extensa is presented. The inference from
the indubitability of thinking and the dubitability of
body is used to conceal the operation of Cartesian automatism
in the rejection of the Aristotelian account of the soul
in favor of the soul as res cogitans. Concerning body,
Cartesian science is responsible for the proof of body
as res extensa since the wax analysis, under the guise
of unbiased phenomenological analysis of perception, repeats
the ontology of the Regulae.

     Chapter 4 argues that Descartes' theological metaphysics
is insincere since God's benevolence, the core of the
Cartesian theodicy, cannot be demonstrated so long as His
will is unintelligible to human reason. The freeing of
reason from theology is also implied by the doctrine of
the divine creation of the eternal truths and the explanation
of its absence from the Meditations. Cartesian rationalism
does not, however, signal the once and for all transition
from metaphysics to science. I therefore take issue with
Caton's claim concerning the insincerity of every metaphysics
subsequent to the Meditations in the light of the redundancy
of the quest for scientific foundations.' According to
Caton, "given that the sciences exist and are certain,
how can it be a reasonable philosophical enterprise to
seek to ground the possibility of something that is actual
especially when that ground must be sought in a domain
that has been rejected as in principle uncertain?"[7] My
response concerning the possibility of philosophy as
metaphysics takes the form of questioning what I take to
be Caton's assimilation of metaphysics to scientific
epistemology. What Caton takes to be an ultimate court
of appeal--the intrinsic validity of clear and distinct
ideas--may be the consequence of a failure to acknowledge
the necessary lack of metaphysical commitment intrinsic

to the Cartesian identification of physics and subjectivity, i.e., the methodic reduction of nature to clear and distinct ideas.

Chapter 5 discusses the tension within Descartes' anthropology between Cartesian science and experience. I argue that Descartes' resolution of the problem of embodiment tends toward epiphenomenalism rather than substantial dualism. This does not prevent the mind, conceived as res cogitans, from receiving its cognitive structure--its powers of sense, imagination, and intellect--in conformity with the structure of what it knows, that is, body as understood by Cartesian science.

I conclude with a summary of the ways in which the Meditations accomplishes its task of the subordination of theology and metaphysics to scientific ontology and epistemology.

To the extent to which the present essay contributes to an understanding of the argument and significance of Descartes' project, it owes much to work already done by others. In addition to the secondary literature referred to throughout the present study, a great debt is owed to Richard Kennington, whose approach to Descartes did much to shape my initial reading of the Meditations. I should also like to thank William T. Bluhm, Hiram Caton, and Stewart Umphrey for their valuable comments on an earlier draft of this essay, President Edward B. Jakubauskas, S.U.N.Y. College at Geneseo, for the sabbatical leave which permitted me to complete the present study, and Mrs. Pamela Thomas, whose typing and overall management of the manuscript was indispensable.

1
THE CARTESIAN ARCHITECTONIC

THE GENESIS OF PHILOSOPHICAL REASON

In the Discourse I and II Descartes presents his scientific method as the final stage of his philosophical coming of age. The emergence of philosophical reason from the prephilosophical is described as a personal "history, or . . . a fable." As we will see, this rhetoric of idiosyncracy is used to soften the impact of Descartes' anti-traditional proposals.

The opening passage, which connects the need for method with mental equality, is problematic. On one level, it is clearly ironic; on another level, it is instructive. In this sense it can be compared to a noble lie, a salutary combination of truth and untruth. Two proofs are given for mental equality:

> Good sense is of all the things in the world the most equally distributed, for everybody thinks himself so abundantly provided with it, that even the most difficult to please in all other matters do not commonly desire more of it than they already possess. It is unlikely that this is an error on their part; it seems rather to be evidence in support of the view that the power of forming a good judgment and of distinguishing the true from the false, which is properly speaking what is called Good sense or Reason, is by nature equal in all men.[1]

This proof initially strikes one as an obvious joke. Surely, Descartes, who repeatedly asserts his mental superiority throughout the Discourse[2], cannot be seriously arguing for equality. The proof defies both logic and common experience. To highly esteem one's own good sense is hardly a proof of its equality to that of others. In many cases self-satisfaction is a sign of inferiority. Descartes warns against such excessive self-estimation, given "how subject we are to delusion in whatever touches ourselves."[3] Mental equality is also contradicted by Descartes' subsequent mental typology.

The second proof of mental equality appears to be more of a joke than the first:

> For as to reason or good sense, inasmuch as it is the only thing that constitutes us men and distinguishes us from the brutes, I would fain believe that it is to be found complete in each individual, and in this I follow the common opinion of the philosophers, who say that the question of more or less occurs only in the sphere of the accidents and does not affect the forms or natures of the individuals in the same species.[4]

It is clear from every Cartesian text that this appeal to species form and "the common opinion of the philosophers" is not serious. For example, in Discourse V species form, presumably needed for the immortality of the soul, is not used to distinguish man from brute. And in Meditation II man as "rational animal" is rejected when Descartes explicates the meaning of "my nature."

The argument is instructive when read in the context of the transition from the prephilosophical to the philosophical-methodic. Descartes means to disclose an equality below the level of the natural light. The equality of "good sense or reason" refers to prephilosophical, or practical, reason. Practical reason is reason concerning "whatever touches ourselves." At this level we are likely to find equality because practical reason is self-correcting. As Descartes says, "I might meet with much more truth in the reasonings that each man makes on the matters that specially concern him, and the issue of which would very soon punish him if he made a wrong judgment, than in the case of those made by a man of letters in his study touching speculations which lead to no result."[5] The ground of the equality of practical judgment is a more fundamental equality--an equality of self-concern. As Richard Kennington observes, "natural egoism is the best distributed thing in the world."[6] The pleasure-pain calculus of good sense is nonetheless fallible. In addition to problems concerning the will and self-deception, there is the problem of transforming corrigibility into certainty. This is solvable only by the unequally distributed natural light, that is,

Descartes' devising of the proper scientific method.

The need for method is in fact neutral to the question of the equality of reason. The goal of the method is not to make unequal minds equal but rather to replace opinion with knowledge. Method is necessary for all minds since differences of opinion result from our thoughts taking different paths and thereby considering different things. Progress is possible only if all minds follow the correct course of inquiry. The devising of the method is not lacking in political symbolism. The results of the method are democratic; all will benefit, though perhaps in proportion to their natural inequalities. Descartes, the maker of the method, assumes the role of aristocratic benefactor.

He presents the discovery of his method through a rhetoric of idiosyncracy. The journey from childhood through education to method is "simply . . . a history, or, if you prefer it, a fable," which one is free to follow or reject due to its purely personal character.[7] By means of such rhetoric Descartes encourages proper emulators and dissuades those unprepared to follow. The latter intent is apparent from the use of the fable metaphor. As the sequel explains, fables, along with histories, are far from reliable sources of instruction. The equating of history and fable is deceptive, however, since Descartes' fable is reliable personal history. He hopes that "all will thank me for my frankness,"[8] but speaks equivocally. Descartes' act of publication is his putting forth of the method as the model to be imitated since it is the only way of "rightly conducting the reason and seeking for truth in the sciences."[9] To those who are capable the Discourse is a genuine invitation to follow.

He begins with his education, the body of knowledge transmitted by the pagan and scholastic traditions. These traditions are found wanting because they have not yielded "clear and certain knowledge . . . of all that is useful in life."[10] Traditional knowledge is evaluated in terms of utility. Knowledge is pursued as a means rather than an end.

The rhetoric of idiosyncracy culminates in Descartes' own judgment as the arbiter concerning traditional learning. He offers the following "syllogism": La Fleche is the tradition. The seventeenth century is the equal of any in the production of great minds. His fellow students will be among its great minds. His mind is considered the equal of theirs. Consequently, "this made me take the liberty of judging all others by myself and of coming to the conclusion that there was no learning in the world such as I was formerly led to believe it to be."[11]

Ancient literature fares no better. Its fables and histories help us to form sound judgments only "when read with discretion." Since even the best histories "omit in them all the circumstances which are basest and least notable,"[12] to emulate such moral caricatures at face value leads one into excesses. In addition, a preoccupation with historical example serves only to produce self-estrangement. This critique of ancient literature is Descartes' warning to unfit emulators not to "form projects beyond their power of performance."[13]

Concerning the various disciplines, Descartes is cautious when discussing scholastic moral philosophy, saying only that it is instructive because it contains useful moral persuasion. The ancient pagans, however, construct moral "palaces most superb and magnificent, which are yet built on sand and mud alone."[14] They praise virtue but are ignorant of its nature because they falsely oppose virtue and passion. This error Descartes traces to a more fundamental mistake--the belief that the soul moves the body, that is, that moral persuasion can affect behavior.[15] This same criticism, of course, applies also to scholastic moral philosophy. As the Passions explains, virtue must be understood in terms of passion in order to overcome the false and thereby ineffectual dichotomy of higher and lower parts of the soul.

When discussing theology Descartes diplomatically suggests a division of labor:

> I honoured our Theology and aspired
> as much as anyone to reach heaven,
> but having learned to regard it as
> a most highly assured fact that the
> road is not less open to the most
> ignorant than to the most learned,
> and that the revealed truths which
> conduct thither are quite above our
> intelligence, I should not have dared
> to submit them to the feebleness of
> my reasonings; and I thought that,
> in order to undertake to examine them
> and succeed in so doing, it was necessary
> to have some extraordinary assistance
> from above and to be more than a mere
> man.[16]

The philosophical-theological division of labor is the following. Theology concerns revealed truth, which transcends human reason. The goal of theology is heaven, whereas the goal of "clear and assured knowledge" is "to learn to distinguish the true from the false, in order to see clearly in my actions and to walk with confidence in this life."[17] Philosophy concerns the terrestrial, yet its inability to comprehend theological truth is not without its theological consequences. Although this inability is presumably not a theological concern since the ignorant and the learned have equal access to heaven, what are we to make of the subsequent attempt at rational theological metaphysics in the Meditations?

Returning to the philosophical tradition, it is not only barren of utility but full of conflicting opinions. This renders every opinion suspect. Anticipating Meditation I, the doubtful is to be considered the equivalent to the false: "Considering how many conflicting opinions . . . may be . . . supported by learned people, while there can never be more than one which is true, I esteemed as well-nigh false all that only went as far as being probable."[18] For Descartes truth is one and indubitable. Adherence to Cartesian method will therefore render legitimate disagreement impossible.

Discourse I is mainly negative, a destruction of everything preventing the development of the proper method. The one traditional discipline which escapes critique is mathematics:

> Most of all was I delighted with Mathematics because of the certainty of its demonstrations and the evidence of its reasoning; but I did not understand its true use, and, believing that it was of service only in the mechanical arts, I was astonished that, seeing how firm and solid was its basis, no loftier edifice had been reared thereupon.[19]

In Discourse II we learn of this edifice. Mathematics is what accounts for the identity of Cartesian method and physics.

With the exception of mathematics, the bankruptcy of the traditional disciplines leaves Descartes with the following alternative. He resolves "to seek no other science than that which could be found in myself, or at least in the great book of the world."[20] What is learned from the great book of the world is that the variety of custom is nearly the equal to the variety of philosophical opinions. Self-discipline remains as the only discipline capable of enhancing his reason. He accordingly resolves to look inward.

To summarize the results of Discourse I, it contains a critique of whatever stands in the way of self-instruction and begins to illuminate the goal of the Cartesian project by revealing something about the origin of Cartesian philosophizing. Since the obstacle to self-instruction is the heteronomy of the teachings and practices of others, the hallmark of Descartes' self-instruction is rational autonomy. His goal is not to become part of an asymptotic progress toward truth, but rather to establish a definitive, ahistorical, unalterable new beginning--"firm and lasting" foundations.[21] Descartes' move to rational autonomy testifies to his virtue, his generosity. True generosity, Descartes explains in the Passions, "consists alone partly in the

fact that he knows that there is nothing that truly pertains
to him but this free disposition of his will, and . . .
a firm and constant resolution to use it well, that is
to say, never to fail of his own will to undertake and
execute all the things which he judges to be the best--which
is to follow perfectly after virtue."[22] What is arrogance
for those prone to excessive self-estimation is for Descartes
the perfect virtue of proper self-esteem. Such self-esteem,
as we have seen, is innate in the prephilosophical soul,
and explains both the origin and goal of philosophy. This
becomes evident when we connect the discussion of wonder
in the Passions to the discussion of Descartes' reason
for publication in Discourse VI.

     In the Passions the source of our interest in the
world is traced to the passion of wonder, "the first of
all the passions." But Cartesian wonder does not satisfy
the intellect's natural desire to know. It is passionate
and radically egocentric. Objects inspire wonder insofar
as they benefit or harm us. Wonder thus divides naturally
into esteem and disdain. And the primary object of esteem
or disdain is the self. Esteem and disdain "are chiefly
remarkable when we relate them to ourselves, i.e., when
it is our own merit that we esteem or despise."[23] In other
words, the prephilosophical soul relates to the world as
matter for its own enhancement. An adversary relation
obtains between self and world. It is this relation which
links the discussion of the prephilosophical soul to the
goal of Cartesian science in Discourse VI.

     In Discourse VI Descartes states that his reluctance
to publish was overcome by duty. As he says, "I believe
that I could not keep [my findings] concealed without greatly
sinning against the law which obliges us to procure, as
much as lies in us, the general good of all mankind."[24]
As Richard Kennington points out, "This law, the only
categorical obligation ever asserted by Descartes, is stated
but once in his writings, and no argument is ever given
for it."[25] The argument for it, it appears, is Descartes'
egocentrism, which manifests itself, as we have seen, as
rational resolve. By exercising the passion-virtue of
generosity, Descartes can rightly esteem himself as the
benefactor of the entire human race. For as he explains:

               So soon as I had acquired some general
               notions concerning Physics . . . they
               caused me to see that it is possible
               to attain knowledge which is very useful
               in life, and that, instead of that
               speculative philosophy which is taught
               in the Schools, we may find a practical
               philosophy by means of which . . .
               we can . . . render ourselves the
               masters and possessors of nature.[26]

The goal of mastery is the rationale for the utility of physics. Applied science rather than speculative philosophy promotes the human good. Descartes' project shows the attitude of benevolence that philosophy-science has concerning society, such that the Discourse is literally a public relations work. The mastery of nature reiterates Francis Bacon's "relief of man's estate," both of which inaugurate the Enlightenment notion of a science-society harmony dedicated to perpetual progress.[27] Descartes explains that the completion of the project lies in the future because of the multitude of experiments required. Nonetheless, the program is clear, anchored as it is in man's nature.

Discourse II completes the development of philosophical reason. Descartes' resolve to engage in self-study is reinforced by his reading of the book of the world and made possible by fortune. As he says, "fortunately I had also no cares or passions to trouble me."[28] This same freedom from passion is mentioned in Meditation I. In neither case are the passions overcome by rational or willful control. Descartes credits fortune (at least until the perfect moral science is completed). But even in the Passions, if you grant that the powerlessness of the soul with respect to the body is remedied, it is never a question of the kind of deliverance from passion that Descartes speaks of in the present context. In Meditation I the deliverance from passion affords Descartes the leisure to resolve to doubt. Here in Discourse II it permits self-examination.

One of the first results of self-reflection was the notion "that there is very often less perfection in works composed of several portions, and carried out by the hands of various masters, than in those on which one individual alone has worked."[29] The examples Descartes gives indicate that this principle was learned from the book of the world. We can call it the unity-perfection principle--the perfection of a work depends upon a unitary source. The principle is not absolute. When and where it is the case is cautiously explained by a series of examples which culminates in the superiority of the Cartesian method and the way of life of the philosopher-scientist. The examples are increasingly comprehensive and exalted concerning the regulation of human affairs--the construction of buildings, cities, constitutions, divine laws. A poorly planned city, for example, more closely resembles a product of "chance rather than the will of men guided by reason."[30] We have referred to the opposition between fortune (unmastered nature) and human resolve. The unity-perfection principle also applies to constitutions, namely, those constructed by one prudent legislator rather than those arising gradually over time. Even though many of its particular laws were "quite strange and even contrary to good morals," pagan Sparta's constitution deserves praise because of its single author.

It is likewise with Christianity, because its rules came from one god.

The unity-perfection principle applies to theoretical works as well:

> And similarly I thought that the sciences found in books--in those at least whose reasonings are only probable and which have no demonstrations, composed as they are of the gradually accumulated opinions of many different individuals--do not approach so near to the truth as the simple reasoning which a man of common sense can quite naturally carry out respecting the things which come immediately before him.[31]

This comparison is a deceptive restatement of the similar contrast in _Discourse_ I. The unity-perfection principle is used here to show the superiority of the practical "good sense" of one man to the "theoretical sense" which is a joint enterprise. But solitary good sense has a severe natural limitation (which Descartes, as we have seen, is transcending by fortune and resolve). It must free itself from the body:

> Since we have all been children before being men, and since it has for long fallen to us to be governed by our appetites . . . it is almost impossible that our judgments should be so excellent or solid as they should have been had we complete use of our reason since our birth, and had we been guided by its means alone.[32]

Egoism and appetite are coeval with man, whereas reason is developmental. _Discourse_ I has spoken of the pleasure-pain epistemology of good sense. Here Descartes is preparing the transition from childhood egoism to philosophical reason. He elaborates on the prejudices of childhood in the _Principles_. Their source is the union of the mind with the body, in which the body forces the mind to understand the world in utilitarian, naive realist terms: "And as all other things were only considered in as far as they served for the use of the body in which it was immersed, mind judged that there was more or less reality in each body, according as the impressions made on body were more or less strong."[33] Childhood is the source of "the natural attitude."

Descartes draws back from the more obvious political implications of the emancipation of individual reason.

His example, he says, is not to be followed by political revolutionaries, "those turbulent and unrestful spirits who, being called neither by birth nor fortune to the management of public affairs, never fail to have always in their minds some new reforms."[34] Descartes adds the requirement of an innately strong mind--generosity--to that of fortune. This type of political revolutionary is not dissuaded, though Descartes reiterates his rhetoric of idiosyncracy and claims to prefer custom, stability, etc. to the chaos and instability of sudden reform. Surely Descartes' philosophical-scientific revolution is meant to have political consequences since the technological mastery of nature requires a favorable relation between science and society.

The first step in Descartes' revolution is "the simple resolve to strip oneself of all opinions and beliefs formerly received."[35] Since this is risky, Descartes provides a typology of souls so that proper and improper emulators can be distinguished. The world is "mainly composed of two classes of minds,"[36] neither of which should resolve to overthrow all opinion. Those overestimating their minds end in skepticism and uncertainty when challenging all opinion. Those having a justifiably modest opinion of their ability rightly follow the ideas of others. Since these two types do not exhaust the world's mentality, a third type, an exceedingly small minority, is implied. The few generous minds are therefore encouraged to follow Descartes' procedure as a true account of the genesis of philosophical reason as such. Concerning this third type, "Those who are generous . . . are naturally impelled to do great things and at the same time to undertake nothing of which they do not feel themselves capable."[37] What achievement can rival the conquest of nature and the elimination of victimization by natural necessity?

Nature is to be mastered in a double sense. The first concerns the invention of an infinitude of devices so that we can painlessly enjoy all that the earth has to offer. Though realized in the future, it ushers in a new beginning for man. As Joseph Cropsey observes, "what he holds up to view is a new and better Eden, one in which man will enjoy all things without pain and trouble not under the condition of ignorance but in enjoyment also of the fruit of the tree of knowledge: a philanthropic Eden at least."[38]

The conquest of nature has a reflexive component. Our own nature can be mastered, that is, improved, and because of its most natural aspect, its corporeality. The epitome of applied science is medicine, which puts within reach the "preservation of health, which is without doubt the chief blessing and the foundation of all other blessings in this life."[39] Medicine is foundational because "the mind depends so much on the temperament and disposition of the bodily organs," such that "if it is possible to find a means of rendering men wiser and cleverer than they

have hitherto been, I believe that it is in medicine that
it must be sought."[40] Medicine compensates for natural
gifts and fortune. Descartes envisions a physiologically
based psychiatry since, in addition to freedom from the
disabilities of age, "we could be free from an infinitude
of maladies both of body and mind."[41] Descartes' new Eden
includes not only the tree of knowledge but thereby the
tree of life.

The road to the new Eden commences with method. The
method is a synthesis of algebra and geometry. Traditional
logic is dropped because the syllogism merely rearranges
what one already knows instead of discovering something
new. Descartes' method is for the purpose of generating
new truths (premises) as the basis for the deduction of
others. The Discourse II account of the Regulae summarizes
what has been demonstrated in the latter, that for Descartes
method, mathematics, and physics comprise one science.
The comprehensiveness of this science extends horizontally
and vertically. Since whatever man's mind can comprehend
is part of an interconnected order, if we adhere to this
order, "there can be nothing so remote that we cannot reach
it, nor so recondite that we cannot discover it."[42] And
since the method reflects the nature of mathematical
thinking, this testifies to Descartes' conviction that
the order of human reason mirrors the order of nature.
Only the mathematicians have produced "evident and certain"
demonstrations which satisfy the first precept of method,
"to accept nothing more than what was presented to my mind
so clearly and distinctly that I could have no occasion
to doubt it."[43] To see the way in which mathematics mediates
method and ontology we should consult Regulae XII and XIV.

Regulae XII, which "states the conclusion of all that
we said before," presents a theory of cognition in terms
of the relation between "ourselves who know and the objects
themselves which are to be known."[44] Descartes gives a
twofold enumeration of objects and cognitive faculties.
There is a perfect fit between the two because the various
cognitive functions are understood in terms of their
respective objects. The overall goal is to establish,
on the basis of methodological considerations, an identity
between the objects of pure mathematics and the physical
objects in the world. This is the rationale for Descartes'
use of "suppositions."

The first supposition concerns sense perception:

> Let us then conceive of the matter
> as follows:--all our external senses,
> in so far as they are part of the body,
> and despite the fact that we direct
> them toward objects, so manifesting
> activity, viz. a movement in space,
> nevertheless properly speaking perceive
> in virtue of passivity alone, just

> in the way the wax receives an impression
> from a seal. And it should not be
> thought that all we mean to assert
> is an analogy between the two.[45]

Apart from the distinction between static and dynamic, the relation between sense organ and object is identical to that between wax and seal. In each case what is involved is direct physical contact, the character of the sensory stimulation entirely dependent upon the nature of the physical modification, i.e., figure upon figure. But this supposition is well founded since "the concept of figure is so common and simple that it is involved in every object of sense."[46] Descartes universalizes: "it is certain that the infinitude of figures suffices to express all the differences in sensible things."[47] Because there is this one-to-one correlation throughout nature between figure and sensible quality, our senses are rightly defined as passive figure-receiving parts of the body.

Step two is the communication of the sensory impression to the common sense. The process is still entirely mechanical since the common sense is also bodily. Descartes stresses that this communication occurs "without the passage of any real entity from one to the other."[48] Contrary to the older view, it is bodily motion rather than incorporeal form that is transmitted. Step three, the passage from the common sense to the imagination, repeats the same kind of process. The common sense serves as the seal, the corporeal imagination as the wax. From sense to imagination, then, sense perception involves only extension and the mechanical transmission of motion from the periphery to the brain.

The analysis becomes analogical when the quantum leap is made to the intellect. As with the other faculties, the nature of the intellect conforms to its respective object. The cognitive requirement to grasp the simple natures grounds the dualism between intellect and body, for "that power by which we are properly said to know things, is purely spiritual, and not less distinct from every part of the body than blood from bone, or hand from eye."[49] The "transnatural" intellect (whose problems we will encounter in the Meditations) has the following nature:

> It is a single agency, whether it
> receives impressions from the common
> sense simultaneously with the fancy,
> or applies itself to those that are
> preserved in the memory, or forms new
> ones . . . . In all these operations
> this cognitive power is at one time
> passive, at another active, and resembles
> now the seal and now the wax. But
> the resemblance on this occasion is
> only one of analogy, for among corporeal
> things there is nothing wholly similar
> to this faculty. It is one and the
> same agency which, when applying itself
> along with the imagination to the common

> sense, is said to see, touch, etc.;
> if applying itself to the imagination
> alone in so far as that is endowed
> with diverse impressions, it is said
> to remember; if it turn to the
> imagination in order to create fresh
> impressions, it is said to imagine
> or conceive: finally if it act alone
> it is said to understand.[50]

Our awareness of the existence of bodies is thus the
passive gaze by the intellect upon the figure that the
corporeal imagination receives from the common sense.
The empirical imagination accurately reports existence
(since a prior sensory impression is necessarily involved),
but is questionable concerning essence. The intellect
therefore avoids error if it "refrain from judging that
the imagination faithfully reports the objects of the
senses."[51] Our awareness of the essence of objects (the
simple natures) arises by an act of abstraction from the
imagination on the part of the intellect. Here Descartes
again relies upon "assumptions," heuristic principles.
His account of the simple natures gives the initial (false)
impression that Descartes is going to suggest something
like a proto-Kantian dualism:

> Relatively to our knowledge single
> things should be taken in an order
> different from that in which we should
> regard them when considered in their
> more real nature. . . . we shall treat
> of things only in relation to our
> understanding's awareness of them,
> and shall call those only simple, the
> cognition of which is so clear and
> so distinct that they cannot be analyzed
> by the mind into others more distinctly
> known.[52]

Concerning bodies, he lists "figure, extension, motion,
etc." and their compounds. These are said to be epistemic
rather than ontological simples. As such their simplicity
is grounded in the intuition of the mind reflecting upon
itself. The simple natures are simply discovered to have
natures of their own. They seem independent of sensation
and cannot be generated or altered by the will. In
Meditation III these are called "innate ideas." Since
the simple natures are restricted to reflection, the drawings
of Regulae XII may be no more representative of the real
than the astronomer's epicycles.

The ontological import of Cartesian method derives
from the dual function of the imagination.[53] The imagination
is instrumental in the initial move away from the world
via abstraction and in the return to the world via extension.
Regulae XII abstracts from images to generate symbolic
objects expressing the relations holding between magnitudes
in general. Although no images are involved in the
contemplation of such "objects", the imagination is crucial
in the movement back to the world since geometry is the

ontological science. As Regulae XIV announces, "The same
rule is to be applied also to the real extension of bodies.
It must be set before the imagination by means of mere
figures, for this is the best way to make it clear to the
understanding."[54] The imagination is indispensable because,
in anticipation of Hume, concerning bodies the imagination
is the criterion of existence: "Hence we announce that
by extension we do not here mean anything distinct and
separate from the extended object itself; and we make it
a rule not to recognize those metaphysical entities which
really cannot be presented to the imagination."[55] On the
basis of this equivalence between the imageable and the
existential the universal mathematics retraces its steps
from symbolic understanding of magnitude as such to the
"real extension of bodies":

> We shall, however, even in this case
> [concerning magnitudes in general]
> make use of our imagination, employing
> not the naked understanding but the
> intellect as aided by images of
> particulars depicted on the fancy.
> Finally we must note that nothing can
> be asserted of magnitudes in general
> that cannot also be ascribed to any
> particular instance. This lets us
> easily conclude that there will be
> no slight profit in transferring
> whatsoever we find asserted of magnitudes
> in general to that particular species
> of magnitude which is most easily and
> distinctly depicted in our imagination.
> But it follows from what we stated
> about the twelfth rule that this must
> be the real extension of body abstracted
> from everything else except the fact
> that it has figure, for in that place
> we represented the imagination itself
> along with the ideas it contains as
> nothing more than a really material
> body possessing extension and figure.[56]

As we have seen, figure and extension apart from body
are ontological myths since "whatever our understanding
may believe as to the truth of the matter, those abstract
entities are never given to our imagination as separate
from the objects in which they inhere."[57] That is to say,
what are distinguishable by the intellect--the concepts
of body and extension--are inseparable to the imagination.
Consequently, the imagination which helps the intellect
produce symbolic figure is indispensable for the
representation of embodied figure as the essence of physical
reality.

This completes the ontic-epistemic correlation of objects and cognitive faculties which constitutes the basis of the method. The dual status of extension (or figure) and the imagination accounts for the coalescence of method, psychology, and ontology. Extension is simultaneously simple nature and real existence. The imagination, necessary for the theories of perception and abstraction, is the intersection of the symbolic and the real because its images in the brain, the material for abstraction, are real impressions of corporeal extension. It appears that what is summarized in Discourse II is physics as method, the reduction of the world to pure mathematics. And since the image is the link between the symbolic and the existential, it appears that the faculty of the imagination is perhaps the place to look for the "metaphysical" foundations of science. As Descartes says in response to the charge that his physics was but "imaginary and fictitious," "my critics here conjoin my Physics with pure Mathematics, which is my deepest wish my Physics should resemble."[58]

THE MORAL COMPONENT

We have seen that the goal of mastery originates in the natural egoism of the prephilosophical soul, but the practice of such mastery must wait until science completes its task. It would appear, then, that any present system of morals must be provisional. This seems to be the case since it is in the Passions that Descartes erects his perfect moral science on a foundation of a completed science of the human composite. However, when it comes to the content of such a definitive morals, it is strikingly similar to the provisional morals of Discourse III. This suggests that the provisional morals be read as indicating the ultimate moral directives that Descartes wishes to give. Discourse I and II have shown the cement binding the theoretical and practical components of Cartesian philosophy to be resolve born of generosity--the willful assertion of unaided reason in all matters. As Descartes states in Discourse V (which presents a summary of the science of the mind-body composite), "reason is a universal instrument."[59] By grounding virtue on such resolve, "I think I can reconcile the most opposed and famous opinions of the ancient philosophers, that of Zeno who thought virtue or honor the supreme good, and that of Epicurus, who thought the supreme good was contentment, to which he gave the name of pleasure."[60] No other philosophers or the church are serious moral contenders.

Descartes' first maxim is the following:

> To obey the laws and customs of my
> country, adhering constantly to the

> religion in which by God's grace I
> had been instructed since my childhood,
> and in all other things directing my
> conduct by opinions the most moderate
> in nature, and the farthest removed
> from excess in all those which are
> commonly received and acted on by the
> most judicious of those with whom I
> might come in contact.[61]

This combination of religious-political orthodoxy and
moderation is clearly prudential and provisional. The
warrant for such conformism is childhood experience, which
we have seen exposed as the original prerational home of
prejudice. The moderation component is also provisional,
but less obviously so. The call for moderation masks a
call for a new type of extremism. Pragmatism requires
moderation since "all excess has a tendency to be bad."[62]
However, bad consequences can be prevented if this tendency
is eliminated. In the light of the projected science,
whose index is certitude, the tendency of excess to be
bad is not due to the vice of extremism but rather to
ignorance. To anticipate a later discussion, we can ask:
If the vice of extremism reduces to ignorance and the virtue
of moderation gives way to certainty, does this mean that
Cartesian virtue is a species of knowledge and vice a species
of error? In the present context the transformation of
one's judgments from the probable to the certain renders
moderation superfluous. Pursuing the correct extreme
eliminates the lack of decisiveness which characterizes
moderation. As Cropsey points out, the Cartesian mean
is Machiavellian rather than Aristotelian[63]--the mean of
the correct extreme, made possible not by the utopian
perfection of one's character but by the projected perfection
of one's knowledge.

The orthodoxy and moderation of the beginning of the
first maxim are in fact contradicted by the introduction
of resolve at the end. As Descartes states, "I also made
a point of counting as excess all the engagements by means
of which we limit in some degree our liberty."[64] The true
excess is the restriction of rational autonomy, which has
replaced traditional orthodoxy and moderation as the true
moderation. Vows and contracts are to cure "the
inconsistancy of feeble souls," i.e., the weak-minded and
the faithful. The man of resolve must retain flexibility
in the face of life's contingencies. Whether or not the
contingent can become a proper object of Cartesian science
(this bears on the Stoicism of the third maxim), what we
learn about the moral component of the Cartesian
architectonic from the first maxim is the provisionality
of its conformism, piety, and moderation, and its adumbration
of rational autonomy as a core component of the perfected
morals.

Whereas in the first maxim a feature of the final morals emerges by opposition to its provisionality, in the second maxim the relation between provisionality and finality is a matter of degree:

> My second maxim was that of being as firm and resolute in my actions as I could be, and not to follow less faithfully opinions the most dubious, when my mind was once made up regarding them, than if these had been beyond doubt.[65]

What is provisional here is not the equation of the dubitable with the certain, but rather the continuance of the dubitable. That is to say, the provisional character of this maxim does not concern the requirement that one be resolved in following one's mind once a decision has been reached, but the circumstance in which such decisions are not free of uncertainty. Once Cartesian science replaces opinion with knowledge, the "as if" nature of the equation of the dubitable with the certain drops out and along with it the "penitence and remorse . . . of those weak and vacillating creatures"[66] (a second reference to the weak and faithful). The final morals will ground resolve in certainty, that is, indubitability.

Thus far traditional pagan and Christian notions of virtue and dubious moral opinions have given way to resolve and certitude. Descartes then introduces stoicism:

> My third maxim was to try always to conquer myself rather than fortune, and to alter my desires rather than change the world, and generally to accustom myself to believe that there is nothing entirely within our power but our own thoughts.[67]

This maxim appears not only provisional but incongruous with the others. Yet it is retained in the Passions. Caton sees this retention as "a basic inconsistency in Descartes' moral position."[68] The only way to remedy this inconsistency is to argue that the Passions is as provisional as the Discourse (which does not work since the contradiction is merely doubled) or to argue that Descartes regarded the recalcitrance of the contingent as a permanent possibility. But this goes against the entire spirit of his project.

Another way to reconcile the inconsistency is to remember that the project of mastery also pertains to self-mastery. The control over one's thoughts is a requirement of Cartesian method. Theoretical stoicism frees the intellect to construct the science that eliminates

practical stoicism. Consequently, Descartes' advice, "making
what is called a virtue out of a necessity, we should no
more desire to be well if ill, or free, if in prison, than
we now do to have wings to fly like birds,"[69] is doubly
misleading. Claiming that the elimination of sickness
is as remote as flight like birds and incorruptible bodies
is an obvious misrepresentation of the Cartesian enterprise.
And given the infinite horizon that Descartes envisions,
even these latter two objectives cannot be ruled out.
To posit perpetual progress, an "infinitude of arts and
science", is to see time as an ally in the struggle against
nature. Such an open-ended horizon makes resignation
perpetually premature, except during the finite time of
individuals. Since stoic resignation is appropriate only
in the short run, stoicism as rational autonomy (and its
practical consequences) is intended as a permanent feature
of Cartesian morals.

The first three maxims converge toward the fourth--the
life of the philosopher-scientist as the paradigm of
theoretical and practical autonomy. Descartes' fable is
thus the true story of the genesis of the philosopher.
The desire for knowledge, rooted in the passion to overcome,
gives the sense of the fourth maxim as the rationale for
the preceding three. The life of rational self-instruction
is choiceworthy since it alone can guarantee "the acquisition
of all the virtues and all the other good things that it
is possible to obtain."[70] As Descartes reiterates in the
sequel, it is the practical concern that motivates the
resolve to overthrow all of his former opinions.

THE HERMENEUTIC PROBLEM OF THE MEDITATIONS

The hermeneutic problem of the Meditations is generated
by the way in which the parts of the architectonic are
juxtaposed in the Discourse. Discourse I and II trace
the evolution of philosophical reason from its beginnings
in prejudice to its fulfillment as method. This evolution
supplements the "unnatural" beginning of the Regulae, in
which the natural light is a given, and the Meditations,
in which res cogitans is the corollary of bodily doubt.
Method requires a prior emancipation of reason from nature.
But such an emancipated reason is nonerotic because
nonbodily. The telos of knowledge must therefore be sought
in the mind-body complex, whose nature is passion, or eros.
As Descartes says in the Passions, "the principal effect
of all the passions in men is that they incite and dispose
their soul to desire those things for which they prepare
their body."[71] Anthropologically, the congenital and
irremovable egoism of all men is the basis of the desire
for mastery. Epistemically, the common genealogy of method
and science is the overcoming of the "natural attitude"
of the life-world. Cartesian resolve, the reason-will

complex, performs such an emancipation of reason, whose first act is the resolve to doubt. Since such resolve is to be practiced in all areas (witness the major otcpo in the Discourse and Meditations prefaced by resolve), the traditional dichotomy of theoretical and practical philosophy is to be overcome. Since the problem concerning the prephilosophical is epistemic rather than moral, Descartes proposes a novel theory-practice composite. He wants a practical philosophy grounded in certainty, a moral science modelled on natural science, whereby the contingent and recalcitrant aspects of the human condition surrender to technical control. The Meditations' concern with epistemology (theory of science) is therefore centrally located within the Cartesian architectonic. The hermeneutic problem of the Meditations concerns the thorny question of the true foundations of Descartes' theory of knowledge, i.e., the theoretical supremacy of Cartesian physics or metaphysics. This question of supremacy arises because of the nature of the second sailing undertaken in Discourse IV.

Discourse IV claims that the sciences need metaphysical foundations--God and the nonbodily soul. Just as in the Meditations, these metaphysical foundations would appear to make use of nothing imageable. Discourse V summarizes Cartesian physics (Le Monde) as following from such a purely noetic metaphysics. This produces the following architectonic order: method, metaphysics, physics. If the method were ontologically noncommital this order would seem initially plausible, that is, noncircular. But the Regulae has shown that method is not ontically neutral; consequently, the order of presentation of Discourse IV and V is suspect.

In the Regulae an identity between method and physics was based on the epistemic-ontic correlation. The imagination played the pivotal role as the link between pure intellect and pure extension on the one hand and sensation and extended body on the other. That is, the foundations of physics seem none other than the maligned images of Discourse IV and the Meditations. Given what therefore amounts to a superfluous metaphysical foundation, the second sailing appears redundant and the true architectonic order becomes: method, physics, and so on. That is, the metaphysical roots of the tree of philosophy are replaced by method, thereby resolving the issue of the priority of physics or metaphysics in favor of physics.

The same conclusion is suggested by the progression in Discourse IV and V, in which Descartes claims that his study of mathematics and physics followed upon his metaphysical meditations. As he puts it in Discourse IV:

> After that I desired to seek for other
> truths, and having put before myself
> the object of the geometricians, which

> I conceived to be a continuous body,
> or a space indefinitely extended in
> length, breadth, height or depth, which
> was divisible into various parts, and
> which might have various figures and
> sizes, and might be moved or transposed
> in all sorts of ways (for all this
> the geometricians suppose to be in
> the object of their contemplation),
> I went through some of their simplest
> demonstrations, and having noticed
> that this great certainty which everyone
> attributes to these demonstrations
> is founded solely on the fact that
> they are conceived of with clearness,
> in accordance with the rule which I
> have just laid down, I also noticed
> that there was nothing at all in them
> to assure me of the existence of their
> object.[72]

In the first place this order departs from the actual order of his self-instruction.[73] In the second place there is an equivocation concerning the status of the objects of geometrical physics. The shift from actual to imagined figures, whereby, as the sequel makes clear, the objects of geometry get assimilated to dream objects, belies the epistemic-ontic correlation of the Regulae summarized in Discourse II. This bifurcation of essence and existence is likewise in tension with the earlier remark about the foundational potential of mathematics.

In Discourse V the derivation of physics from metaphysics is depicted in the form of a cosmogonic fable. This fabulous new Genesis prepares the new technical Eden since neither contains "those forms or qualities which are so debated in the Schools."[74] Contrary to the Meditations, it appears that the removal of final cause permits an argument from nature as effect to God as cause since Descartes "observed certain laws which God has so established in Nature, and of which He has imprinted such ideas on our minds, that, after having reflected sufficiently upon the matter, we cannot doubt their being accurately observed in all that exists or is done in the world."[75] The fable instructs us to consider:

> What would happen in a new world if
> God now created, somewhere in an
> imaginary space, matter sufficient
> wherewith to form it, and if He agitated
> in diverse ways, and without any order,
> the diverse portions of this matter,
> so that there resulted a chaos as
> confused as the poets ever feigned,

> and concluded His work by merely lending
> His concurrence to Nature in the usual
> way, leaving her to act in accordance
> with the laws which He had established.[76]

The outcome is the universe of mechanics, whose derivation
from God is the following:

> Further I pointed out what are the
> laws of Nature, and, without resting
> my reasons on any other principle than
> the infinite perfections of God, I
> tried to demonstrate all those of which
> one could have any doubt, and to show
> that they are of such a nature that
> even if God had created other worlds,
> He could not have created any in which
> these laws would fail to be observed.[77]

This fable, which seems to be another noble lie, raises
the following issues. God is said to be the author of
the laws of mechanics, yet his will is subservient to such
laws since such laws must hold in all possible worlds.
(The doctrine of the divine creation of the eternal truths
will be discussed in conjunction with the theodicy of the
Meditations.) The present passage suggests a possibly
deliberate ambiguity in the relation between God's will
and the laws of nature. In Le Monde (which Discourse V
summarizes, again contradicting the order of self-instruction
mentioned in Discourse IV since Le Monde was written prior
to those metaphysical meditations of Discourse IV) this
ambiguity is apparently resolved in favor of God. God's
will is not subservient to laws of nature; such laws are
grounded in God's immutability. The single divine perfection
of immutability can perhaps explain the eternality and
immutability of such laws; however, it in no way implies
a preference for either mechanical or teleological physics.
In the Meditations' theodicy the issue concerns the relation
between divine inscrutability and mechanical physics.
In Discourse V a compatibilism between biblical and Cartesian
creation is rejected by the either-or character of the
following remark:

> I did not at the same time wish to
> infer from all these facts that this
> world has been created in the manner
> which I described; for it is much more
> probable that at the beginning God
> made it such as it was to be . . .
> . [However], we may well believe,
> without doing outrage to the miracle
> of creation, that . . . all things
> which are purely material might in

> course of time have become such as
> we observe them to be at present; and
> their nature is much easier to understand
> when we see them coming to pass little
> by little . . . than were we to consider
> them as all complete to begin with.[78]

The tension between the probable biblical account and the
more understandable (more rational) Cartesian account is
inferred from the dynamics of nature itself, the implication
being that what is fabulous in the new Genesis is precisely
its biblical component.

Our suspicion concerning the self-grounding character
of physics and consequent opposition to theological orthodoxy
is increased by Descartes' reiteration of the necessity
of an oblique versus frontal viewing of his metaphysics
and physics. He begins Discourse IV by saying that his
foundations are "so metaphysical and so unusual that they
may perhaps not be acceptable to everyone."[79] The
introduction to Discourse V tells more. The reason for
the fabulous cosmogony is that if Descartes were to present
the entirety of his physics, "it would have been necessary
now to speak of many matters of dispute among the learned,
with whom I have no desire to embroil myself."[80] The root
of his conflict with the learned is his endorsement of
Galileo, which, upon Descartes' learning of Galileo's fate,
caused his nonpublication of Le Monde. The fabulous
cosmogony is thus a way of "putting all these topics somewhat
in shadow, and being able to express myself freely about
them, without being obliged to adopt or refute the opinions
which are accepted by the learned."[81] Descartes' obliqueness
goes so far as to imply that the usefulness of his science
can be separated from the question of its truth. In
Discourse VI, when referring to his suppression of Le Monde
because of the church's disapproval of Galileo, Descartes
states his relation to the religious and civil authorities
in terms of thoughts and actions. The authorities "cannot
have less weight with my actions than my own reason has
over my thoughts."[82] Descartes defers to authority
concerning publication but not concerning truth. The
suppressed Le Monde was true because of "the great care
which I have always taken not to accept any new beliefs
unless I had very certain proof of their truth."[83] At
the same time, he refrains from saying he agrees with
Galileo: "I will not say that I agreed with this opinion
[of the moving earth], but only that before their censure
I observed in it nothing which I could possibly imagine
to be prejudicial either to Religion or the State, or
consequently which could have prevented me from giving
expression to it in writing, if my reason had persuaded
me to do so."[84] We are asked to believe that Descartes
withheld Le Monde because the religious and civil authorities
mistakenly saw a conflict with Galileo, that the issue

of publication becomes one of pragmatics rather than truth.
But as we saw at the outset, Descartes paraded the "infinity
of arts and crafts" to be derived from his science as the
reason for publication. This practical human gain is what
avoids the disputes with the learned. Since a separation
of utility from truth is impossible for Descartes, the
prudential character of the explanation for publication,
on top of the misrepresentation of the doctrinal order
of the second sailing, warrants a healthy scepticism
concerning the possibility of peaceful coexistence between
reason and religion.

The initial evidence of Cartesian iconoclasm in the
Meditations is the prudentially written Letter to the
Sorbonne, the leader of the learned with whom Descartes
wished to avoid dispute. The letter establishes the
following three disinctions: 1) the Discourse division
of labor between philosophy and religion, 2) a metaphysics
of science as opposed to a metaphysics of piety, and 3)
a lack of identity between religion and moral virtue.

The appeal for Sorbonne protection, says Descartes,
is justified in terms of the purely theological benefits
of the Meditations--a demonstration by natural reason that
God exists and that the soul does not perish with the body,
for the purpose of converting the infidels. Although the
immortality of the soul is not demonstrated in the
Meditations (the Letter speaks merely of its precondition),
Descartes cites the Lateran Council under Leo X as requiring
such a demonstration.

Since the atheists rather than the faithful are to
be convinced, the proofs of God and immortality of the
soul must be accomplished by natural reason rather than
faith. To the atheist the faith proof--the dialectic of
faith as ratio cognoscendi of God and God as ratio essendi
of faith--is circular reasoning. The audience for the
proofs are thus those atheists who are among the rational.
Since natural reason speaks to natural reason the Meditations
is a philosophical rather than a theological work, though
still, apparently, for the purpose of apologetics. But
since, according to the Discourse, theology concerns
transrational revealed truth, the Meditations' apology
is suspect.

The shift from theology to philosophy concerning both
method and objective is made explicit when the atheists
are dropped as the audience. Because "there are not so
many in the world who are fitted for metaphysical
speculations,"[85] Descartes writes to the "few [who] give
themselves to the search after truth" rather than "the
greater number [who] arrogantly combat the most important
of truths."[86] The division between the few rational and
many nonrational replaces that between the atheistic rational
and faithful nonrational. This mental typology is analogous
to that concerning Descartes' imitators in the Discourse.
Since the atheists qua atheists are no longer addressed,

the rational proofs of God and of the immortal soul cannot
be for the purpose of conversion. Such proofs are apparently
for the purpose of scientific foundations, though it is
hard to see the relation between the soul's immortality
and the philosophy of science.

The letter concludes by giving two "justifications"
for Sorbonne protection of the apologetic Meditations.
Descartes collapses the philosophy (reason)-theology (faith)
division of labor and misstates the relation between the
Sorbonne and the atheists. He says that the Sorbonne's
imprimator is necessary because, next to the Sacred Councils,
the Sorbonne exerts the greatest possible authority, "not
only in what concerns the faith, but also in what regards
human philosophy as well."[87] Descartes goes so far as
to request corrections from the Sorbonne. Given what we
have seen concerning Descartes' estimate of critics, this
request is surely prudential. And to claim that the Sorbonne
exerts philosophical authority is not to claim that it
possesses philosophical truth. The irony continues when
he tells the Sorbonne that "your authority will cause the
atheists, who are usually more arrogant than learned or
judicious, to rid themselves of their spirit of
contradiction."[88] In addition to the hyperbolic statement
of Sorbonne authority (for it is still a question of thought
versus action), this passage completes the transition from
the original distinction of atheists-faithful to few
rational-many nonrational by grouping the atheists among
the nonrational many. The Meditations is thus dedicated
to the few rational, those free thinkers who are not
influenced by Sorbonne authority. To request the protection
of the Sorbonne is to request protection from those who
are so influenced--the faithful learned, the chief organ
for which is the Sorbonne itself. Since the Sorbonne is
the defender of the faith, Descartes seeks its protection
lest it judge the Meditations to contain anything heretical.

The closing flattery concerning Sorbonne authority
over the atheists misrepresents the only kind of appeal
that could be effective given the moral nature of most
men and atheists in particular--rationally grounded fear
and hope. As Descartes says, "inasmuch as often in this
life greater rewards are offered for vice than for virtue,
few would prefer the right to the useful, were they
restrained neither by the fear of God nor the expectation
of another life."[89] The point was made more graphically
in Discourse V: "For next to the error of denying God
. . . there is none which is more effectual in leading
feeble spirits from the straight path of virue, than to
imagine that the soul of the brute is of the same nature
as our own, and that in consequence, after this life we
have nothing to fear or to hope for, any more than the
flies and ants."[90] The Discourse passage derives virtue
from religion. The Sorbonne Letter implies their separation
since natural reason is to persuade infidels "of any

religion, indeed, we may almost say, of any moral virtue."[91]
"Often in this life" refers to the many whose morality
requires pleasures and pains beyond this life, the
implication being that, however seldom, there are the few
whose virtue does not require such religious support.

In the Sorbonne Letter, then, Descartes has prepared
the following reading of the Meditations. It is rationalist
philosophy which potentially conflicts with faith. My
aim in what follows is to show how the heretical potential
of the Meditations is made actual by the way in which its
theological metaphysics deflects from its true metaphysical
foundation as reiteration of the epistemic-ontic correlation
of the Regulae. It is such an epistemic-ontic correlation
which is responsible for what amounts to the self-grounding
of Cartesian physics as method.

2
HYPERBOLIC DOUBT

Cartesian doubt is a method for the overcoming of theoretical prejudices in the interest of establishing solid foundations for the sciences. At the same time, as the enactment of the first rule of method of the Discourse, the launching of the doubt is a practice, a practice made possible by a prior overcoming of that other prejudice--one's prephilosophical soul. Since, as the Discourse has shown, the doubt as a necessary first step is ultimately in the interest of certainty required for action, the beginning of doubt in the Meditations is not pure or originary. Cartesian doubt is thus a theoretical practice. As he says, "I should feel that I was doing wrong were I to occupy in deliberation the time that yet remains to me for action."[1] Doubt requires a certain disposition. As we have seen, the passage from childhood to maturity is not enough. The passions must be mastered. But Descartes attributes his freedom from passions and cares to the fact that he is no longer troubled by them. Apparently nature has favored Descartes with a disposition conducive to philosophizing, i.e., with a willful resolve to transcend the natural attitude and its teachings.

The Cartesian way of doubt is central to the argument for the Cartesian soul as res cogitans (exclusively mind or consciousness). The motive for such a conception is the apparent grounding of objectivity (whose index is mathematical certitude) upon subjectivity. In the interest of a metaphysical, that is, nonscientific, foundation for Cartesian science (which is considered nonexistent during this enterprise) the ego cogito emerges as a successful rejoinder to what appears as a thoroughgoing skepticism at the conclusion of Meditation I. This skepticism is personified by the hypothesis of the evil genius as a presumably omnipotent deceiver. The cogito, in resisting such a deceiver, establishes itself as the desired "Archimedian point" of certainty. This locus of subjective certainty functions as a presuppositionless and indubitable "first principle," on the basis of which can be demonstrated

the existence of a benevolent God, who in turn must provide
the guarantee of Cartesian science by conferring validity
upon "clear and distinct" ideas. Notwithstanding the
well-known difficulties afflicting the theology of the
Meditations (problems concerning the proofs of God and
the much debated issue of epistemic circularity involving
God and the criterion of clarity and distinctness), that
Descartes' strategy involves confronting an omnipotent
deceiver at the inception of Meditation II is agreed upon
by most contemporary commentators.[2] I will try to show
that the majority view is mistaken and consequently fails
to disclose the genuine methodological achievement of
Cartesian doubt and thereby the foundational role of the
cogito. A consistent interpretation of the doubt argument
confronts the following problems surrounding, as well as
within, Meditation I. Concerning the theology of the
Meditations, if we maintain that the doubt is universal,
such that the evil genius is a mythical deceiver-God, the
internal logic of the Meditations is threatened. Given
the fact that the cogito defeats such an omnipotent deceiver,
the reentry of God in Meditation III as a threat to reason
appears, as Kennington points out, redundant.[3] The logic
of the Meditations suggests a) that the deceiver concluding
Meditation I is not omnipotent, b) that the cogito asserts
itself in the face of a nonuniversal doubt, and c) that
the reappearance of God in Meditation III sets the stage
for the true theological problem in the Meditations--the
contest between God and human reason. Without at this
point judging the success or failure of Descartes' theodicy,
it would appear that the opinion of those who assert the
victory of natural reason over God due to the invincibility
of the cogito in the face of an omnipotent God in Meditation
II is premature.

This forces a consideration of the rivalry between
the cogito and God for the title of "first principle,"
for there can be but one Archimedian point, and thus focuses
the issue between the sincerity and insincerity
interpretations. The structure of the doubt bears on this
issue in the following way. If the doubt is not in fact
universal (such that God is removed from Meditation I to
reappear in Meditation III, i.e., on the condition that
the articulation of the cogito must precede this
reappearance) the following is suggested. God must follow
the cogito because the cogito is the principal means of
proving God. This cogito-dependency of God, rather than
a proof of God from nature (which, as Meditation IV explains,
is not possible because it depends upon fathoming God's
inscrutable will) implies that the cogito is the true "first
principle" (not to mention the fact, as we have seen, that
even according to the more orthodox view the cogito resists
an omnipotent deceiver). But this conclusion is also
premature, for the precise meaning of "first principle"
is as yet unclarified. Does Descartes mean by a "principle"

that which is "first for us" ("first for me" is more accurate concerning the cogito) or "first by nature"? As we have seen, the difficulty concerning the status of the cogito as a principle is illustrated by the tree of philosophy in the preface to the Principles, where both God and the human soul ambiguously function as metaphysical roots. Is Descartes' Archimedian point epistemological or ontological? The distinction between the orders of knowing and being thus bears heavily on fixing the status of the cogito as "first principle."

Concerning the necessity of the doubt argument in the first place, if the cogito is truly a first principle whose intuitive self-certainty is irrefutable, why must it emerge from a discursive argument concerning dubitables? Perhaps the need for the doubt lies not ·so much in its role as the revealer of the cogito but in its relation to the subsequent question concerning the nature of what is revealed, the "what I am" rather than the "that I am."

What prevents such a doubt--such a severe criterion of indubitability--from being sterile? Why does Descartes appear to run the risk of total skepticism on the one hand or the discovery of an indubitable but perhaps trivial or barren first truth on the other? That this truth is indeed a first principle raises the suspicion that the structure of the doubt is guided by its conclusion--an incorporeal, cognitively pure res cogitans.

Cartesian doubt should not be construed as either a genuine or methodological skepticism, although this is the predominant view. Bernard Williams writes:

> The doubt about the possibility of knowledge will be a sceptical doubt, and seen as a response to this, the Method of Doubt takes on the form of pre-emptive scepticism, which serves the aim of answering sceptical doubts by taking them as far as they can be taken and coming out on the other side. . . . [It is] important that this should not be seen as a purely gratuitous demand, a merely obsessional concern with an artificial scepticism.[4]

Descartes distinguishes his doubt from skepticism in several ways, such that the overcoming of doubt by the cogito is not a refuge from skepticism. Unlike the Skeptics, who doubt all for the sake of uncertainty, Descartes resolves to doubt to achieve certainty. He doubts to show the limitations inherent in the attempt. In a letter to Hyperaspistes, Descartes says of the Skeptics that "It is only in name, and perhaps in intention and resolve, that they adhere to their heresy of doubting everything."[5]

Total skepticism can be but a pretense because of its self-refuting character. In the same letter: "certainly I have never denied that the Skeptics themselves, as long as they clearly perceive some truth, spontaneously assent to it."[6] Socratic ignorance is also suspect because "If Socrates says he doubts everything, it follows necessarily that he knows this at least--that he doubts. Likewise he knows that something can be either true or false, and so on, for all those consequences necessarily attach to the nature of doubt."[7] In the Search After Truth Descartes links Socratic ignorance to Pyrrhonism, "water so deep that one cannot find any footing in it."[8] A truly universal skepticism, it would appear, is both impossible and pointless.

Cartesian doubt is not a gradual transition from uncertainty, or opinion, to certainty, or knowledge. The doubt sublimates from ignorance (the dubitable equated with the false) to knowledge (truth as indubitability). Certainty does not evolve from the purging of uncertainty; it confronts it as an immovable object. Consequently, there is no Cartesian counterpart to Platonic true opinion or the Aristotelian naturally constituted way from what is first for us to what is first by nature. The cogito of Meditation II is presented as an unmediated truth.

The genuine methodological significance of the doubt is revealed in the way in which it accomplishes the critique of prescientific experience. The issue concerns the extent to which the critique of the cognitive faculties depends upon the prior Cartesian notion of body as mathematical extendedness. In what follows I try to show how the doubt embodies a dogmatic intrusion of Cartesian science at pivotal points into the critique of prescientific experience. I will argue that a Cartesian circle of the following type infects the presumably presuppositionless doubt procedure. The doubt procedure requires that Cartesian science be considered nonexistent during the search for its foundations. However, its doctrines are used to drive the critique of the cognitive faculties from sense to imagination to intellect. There occurs an epistemic-ontic regression (which shows Meditation I as the reiteration of the Regulae XII epistemic-ontic correlation) in which the order of the cognitive faculties parallels the order and dependence of their respective objects. That is to say, the separation of the soul into the cognitive powers of sense, imagination, and intellect is the correlate of a prior ontic stratification of sensory properties, pure images, and ultimately res extensa. The fulcrum about which this epistemic-ontic regression revolves is the transformation of perceptions into images by the dream hypothesis. This in turn facilitates the reduction of the essence of body to mathematically understood extension. And since the mathematicals resist the evil genius, there results the

Cartesian circle of a presumably nonexistent science serving as the rationale for the critique of prescientific experience.

As Descartes explains in the synopsis of Meditation I, the purpose of the doubt is to detach the mind from the senses. The importance of such detachment is reiterated to Pierre Gassendi: "My statement that the entire testimony of the senses must be considered to be uncertain, nay, even false, is quite serious and so necessary for the comprehension of my meditations that he who will not or cannot admit that, is unfit to urge any objection to them."[9] In the Principles, as we have seen, sense testimony is said to be the "first and principal of our errors."[10] The doubt is thus a means of cognitive liberation intended to disclose a domain of theoretical purity--a region of thinking unencumbered by sensory prejudice--and in a twofold manner: internally (epistemically) by transcending the senses and passions as the ways in which the prephilosophical, embodied soul is prejudiced by such embodiment; externally (ontically) by casting doubt on the existence of sensory objects, significantly including the body of the doubter. This dual critique prepares the nonbodily res cogitans cognizing apparently incorporeal objects, the "ideas" of Meditation III. The clue to the doubt is thus the suppression of bodily existence, which in turn permits the cogito to emerge as a first principle--a region of thinking, but one whose genesis or possible dependence upon body is left indeterminate, or metaphysically neutral.

The rhetorical strategy employed in the doubt argument is that of hyperbole. When in Meditation VI Descartes characterizes the doubt as a whole and its dream phase in particular he concedes that they are "hyperbolical and ridiculous." Yet in neither Meditation I nor VI does he explain the precise nature of the hyperbole. The following have been proposed as hyperbolic indicators. In the first place, if Descartes were seriously concerned about distinguishing wakefulness from dreaming, he would not wait until the conclusion of Meditation VI to resolve the dilemma. Such irresolution on Descartes' part implies, as some have observed, that the metaphysics of the Meditations (the proofs of God and His veracity instrumental to the coherence criteria of wakefulness) is worked out by a dreaming metaphysician.[11] On the other hand, if such a metaphysics has the same type and degree of certainty as mathematical demonstration (which would appear to be a genuinely hyperbolic claim) perhaps this dreaming metaphysics is not undermined, since Descartes claims in Meditation I that the truths of mathematics are neutral to the waking-dreaming distinction. (The relation between dreaming and mathematics will be discussed below.) The critiques of sensation and imagination contain what appear to be 1) an unacknowledged hyperbole (the disproportion between reasons for doubting and reasons for rejecting the senses), 2) the abandonment of an acknowledged hyperbole (the insanity hypothesis), and 3) the hyperboles acknowledged in Meditation VI (the dream doubt in particular and its suspension of bodily existence personified by the evil genius). In what follows I argue that it is the evil genius inspired doubt that testifies to the hyperbolic character of the doubt as a whole and that the hyperbolic insanity hypothesis, withdrawn from the critique of sensation as such, is methodologically reintroduced to make more plausible the assumption of dreaming, which is instrumental to the transition from the critique of sensation to the critique of the imagination.

EPISTEMIC-ONTIC REGRESSION

Doubt of the senses procedes by a dialectical examination (reason for doubting countered by reason for believing countered by reason for rejection) to show that sensing is dependent upon imaging. What appears as the initial hyperbole involves the move from sometimes deception to total rejection of the senses. Although the rationale of doubt of never trusting what has proven fallible seems plausible considering the rigorous demand of indubitability, as a strict rule of inference it appears hyperbolic. According to Leibniz the doubt rationale, to be more precise, should read: "it is necessary, with regard to each thing, to consider the degree of assent or reserve that it merits, or, more simply, it is necessary to examine the reasons for each assertion."[12] Kennington offers the following response to the charge of hyperbole:

> Doubt partakes of the practical character of natural reason; 'reason is a universal instrument' (Discourse V, para. 10). It is 'prudent', says Descartes, 'not to trust entirely to anything by which we have been deceived,' and the senses deceive. . . . Cartesian doubt demands that if there is some one reason for doubting a thing, it must be totally rejected. Its rationality is the requirement that a ratio dubitandi be present. The inference from the ratio dubitandi to the total rejection is hyperbolic and arbitrary until the underlying practical intention is recognized. Ultimately, all things will be doubted which can be denied without contradiction. All the sensible or factual will be doubted for, as with Hume, 'the contrary of every matter of fact is still possible . . . it

> can never imply a contradiction.' For
> Descartes one existent will resist
> this test of logical possibility.[13]

Kennington's point is well taken. The rationale of doubt,
that "all things will be doubted which can be denied without
contradiction," is nonhyperbolic. Yet Descartes does not
consistently apply it. If wholesale sensory rejection
and the assumption of dreaming are not hyperbolic because
noncontradictory, why not apply the same principle to the
madness hypothesis that follows? Descartes' only response
to the possibility that he is like the insane, "whose
cerebella are so troubled by the violent vapours of black
bile," is to say "they are mad, and I should not be any
less insane were I to follow examples so extravagant."[14]
Descartes rejects the hypothesis of madness as hyperbolic.
Although it is true that the assumption of madness, because
of its consequences for the reliability of reason, is more
detrimental to the course of inquiry than the complete
rejection of sensation, and although it is true that the
ratio dubitandi of sanity is weaker than that of sensation
and wakefulness, the logically consistent application of
the rationale of doubt requires the assumption of madness.
No matter how slight the ratio dubitandi of sanity, to
assume madness is not to contradict oneself. The
nonapplication of the doubt rationale to the madness aporia
therefore shows a perhaps necessary asymmetry (to avoid
bringing the inquiry to a halt through an assumption of
incorrigible irrationality and sensory deception) in the
ratio dubitandi-ratio credendi dialectic. At the same
time, Descartes will do partial justice to the madness
aporia by employing it within the dream doubt.

THE DREAM ARGUMENT

Hyperbolic or not, the initial total rejection of
sensation is amended in favor of size-distance corrigibility.
The Leibniz suggestion of a discursive approach to sensory
deception would be necessary if it really were a question
of determining which sensory opinions are reliable. But
since Descartes' purpose is to discredit sensation as such
as a valid cognitive principle, if the principle underlying
both deceptive and veridical sensory opinions is found
defective the senses fall in toto and the Leibniz critique
is undercut. The senses are eliminated not due to problems
of range or precision, but due to the conditions under
which they may be operating--physiologically based insanity
and dreaming. Following the dismissal of the insanity
hypothesis as hyperbolic, Descartes presents what I will
refer to as the dream doubt proper:

> At the same time I must remember that
> I am a man, and that consequently I
> am in the habit of sleeping, and in
> my dreams representing to myself the
> same things or sometimes even less
> probable things, than do those who
> are insane in their waking moments.
> How often has it happened to me that
> in the night I dreamt that I found
> myself in this particular place, that
> I was dressed and seated near the fire,
> whilst in reality I was lying undressed
> in bed! At this moment it does indeed
> seem to me that it is with eyes awake
> that I am looking at this paper; that
> this head which I move is not asleep,
> that it is deliberately and of set
> purpose that I extend my hand and
> perceive it; what happens in sleep
> does not appear so clear nor so distinct
> as does all this. But in thinking
> over this I remind myself that on many
> occasions I have in sleep been deceived
> by similar illusions, and in dwelling
> carefully on this reflection I see
> so manifestly that there are no certain
> indications by which we may clearly
> distinguish wakefulness from sleep
> that I am lost in astonishment. And
> my astonishment is such that it is
> almost capable of persuading me that
> I now dream.[15]

Descartes' extremely compressed argument aims to
establish that there are no signs of a content or qualitative
nature to distinguish dreaming from wakefulness when isolated
episodes are compared, thereby precluding the Meditation
VI proofs of such a distinction. In order to make the
strongest case for the rejection of the content criterion,
however, he must make use of the possibility of insanity
initially dismissed as hyperbolic. If wakefulness were
restricted to the psychologically (that is, physiologically)
normal, the occurrence of bizarre dreams differentiates
the waking and dreaming states. If wakefulness also includes
the insane, the bizarre dreams of the sane cannot
differentiate the two states. As long as waking insanity
remains a possibility, every conceivable dream, regardless
of content, can have a waking counterpart. A bizarre
experience can testify to Descartes' normal dreaming or
insane wakefulness, even though the latter possibility
reintroduces irremedial skepticism. But we must remember
that Descartes wants to give only the impression that,
insofar as isolated dream and waking episodes are compared,

wakefulness and dreaming cannot be distinguished. His motive for this seeming aporia becomes clear from the sequel.

After observing that he cannot distinguish between all such episodes in terms of clarity and distinctness, Descartes confesses to be "lost in astonishment." The insanity option is instrumental in producing Descartes' astonishment; however, its use produces a troublesome ambiguity concerning the status of the doubter in Meditation I. On the one hand, the nature of the doubter-dreamer appears unproblematic. It is clearly the mind-body composite, the "true man" of the Discourse. On the other hand, the doubter can be construed as res cogitans, which precludes an assumption of physiologically based insanity whether hyperbolic or reasonable. Leon Pearl presents the "true man" account:

> Descartes is presenting a person who is philosophizing for the first time. When such a person first entertains the possibility that he may never have been awake, he does not immediately conceive himself to be a disembodied mind fabricating dreams, but rather a living human, which includes his body, sleeping throughout a lifetime with his body supplying his imagination with data for the construction of his dreams. . . . at no point does he consider his own mind as the possible agent, for he has not yet developed a concept of mind as a result of which he could entertain this as a possibility. He does not articulate such a concept until the Second Meditation . . . . since he has yet no conception of himself as distinct from his body, in the doubting the existence of the physical world, he is indirectly doubting his own existence.[16]

Pearl equates Descartes' order of presentation with the order of the argument. That this is not the case is indicated by the way in which res cogitans can be seen inhabiting Meditation I. In Meditation II Descartes describes the res cogitans as "a thing which doubts, understands, [conceives], affirms, denies, wills, refuses, which also imagines and feels."[17] In the sequel he explains the different senses in which "imagines and feels" refer to mind and body. The attribute of "doubts" (indeed, all the rest) is unequivocally mental. The implication that the doubting Descartes must be in some sense abstracted from his body is made explicit in The Search After Truth

when he says, "what I am, inasmuch as I doubt, is in no
wise what I call my body."[18] The suppression of body in
favor of res cogitans is in fact the core of the doubt
from its inception, since "doubting of my body, I should
at the same time doubt of myself, and this I cannot do."[19]
In this sense Descartes' subsequent presentation of the
res cogitans as surviving bodily doubt is question-begging
since doubting presupposes res cogitans. That the evil
genius has not yet rendered body doubtful is also beside
the point since the activity of doubting, regardless of
its object, is an implicit body denial concerning the
doubter. At the same time, the activities of sensing,
imaging, and dreaming, as well as the earlier reference
to Descartes' control over his cares and passions, clearly
attest to the presence of the "true man" in Meditation
I, such that a methodological ambiguity concerning the
status of the doubter and the res cogitans persists through
the first two Meditations. The relevance of this ambiguity
in the present context concerns the legitimacy of the bodily
based insanity hypothesis.   Given   the   above   difficulty
with the insanity hypothesis, why must Descartes include
it? As we have seen, it is instrumental in establishing
a one-to-one correspondence between any conceivable dreaming
and waking content. According to Anthony Kenny, "The
question, 'How do I know that I am not mad?' is one of
great philosophical interest. It is not pursued, possibly
because it might seem offensive to the reader (AT X, 510;
HRI, 314), but is replaced by the question, 'How do I know
that I am not dreaming'?."[20] A more plausible reason is
given by Harry G. Frankfurt. "His point is clearly that
dreaming is a nonpathological equivalent of madness.
Descartes recognizes that it is not appropriate for him
to attack the testimony of his senses with the suggestion
that he may be abnormal. So he considers an analogue of
madness that involves no abnormality."[21] While this may
be Descartes' intent, it appears that his insanity must
logically remain a possibility in order for the argument
to be comprehensive (even though the ratio dubitandi of
wakefulness, as we have seen, does not have to be this
strong). For as we have seen, a comparison between the
dreams of the sane and the wakefulness of the sane produces
a waking-dreaming distinction when bizarre dreams are
considered since sane dream life comprises the entirety
of sane waking life plus the bizarre (the extremely unlikely
and the physically, though not perhaps the logically,
impossible so long as only dream images are considered).
To eliminate bizarre experiences as a criterion of dreaming,
Descartes' insanity must remain an alternative. If not,
he could not summarily be "lost in astonishment." Unless
insanity remains a possibility, all that one could say
is that every waking experience has a dreamt correlate,
but that the correlation in the reverse direction breaks
down in the face of the bizarre.

As far as Descartes' objective in <u>Meditation</u> I of discrediting the senses is concerned, however, it would appear that all that is required is the correlation from wakefulness to dreams. And this is done in <u>Meditation</u> VI. Ostensibly rehearsing the dream argument, Descartes states that "I never have believed myself to feel anything in waking moments which I cannot also sometimes believe myself to feel when I sleep."[22] The insanity reference is dropped. Since this correlation from waking to dream life is sufficient to cast doubt on sane waking testimony, and establishes sane bizarre dreams as distinguishable from sane wakefulness, why does Descartes employ the more comprehensive sane dream-insane wakefulness comparison in <u>Meditation</u> I? My suggestion is that the intent of the dream doubt in <u>Meditation</u> I is other than that in <u>Meditation</u> VI. The <u>Meditation</u> VI account uses dream experience to doubt bodily existence by generating a doubt concerning the cause-and-effect relation between bodies and perceptions. As Descartes says, "as I do not think that these things which I seem to feel in sleep proceed from objects outside of me, I do not see any reason why I should have this belief regarding objects which I seem to perceive while awake."[23] That is, whereas our senses are not stimulated during dreams yet dream images arise, perhaps we spontaneously generate (by some hidden faculty) perceptions during wakefulness. In <u>Meditation</u> I, however, the senses and imagination are not completely severed from bodies during dreams because the relation of copy to original replaces the relation of cause and effect between images and bodies.

We have reached the point at which Descartes, though not totally convinced that he is dreaming ("my astonishment is such that it is almost capable of persuading me that I now dream"), allows his astonishment to go unresolved in order to continue the epistemic-ontic regression. By so doing he adumbrates a similar strategy employed in <u>Meditation</u> II. After recounting his predoubt conception of body as thoughtless and lifeless, Descartes says, "on the contrary, I was rather astonished to find that faculties similar to them existed in some bodies."[24] He refrains from resolving the soul-body <u>aporia</u> in <u>Meditation</u> II in order to explicate the nature of the soul in abstraction from the body. Analogously, in <u>Meditation</u> I the unresolved dream <u>aporia</u> is the first stage of an explication of the nature of the essence of body which begins by abstracting images from their sensory origin. That the astonishment in <u>Meditations</u> I and II is rhetorical rather than sincere is evident from Descartes' account of "astonishment" in the <u>Passions</u> as "an excess of wonder which can never be otherwise than bad"[25] because it produces irresolution. However, irresolution is valuable (so long as it lasts no longer than necessary) because it permits time for deliberation.[26] In <u>Meditation</u> I such irresolution is temporarily in order because it facilitates the move from sensing to imaging.

Following the dream doubt proper Descartes says "Now let us assume that we are asleep [rather than the equally logically possible awake but insane] and that all these particulars, e.g., that we open our eyes, shake our head, extend our hands, and so on, are but false delusions; and let us reflect that possibly neither our hands nor our whole body are such as they appear to us to be."[27] This hypothesis of an incorporeal dreamer implies the causal break between bodies and images made explicit in Meditation VI, but such a hypothesis is provisional at this stage of Meditation I.

Thus far the heterogeneity between perceptions and bodies rests on the assumption of dreaming and its transformation of the perceptions of the dreamer's own body into autonomously generated dream images. However, their autonomous genesis does not preclude a dependence concerning their content. As Descartes explains, "At the same time we must at least confess that the things which are represented to us in sleep are like painted representations which can only have been formed as the counterparts of something real and true, and that in this way those general things at least, i.e., eyes, a head, hands, and a whole body, are not imaginary things, but things really existent."[28] Since copies require originals, the dream assumption, while serving its purpose of metaphorically drawing attention to the image character of perceptions, does not as such jeopardize material existence. It would appear that the dream imagination is equivalent to the empirical imagination of Meditation II, which "is nothing else than to contemplate the figure or image of a corporeal thing."[29]

The nagging dependence of such images on existent bodies is removed by the transition from the empirically based dream imagination to the pure imagination of (nondreaming) painters. The dream doubt proper is temporarily bracketed and the analysis turns from the question of the relation of copy (images) to original (bodies) to the nature of the limits of the nonempirical, creative imagination. These limits turn out to be synonymous with the res extensa of Cartesian science. The creative imagination is limited first by sensed particulars (novel composites require previously sensed particulars) and then by color. And color and the general things (eyes, heads, hands, and the like) in turn depend upon "other objects yet more simple and more universal, which are real and true . . . and of these . . . all these images . . . whether true and real or false and fantastic, are formed."[30] The sequel unambiguously asserts that the imagination and its images, whether empirical or a priori, are grounded in the simple natures constituting Cartesian science:

> To such a class of things pertains
> corporeal nature in general, and its
> extension, the figure of extended things,
> their quantity or magnitude and number,
> as also the place in which they are,
> the time which measures their duration,
> and so on.[31]

Pearl, who fails to appreciate the temporary _epoche_ of
the dream assumption at this point, refers to the "crucial
difference between the introduction of the simples in the
Regulae and in the _First Meditation_":

> In the former work they are the objects
> of intellectual intuition, whereas
> in the _First Meditation_ Descartes
> discovers them by inspecting what he
> considers might possibly be dream objects
> and events. . . . in the _First
> Meditation_, the fact that these simple
> natures are found together and are
> the ultimate elements of physical
> existence is a contingent truth which
> might have been otherwise.[32]

Since Descartes says that images, "whether true and real
or false and fantastic," depend upon the simple natures,
it is clear that the simple natures represent the _a priori_
possibilities of objects as such.[33] The ontology of _Regulae_
XII, in which Descartes argues that "it is certain that
the infinitude of figures suffices to express all the
differences in sensible things,"[34] is dogmatically asserted
here in _Meditation_ I and implicitly resolves the doubt
concerning the causal connection between perceptions and
bodies subsequently raised in _Meditations_ I and VI.
Cartesian science does double duty in _Meditation_ I. The
ultimate _ratio dubitandi_ of perception is the essence of
body as _res extensa_. And, as the mechanical theory of
perception in _Meditation_ VI shows, it is as the effects
of _res extensa_ upon our sense organs that perceptions arise.

INTELLECT AND MATHEMATICS

The Cartesian universals and the pure intellect have
thus far escaped doubt due to their nonempirical and
apparently self-evident nature. The question about reason
and mathematics thus becomes one of origins rather than
contents _per se_. Instead of a critical analysis of reason
and its truths, the argument shifts from epistemology and
ontology to anthropology ("the author of my being"). The
final phase of doubt progresses from a theistic account
of Descartes' origin, which is replaced by an atheistic

account, which in turn is replaced by the evil genius. The threat to reason turns on the relation between these components of the final doubt phase, specifically the identity of the evil genius. Does the evil genius represent the malevolent God, atheistic materialism, or something else?

After stating the belief (i.e., the opinion, which would seem to disqualify this belief in conformity with the requirement of doubt) that he has been created as he is by an all-powerful God, Descartes raises the possibility of the fallibility of reason in the form of systematic and total deception concerning both mathematics and material existence. God may have created us prone to such errors if He is all-powerful and evil. Our being deceived is taken as the anthropocentric sign of God's possible malevolence. As Descartes says:

> But possibly God has not desired that
> I should be thus deceived, for He is
> said to be supremely good. If, however,
> it is contrary to this goodness to
> have made me such that I constantly
> deceive myself, it would also appear
> contrary to His goodness to permit
> me to be sometimes deceived, and
> nevertheless I cannot doubt that he
> does permit this.[43]

Reason is dubitable if God's power is in the service of an evil will. Differently stated, God's goodness is not an attribute that analytically inheres in the concept of God as do omnipotence, omniscience, and creativity. The possibility of God's evil is indicated in two ways. First, God is said, not known, to be good; His goodness is merely hearsay. Second, since the permissibility of deception at some times attests to God's malevolence, what prevents the deception by one so powerful from being total? If reason is created by such an omnipotent and evil God, it errs systematically.

But to understand the precise mode of its errors we must be aware of that other question of origins, that concerning the mathematical truths themselves, for God is said to be the creator of the epistemic-ontic dyad reason-mathematics. That the mathematical truths have an origin is indicated by Descartes not in the <u>Meditations</u> but in the Correspondence and Replies. While the absence of the doctrine of the divine creation of the eternal truths in <u>Meditation</u> I is plausible since the theology upon which it depends (the goodness of God's will) has yet to be argued, the challenge to reason of the created status of such truths would appear to be the following. If God arbitrarily creates the eternal truths and his will is not known to be benevolent in creating our intellects, how can we claim that our logical

and mathematical thinking is in accord with these divinely
decreed truths? What is contradictory or clear and distinct
to human reason may in fact not be so. An omnipotent God
may desire to create truths judged contradictory by human
reason. The absence of the doctrine of the divine creation
of the external truths means that the intrinsic cogency
or self-evidence of mathematics to human reason is never
directly questioned. To human reason these are the simplest
things conceivable. Hence the critique takes the form
of a suspicion concerning the origin of the faculty. The
vindication of the faculty vindicates its "subjectively"
certain truths. But the vindication via a proof of a good
God is not immediately forthcoming. Instead, in the name
of piety and at the same time to confront the atheists
referred to in the Letter to the Sorbonne, the supposition
of an all-powerful (and perhaps evil) God is retracted
(not to reappear until Meditation III) and its place is
taken by the atheistic supposition regarding the origin
and status of human reason.

The suggestion of an omnipotent but perhaps evil God
is to be regarded as a fable and therefore replaced as
the ratio dubitandi of reason by the atheistic suggestion
that reason's origin is materialistic. Referring to the
atheists:

> nevertheless in whatever way they suppose
> that I have arrived at the state of
> being that I have reached--whether
> they attribute it to fate or to accident,
> or make out that it is by a continual
> succession of antecedents, or by some
> other method--since to err and deceive
> myself is a defect, it is clear that
> the greater will be the probability
> of my being so imperfect as to deceive
> myself ever, as is the author to whom
> they assign my origin the less
> powerful.[44]

Anticipating the ontological proportionality of cause and
effect employed in Meditation III, what is asserted is
an inverse relation between the power causing his origin
and the likelihood of deception, in which the least powerful
origin of his being entails the greatest likelihood of
perpetual deception. Descartes' anthropology enters as
the threat to reason via its perhaps corporeal origin,
which is said to be more threatening than creation by an
omnipotent evil God. If not an omnipotent and veracious
God (the most powerful and intelligent cause of my being),
but the chance interplay of mechanical and blind matter
(the least powerful and intelligent cause of my being)
is the source of my coming into being and attaining my

present status (we have pointed to the "true man"-res
cogitans ambiguity in Meditation I), the threat to reason
becomes twofold. On the one hand, the very existence of
mind is jeopardized; on the other hand, its claim to
cognitive validity is dubitable. If matter is my origin
it is hard to explain the being of mind as more than
epiphenomenal. The transnatural status of the intellect
required for cognitive purity is hard to account for on
a material base. Apart from the question of mind coming
from nonmind, the nonintelligent and blind nature of this
originating matter makes it sheer chance that there can
be a correspondence between human reason as clear and
distinct cognition and the ultimate being of nature.

     This materialistic hypothesis is actually a compound
of three subhypotheses of varying meaning. As Descartes
puts it, "fate . . . accident, or . . . a continual
succession of antecedents" perhaps brings him into being.
This atheistic materialism thus includes fatalism, chance,
and mechanical necessity. Kennington stresses the link
between fate and chance, regarding this materialism as
Lucretian and hence detrimental to reason, while Caton
stresses the connection between fate and necessity, judging
this materialism to be Stoic providence and hence favorable
to reason.[45] Though the Kennington view would appear to
be more plausible since the atheistic hypothesis is
introduced as the more damaging to reason, Descartes himself
does not distinguish between or indicate a preference for
one of the three subhypotheses. In Meditation I none of
these various atheisms is pursued. Instead, it is at this
point that the celebrated evil genius makes his appearance.

THE EVIL GENIUS

     The replacement of the theistic and the atheistic
hypotheses by that of the evil genius is the key to the
final stage of doubt and determines to some extent the
cogito and theodicy discussions that follow. A first clue
to the identity of the evil genius is its place within
the argument. It follows the atheistic account of genesis,
appearing perhaps as its continuation. At the same time,
God (whether malevolent or beneficent) has been removed
from Meditation I. As Descartes says when he proposes
the materialistic hypothesis, "There may indeed be those
who would prefer to deny the existence of a God so powerful,
rather than believe that all other things are uncertain.
But let us not oppose them for the present, and grant that
all that is here said of a god is a fable."[46] This suggests,
contrary to the view of L. J. Beck and others,[47] that the
evil genius is not the nonheretical personification of
an omnipotent but evil God, but perhaps the personification
of the atheistic alternative. This is the view of

Kennington, who identifies the evil genius with Cartesian nature.[48]

The more conclusive evidence as to the meaning of the evil genius is the characterization of his degree of power and its correlation with the list of dubitables. Following the interpretation of Kennington (see note 2), I maintain that the evil genius is not synonymous with divine, all-powerful deception because his power is finite since what he renders dubious is limited. Descartes presents the evil genius as follows:

> Therefore I shall suppose, not that the supremely good God, the fountain of truth, but that some evil genius, at the same time extremely powerful and deceiving, has employed all of his efforts in order to deceive me.[49]

Concerning the power of the evil genius, he is not claimed to be omnipotent or a creator in any of his characterizations throughout Meditations I and II. However, it is the correlation between deception and power on the basis of the products of his deception, the revised list of dubitables following the appearance of the evil genius in Meditation I and its reiteration at the beginning of Meditation II, which settles the issue. Neither list mentions mathematics. This omission is crucial since God was introduced to cast doubt not only on all worldly entities but particularly mathematics. The exemption of mathematics implies the finitude of the evil genius and the restriction of doubt to the corporeal.

In line with the rationale of doubt, the exemption of mathematics from doubt implies that the denial of mathematics is contradictory. This is confirmed by Descartes' proclamation in Meditation III in response to a possibly omnipotent evil God: "Let who will deceive me, He can never cause me to be nothing while I think that I am, or some day cause it to be true to say that I have never been, it being true now to say that I am, or that two and three make more or less than five, or any such thing in which I see a manifest contradiction."[50] The reappearance of God renews the threat posed by an omnipotent and perhaps evil deceiver to the validity of human reason. For if the cogito, the paradigm of clear and distinct cognition, overcomes such a deceiver at the beginning of Meditation II, why should an identical deceiver be reintroduced in Meditation III to pose a previously overcome challenge? This does violence to both the logic of the argument and the nature of the theological problem in the latter portions of the Meditations. As Kennington points out, if the evil genius were omnipotent (a mythical evil God), the law of contradiction would be suspended and all

reasoning would come to a halt.[51] The removal of God from
Meditation I is Descartes' postponement of the contest
between God and human reason. And the apparent victory
of reason over God in the passage from Meditation III is
premature prior to a resolution of the question of God's
goodness.

The doubt not intended to be universal, its significance
and the identity of the evil genius are arrived at on the
basis of the list of dubitables. Ontically, what is doubted
is all manner of corporeal existence, including the body
of the doubter. Epistemically, what is rejected is all
testimony regarding body understood by the bodily based
senses and imagination. What are immune from doubt are
the rational truths, the simple natures, apprehended by
the pure intellect.[52] The defect of the faculties of
sensation and imagination consists in their dependence
on such simple natures.[53]

With the removal of God, the rational truths are suspect
if they are thought to reside in an intellect untrustworthy
due to corporeal origins. This suggests, again, that
atheistic materialism, personified by the evil genius,
is the fundamental challenge, which, to repeat, is the
view of Kennington and is based on the finitude of the
evil genius. However, the equation of the evil genius
with atheistic materialism in Meditation I generates a
troublesome paradox concerning the status of body at the
conclusion of the doubt. On such an equation body must
be simultaneously posited and denied since materialism
is said to be responsible for doubt of bodies. Such a
doubt also violates the rationale of doubt concerning the
contradictory. The contradiction concerning the positing
and denying of body is genuine because at this point in
the Meditations the issue is not the likeness of images
to body, which is consistent with an atomism concerning
body, but the very existence of these bodies no matter
how conceived. To save the evil genius from perpetrating
such a contradiction, it seems that an identity other than
omnipotent deceiver and atheistic materialism is necessary
to appreciate the genuine methodological intent of Meditation
I. Remaining faithful to the finitude of the evil genius,
we must identify him with neither God nor nature. The
dream doubt proper had not placed material existence in
doubt, and Cartesian science as the essence of body merely
denies the claim of a likeness between perceptions and
bodies. The evil genius is rather the personification
of bodily doubt by extending the dream assumption. As
Descartes says, "I shall consider that the heavens, the
earth, colours, figures, sound, and all other external
things are nought but the illusions and dreams of which
this genius has availed himself in order to lay traps for
my credulity."[54] The exclusion of mathematics is just
its presuppositionality throughout Meditation I. Although,
as Descartes explains in the synopsis of Meditation VI,

"that there is in truth a world, that men possess bodies
. . . have never been doubted by anyone of sense,"[55] it
is the strategic relation between the doubt and the cogito
which explains the presence of the evil genius in Meditation
I. The denial of body sets the stage for the explication
of the res cogitans as a metaphysically, that is, bodily,
neutral epistemic first principle.

CRITIQUE OF CONTEMPORARY ACCOUNTS

The failure to appreciate Cartesian doubt as an amalgam
of scientific dogmatics and hyperbolic rhetoric has produced
the following accounts of Descartes' doubt strategy.

Sincere Skepticism

The most extreme view of the dream doubt and the view
which most violates the text claims that the dream aporia
is not only sincere but persuasive. David and Jean Beer
Blumenfeld, after reviewing various objections to the dream
argument, conclude that "The dreaming argument is actually
quite strong and it continues to present a serious challenge
to our supposed knowledge of the external world."[56] And
George Nakhnikian states that "I accept the conclusions
of the dream argument. If these conclusions are, indeed,
acceptable, then Descartes' metaphysical defense of
perceptual knowledge is unsuccessful. Hence, his solution
of the problem of the transcendence of the physical world
(and of other minds) is unsuccessful."[57] To read the dream
doubt as a genuine aporia not only ignores the Meditation
I context but contradicts Descartes' explicit statements.
Toward the end of Meditation I Descartes retracts the dream
aporia and in Meditation VI, as we have seen, characterizes
the dream doubt as "hyperbolic and ridiculous." Sensitivity
to Descartes' rhetoric requires a reading of the dream
argument not in terms of its validity or invalidity but
in terms of its function within the epistemic-ontic
regression characterizing Meditation I. To interpret the
dream doubt as genuine skepticism fails to identify the
proper relation between the hyperbole of the assumption
of dreaming personified by the evil genius and the scientific
dogmatics which the dream doubt proper serves by facilitating
the distinction between the essence and existence of body.

Methodological Skepticism

Most interpreters read the dream doubt as
methodological, a provisional skepticism. According to
Beck, the assumption of dreaming is "a mere cautionary

process." "In the same way as it was suggested that because 'the senses sometimes deceive us', therefore we should consider, provisionally be it said, that 'the senses always deceive us' is the only safe maxim, so that the fact that we are sometimes unable to distinguish a dream sequence from a waking sequence is sufficient ground to throw doubt on the distinction between the two states."[58] James Stuart summarizes recent scholarship by distinguishing between the traditional and Frankfurt interpretations. On the traditional interpretation (endorsed by Frederick Copleston, Richard H. Popkin, Kenny, and James J. Walsh), "The dream argument is intended to introduce the possibility that our lives are a dream; since dreaming and waking cannot be distinguished, we might be dreaming."[59] This view accepts the apparent hyperbole of concluding total rejection from sometime deception. The epistemic consequence of this view is that all possible sensory testimony is considered false; the ontic consequence is the reduction of the material world to the status of illusion. The Frankfurt interpretation (endorsed also by Curley and Williams) "rejects the view that 'life is a dream'. Rather, Descartes is making the point that we cannot discriminate between veridical and nonveridical sensory experiences, since we cannot distinguish the dream state from the waking state. Thus instead of the possibility that we might be dreaming all the time, he is raising the possibility that we might be dreaming at <u>any</u> time."[60] This view sees the dream argument doubting whether the senses experience the world rather than doubting worldly existence itself. I agree with Frankfurt that the initial dream argument does not involve denying material existence, though I have argued this on different grounds. Frankfurt distinguishes the dream and evil genius phases of doubt, whereas I read them as the two phases of dream doubt in <u>Meditation</u> I corresponding to the twofold objective concerning the status of sensation and body. The dream doubt proper, the initial dream assumption, prepares the analysis of the essence of body. The reintroduction of the dream assumption in the figure of the evil genius is for the purpose of the hyperbolic denial of material existence. Concerning the question of the scope of the dream doubt, whether it posits the possibility of dreaming all the time versus dreaming at any time, Descartes confirms the traditional interpretation when he says, in <u>Meditation</u> II, "Even though I should always sleep."[61] And this, I take it, is in keeping with the nonhyperbolic meaning of the dream assumption as scientific critique of sensation.

Aside from their points of disagreement, what is significant about these two versions of the methodological skepticism interpretation, as Stuart correctly observes, is that they both take seriously the seeming inability to find a criterion distinguishing wakefulness from dreaming. Although the skepticism is seen as methodological rather

than sincere, these versions of the doubt likewise fail
to capture the meaning of Cartesian rhetoric as hyperbolic
entry into scientific dogmatics.

The Causal Interpretation

Taking issue with the traditional and Frankfurt
accounts, Stuart interprets the dream argument as a metaphor
for a lack of causal relation between bodies and perceptions.
He bases his view in part on what he regards as the
nonautonomous character of the Meditation I argument.
Concerning the scope of the dream doubt, Stuart judges
the traditional and Frankfurt interpretations to be equally
plausible readings of Descartes' intentions (in spite of
Descartes' statement in Meditation II about always sleeping)
solely on the basis of Meditation I and other texts. He
therefore consults Meditation VI, where Descartes argues
(after remarking on the involuntary nature of dreams and
their qualitative likeness to waking life) that since we
do not judge that dream images are caused by bodies, why
should we judge waking experiences, qua images, to be so
caused. That is to say, the qualitative and content
indistinguishability of the two states creates the
possibility that if material bodies are not the objects
of dreaming experience, then perhaps material bodies are
not the objects of waking experience. Stuart gives the
following explanation of the relation between the dream
doubt and the critique of sensation:

> Although the problem of knowing whether
> we are awake or dreaming and the
> difficulty of knowing if we are really
> aware of material objects in our waking
> experiences are both present in
> Meditation I, there is nevertheless,
> only one dream argument. This is an
> argument which Descartes regards as
> calling into question the existence
> of the material world. To that extent,
> the traditional interpretation is
> correct. The route by which Descartes
> arrives at this conclusion, however,
> does not involve our inability to tell
> whether we are dreaming or awake, and,
> therefore, not the possibility that
> our lives are a dream. Rather, our
> inability to know that our waking
> experiences are caused by external
> objects, a belief called into question
> by dreaming, is the ground for our
> doubting the existence of the external
> world.[62]

Stuart's argument was anticipated by Williams, who writes concerning the <u>Meditation</u> VI account that "Descartes regards it as self-evident that if I have veridical perceptions, then I have experiences which are caused by things outside myself. This idea--let us label it the 'causal conception of perception'--is built into the hyperbolical doubt. . . . If this proposition is doubtful, then every perceptual judgement is doubtful."[63]

Stuart correctly sees the relatively minor role played by the uncertainty about wakefulness <u>per se</u> concerning the question of bodily existence, observing that "the existence of external objects is established by Descartes independently of establishing that we know whether we are dreaming or awake."[64] My disagreements with Stuart stem from his claim that the arguments of <u>Meditations</u> I and VI are of a piece in using dream experience as the metaphor for a possible causal chasm between bodies and perceptions, <u>Meditation</u> VI doing explicitly what is done less clearly in <u>Meditation</u> I. <u>Meditation</u> VI clearly questions material existence for the reasons given by Stuart. However, it is a mistake to take this as a recapitulation of <u>Meditation</u> I. As I have suggested, Descartes employs the assumption of dreaming for two purposes. What appears to be an argument doubting existence (the dream doubt proper) is but a preparation for a detour to an investigation of essence. Following the analysis of essence, the dream assumption resumes, in the figure of the evil genius, to suspend bodily existence. This accounts in part for the methodic achievement of <u>Meditations</u> I and II concerning mind and body. In <u>Meditation</u> I the essence of body is determined independently of its existence, whereas in <u>Meditation</u> II the existence of mind is discovered prior to the determination of its bodily or nonbodily essence. The complete <u>Meditation</u> I context must be appreciated to grasp the dual significance of its dream component. Stuart does only partial justice to this context since he omits discussing the relation between dreaming and science, Descartes' abandonment of the dream <u>aporia</u> in <u>Meditation</u> I, and the sense in which the dream doubt is designated by Descartes as "hyperbolical and ridiculous."

To remind us of the hyperbolic nature of the evil genius dream personification, Descartes closes <u>Meditation</u> I by comparing his deceptive waking experiences to the pleasant illusions of a dreaming prisoner. Whereas the prisoner is captivated by his freely created dream images, Descartes is the prisoner of involuntary waking images. Both are enslaved, yet Descartes is an unusual natural slave. Since his slavery to reason has thus far not been impugned, Descartes is still convinced that he knows the essence of those bodies whose existence is perhaps a dream.

The methodological achievement of <u>Meditation</u> I can be summarized as follows. With respect to Cartesian science, the epistemic-ontic regression and the finitude of the

evil genius exempts from doubt the essence of body as clear
and distinct cognition.   This produces the circle whereby
Cartesian science is both cause and resolution of the
critique of prescientific experience.   The doubt of body
by the evil genius prepares the epistemological soul of
Meditation II through the suspension of the anthropological
questions of genesis and soul-body relation.   And the lack
of identity between the evil genius and God sets the stage
for the subsequent controversy between faith and reason
in the Meditations theodicy.

3
THE DUAL CRITIQUE
OF ARISTOTLE

In the letter of 28 January 1641 to Marin Mersenne concerning the objectives of the <u>Meditations</u> Descartes explains

> that these six Meditations contain all the foundations of my Physics. But please do not tell people, for that might make it harder for supporters of Aristotle to approve them. I hope that readers will gradually get used to my principles, and recognize their truth, before they notice that they destroy the principles of Aristotle.[1]

The rhetoric involved in such a destruction is revealed in the advice that Descartes gave Henricus Regius, who had offended the Scholastics with his open avowal of Cartesian mechanicism:

> I should like it best if you never put forward any new opinions, but retained all the old ones in name, and merely brought forward new arguments. This is a course of action to which nobody could take exception, 'and yet those who understand your arguments would spontaneously draw from them the conclusions you had in mind. For instance, why did you openly reject substantial forms and real qualities? Do you not remember that on p. 164 of the French edition of my Meteors, I expressly said that I did not at all reject or deny them, but simply found them unnecessary in setting out my explanations. If you had taken this course, everybody in your audience would have rejected them as soon as they saw they were useless, but you would not have become so unpopular with your colleagues.[2]

In _Meditation_ II Descartes employs an analogous strategy
in his rejection of the Aristotelian soul as the form of
a living body in favor of the soul as exclusively mind
or consciousness, and the rejection of substantial forms
and real qualities in favor of body as mathematical
extension. _Meditation_ II makes more explicit the
epistemic-ontic correlation which served as the true _ratio
dubitandi_ of prescientific experience in _Meditation_ I.
Without appearing to rely upon the doctrines of the still
presumably nonexistent Cartesian science, Descartes
establishes a theory of soul which turns out to be perfectly
suited for the establishment of such a science--an
incorporeal _res cogitans_ whose access to body is in terms
of _res extensa_ as clear and distinct idea. From this
bifurcation automatically follows the rejection of the
Aristotelian accounts of soul and body.

The critiques of Aristotle follow from the threefold
articulation of the knowledge of mind--the indubitability
of its existence, its mode of existence as nonbodily, and
its mediated cognitive relation to the world. In what
follows I defend the _ego sum_, _ego existo_ as intuition rather
than inference (whether syllogistic or enthymematic) and
show the way in which the argument employed in the wax
analysis is in conformity with Cartesian ontology.
Concerning the nature of the soul as exclusively mind or
consciousness, the correlative of which is the doctrine
of bodily automatism, I offer an answer to the following
question: Is the automatism of _Meditation_ II a consequence
of a legitimate argument (namely, that since the soul
of a living mind-body composite is equated with mind or
consciousness, the power of self-motion must be located
exclusively in the body), or is it perhaps a suppressed
premise in an enthymematic argument demonstrating the soul
to be exclusively mind or consciousness?

EGO SUM, EGO EXISTO

Descartes' assertion of radical autonomy reiterates
the "one man" principle with which he opened _Discourse_
II. In _Meditation_ II this autonomy resides in the uniquely
first person certainty of the existence of the "I."
Descartes introduces the "I" as the rebuttal to the doubt
of the previous _Meditation_, that my perceptions concerning
both the existence and nature of physical objects are in
error. This egocentric rebuttal to bodily doubt, however,
is not an overthrowing of such a doubt since body continues
to remain doubtful following the existence of the _cogito_.
This raises the question of the genuine significance of
such a doubt and its location in the argument, since for
Descartes it is absolutely necessary that it precede
Meditation II but at the same time is not a threat to the
indubitability of _ego sum_. The significance of bodily
doubt concerns the problematic move from _ego sum_ to _sum
res cogitans_ as incorporeal first principle. Since the
cogito does not have to resist a putative omnipotent
deceiver, bodily doubt turns out to be but a ground clearing
maneuver in the establishing of _sum res cogitans_. Though
the denial of body is presumably essential in clarifying
the _cogito_'s mode of existence (the _cogito_ must be understood

as res cogitans since it is known to exist while body is presumed nonexistent), it is clearly not necessary concerning existence per se. This is because of the intuitive and incorrigible certainty of the knowledge of one's existence. As we have seen, the nonbodily truths (including the cogito) were removed from doubt with the removal of God from Meditation I. There is also the fact that Cartesian self-certainty, unlike the certainty concerning body and the rational truths, is not faced with a subject-object split. It is more properly an act of reflection. While it appears plausible (though illegitimate, as we will see) to go from the existence of the ego sum and the presumptive nonexistence of body to the incorporeality of the ego sum, mere existence is not and cannot be such an inference since the only inference from the dubiety of body is modal rather than existential. The assertion of the cogito is consistent with the prior doubt of body, but this is because nothing follows concerning the existence of anything else solely from the claim that bodies are nonexistent. The indubitability of the cogito does not follow from the suspension of body; it asserts its indubitability independently of the existential status of body. It is precisely this ontological indifference of the cogito that permits it to be a response to the doubt of Meditation I. The doubt of body is nonetheless used to prepare the subsequent modal inference to the cognitively pure res cogitans. After all, to paraphrase what Descartes explains to Andreas Colvius,[3] anyone can make the leap from the fact of doubting to the necessity of existing. The point about the relation of the ego sum to the bodily doubt is not that its existence follows from such a doubt, but that its mode of existence avoids corporeality. It is thus not necessary to infer existence from one such doubt. Since any act of doubting is sufficient to demonstrate the existence of the ego sum, the route through bodily doubt reveals its meaning by readying the move to the modal res cogitans. However, we have already seen the conflation between the "true man" and res cogitans in the ambiguous anthropology of Meditation I. Since the act of doubting presupposes rather than establishes that mind must be in some sense nonbodily, there arises the suspicion that bodily doubt is as irrelevant to the question of mode as it is concerning the question of the indubitability of ego sum. This suspicion will be borne out when we examine Descartes' argument for sum res cogitans. Thus far we have been given two explanations of the transnatural status of mind--a pretheoretical willful resolve, and, as we are about to see in Meditation II, a consequence of the method of bodily doubt. However, since neither explanation establishes a distinction between mind and nature (body) in the order of being, we will have to wait until Meditation VI to see whether Descartes makes good his claim to provide such an account.

The presentations of the cogito as a response to bodily doubt (whatever the cause of such a doubt) indicate that the ego sum, ego existo is in fact synonymous with sum res cogitans. What is genuinely perplexing, however, is the identity of the various rationes dubitandi throughout Meditation II as it bears on the overall strategy of the

Meditations. According to Caton, the deceiver in Meditation I and II is God, such that the indubitability of the cogito represents the triumph of rationalism over theology. He refers to Gerhardt Kruger, who argues that "self-consciousness constitutes itself in defiance of all omnipotence. This is not 'Christian inwardness'; rather, here begins in philosophy as such the rebellion against Christianity that we call Enlightenment."[4] I have been basing my interpretation of the finitude of the evil genius as the ratio dubitandi at the conclusion of Meditation I (following Kennington, who also argues that the Meditation II deceiver is the evil genius as the personification of atheistic nature) on the omission of the nonbodily truths from the list of dubitables in Meditation I following the removal of God. God's delayed reappearance until Meditation III signifies the postponement of the reason-theology contest as a necessarily post-cogito contest given the immunity from doubt of the rational truths and given the dependence of the proof of God on the cogito.

The textual evidence concerning the deceiver in Meditation II is ambiguous, to say the least. Unlike the descriptions distinguishing between God and evil genius in Meditation I, the four accounts of the deceiver in Meditation II give the impression of a deliberate ambiguity on Descartes' part concerning the relation between rationalism and theology.[5] Two descriptions of a deceiver precede the ego sum and two descriptions precede the sum res cogitans. Each pair appears to refer to both evil genius and God.

The initial deceiver is referred to as "some God or some other being by whatever name we call it,"[6] i.e., a disjunction of God or evil genius, used to raise the following questions: Is there not something in addition to body? Is God or some other cause putting false perceptions into my mind? Am I myself producing such deceptions? Regardless of the source of such fallacious perceptions, their existence means that there does exist something in addition to body. As we have seen, and as Descartes explains, the denial of body and all modes of external things is at the same time the argument for the existence of mind:

> But I was persuaded that there was nothing in all the world, that there was no heaven, no earth, that there were no minds, nor any bodies; was I not then likewise persuaded that I did not exist? Not at all; of a surety I myself did exist since I persuaded myself of something [or merely because I thought of something].[7]

At this point I exist qua experiencing thoughts.

The intuition of existence is next presented as the corollary of the evil genius hypothesis:

> But there is some deceiver or other, very powerful and very cunning, who ever employs his ingenuity in deceiving

> me. Then without doubt I exist also
> if he deceives me, and let him deceive
> me as much as he will, he can never
> cause me to be nothing so long as I
> think that I am something. So that
> after having reflected well and carefully
> examined all things, we must come to
> the definite conclusion that this
> proposition: I am, I exist, is
> necessarily true each time that I
> pronounce it, or that I mentally conceive
> it.[8]

Descartes offers a third description of the deceiver just prior to demonstrating _sum res cogitans_. This description also refers to the evil genius:

> But what am I, now that I suppose that
> there is a certain genius which is
> extremely powerful, and, if I may say
> so, malicious, who employs all his
> powers in deceiving me?[9]

But then, again in the context of arguing for _sum res cogitans_, Descartes writes:

> Is there nothing in all this which
> is as true as it is certain that I
> exist, even though I should always
> sleep and though he who has given me
> being employed all his ingenuity in
> deceiving me?[10]

Although this description is a compound of the evil genius (the personification of the dream doubt concerning body) and God, and although the sequel omits a reference to God but retains the threat of dreaming, the possibility of an omnipotent deceiver is nonetheless introduced. In each appearance the putative omnipotent deceiver is resisted by the _cogito_, in the former case as _ego sum_ and in the present case as _sum res cogitans_.

The difficulties involved in resolving the deceiver dilemma along the lines suggested by Kennington are the following. In the first place, the textual reference to God as _ratio dubitandi_ is unmistakable. And in the second place, the reference to the creator of my being cannot be interpreted as the personification of atheistic natural origins given the contradiction this generated in _Meditation_ I concerning the doubt of body on the basis of materialism. The difficulty in accepting the interpretation of Caton, in addition to the linguistic ambiguity in the deceiver's descriptions, concerns what is rendered dubious throughout _Meditation_ II. It appears that _Meditation_ II continues _Meditation_ I in restricting the doubt to every mode of bodily and external existence. If the doubt concerns only body, why use God rather than the evil genius as the cause of such a doubt? If God is the reason for such a doubt, does not his omnipotence also jeopardize the certainty of the cogito, even though, as we will see, the cogito is not, strictly speaking, to be counted as one of the rational truths?

A possible rebuff of an omnipotent deceiver could perhaps be argued as follows. Assuming an omnipotent deceiver, total deception is impossible given that one of the requirements of deception is the existence and awareness of this existence on the part of the deceived. To paraphrase the conclusion of Meditation II, if I am believing wrongly, perceiving wrongly, etc., then whatever I am believing, perceiving, etc., falls victim to doubt. But the believing, perceiving, etc., that is, the mental acts themselves, cannot be subsumed under doubt. Unlike their objects, mental acts cannot be doubted without contradiction since to deny them is to be engaged in them. In this sense a doubt caused by even an omnipotent deceiver is overcome in the very attempt. But such an argument assumes that the law of contradiction is sacrosanct. And as we have seen from Meditation I, God's omnipotence renders nothing sacrosanct. On the assumption of a truly omnipotent deceiver, then, the disconcerting possibility remains that such a deceiver can undercut what appears to be an indubitable certainty concerning the bond between thinking and existing. That is, a truly deceiving God may commit the logical perversion of deceiving me into thinking my existence when I do not exist. Descartes appears to suggest just such a possibility concerning God in Meditation III when he says that "I am constrained to confess that it is easy to Him, if He wishes it, to cause me to err, even in matters in which I believe myself to have the best evidence."[11] The sequel makes it clear that this also includes the cogito. But such a doubt implies a return to the aporia posed by God in Meditation I--the suspension of the law of contradiction and thereby the cessation of rational inquiry--which militates against an omnipotent deceiver in Meditation II. It appears, then, that a coherent account of the deceiver-deceived relation in Meditation II is not possible on either assumption concerning the power of the deceiver. Why, then, does Descartes present us with such an illogic?

My suggestion concerning the significance of Descartes' deliberate ambiguity is the following. On the one hand, although God is mentioned twice, in Meditation II what is rendered doubtful is bodily existence, such that God is employing less than full powers of deception. On the other hand, this permits the establishment of the cogito as the means to subsequently prove God's existence and goodness (i.e., the existence of a God whose inscrutable omnipotence threatens the cogito and thereby any such rational proofs). The only way to explain such illogic, given the care with which Meditation II was written, is to realize that it is used to mask what becomes evident from Meditation III on--the independence of reason from theology.

Intuition vs. Inference

As we have seen, Descartes proclaims the initial certainty of his existence with the following words:

> I am, I exist, is necessarily true each time
> that I pronounce it, or that I mentally conceive
> it.[12]

Despite not even the appearance of an inference or deduction,
and despite Descartes' repeated denials, commentators persist
in defending various versions of the inference interpretation
of the cogito.[13] However, when Meditation II is seen within
the context of the prior doubt argument, as well as the
Cartesian architectonic, the intuitive character of the
certainty of existence becomes apparent. I have already
discussed the former, namely, that the certainty of
Descartes' existence qua thinking that existence receives
its sense from the preceding bodily doubt. The ego sum,
etc., can be read, therefore, as a contraction of "what
I am inasmuch as I doubt, is in no wise what I call my
body. . . . otherwise, doubting of my body I should at
the same time doubt of myself, and this I cannot do."[14]
Since res dubitans is already res cogitans in Meditation
I, the cogito of Meditation II is not a novel discovery;
it is rather an explication of what was the case all along.
        If there is any inference involved in the cogito it
does not pertain to the ego sum. To the extent that the
cogito is preceded by bodily doubt it is possible to construe
the move to sum res cogitans as an inference. But as I
have indicated, Meditation I already contained such an
implicit inference by the presence of the res cogitans
as the initiator of doubt, such that the inference to be
carried out in Meditation II merely repeats and makes
explicit the inference of Meditation I.
        The certainty of the cogito is on the basis of a
reflective awareness that makes explicit the experiential
two-in-one of existence and thought. To capture the intimacy
of the intuitive connection between the two it is perhaps
better to speak of a single thought, a thought which thinks
existence. Descartes' proposition can perhaps be paraphrased
as "I think, I am" or "I exist thinking." So closely are
thinking and existing tied to one another in "I am, I exist
. . . each time . . . I mentally conceive it" that it is
impossible to grant priority to either without losing the
force of the intuition or begging the question. The two
parts of the proposition are not parts in the sense that
they must be combined to form a whole. They are more like
Gestalt "whole-parts," equally fundamental aspects of a
unitary intuition, inseparable. Their inseparability does
not imply, of course, anything like the connection between
premise and conclusion of traditional logic. Such a relation
is absent from Meditation II, is denied by Descartes, and
goes contrary to his critique of the traditional logic.
For these reasons the cogito ergo sum of the Discourse
and Principles must be distinguished from the alogical
ego sum, ego existo of Meditation II.
        Descartes' perhaps most emphatic repudiation of the
inference interpretation occurs in the Replies to the Second
Objections:

> But when we become aware that we are
> thinking beings, this is a primitive
> act of knowledge derived from no

syllogistic reasoning. He who says,
'I think, hence I am, or exist,' does
not deduce existence from thought by
a syllogism, but, by a simple act of
mental vision, recognizes it as if
it were a thing that is known per se.
This is evident from the fact that
if it were syllogistically deduced,
the major premise, that everything
that thinks is, or exists, would have
to be known previously; but yet that
has rather been learned from the
experience of the individual--that
unless he exists he cannot think.[15]

The proposition "I think, therefore I am" is thus either
an illegitimate syllogism because of a missing major premise,
or an exercise in question-begging if this premise is
supplied since the ground of the premise is precisely what
is in need of demonstration. But what is in need of
demonstration is not demonstrated at all; it is indubitably
intuited as an unshakable first-person certainty, the only
kind of certainty Descartes acknowledges. To this extent
the certainty of the cogito and of the rational truths
generally does not differ.

Descartes readily concedes that there are numerous
logical truths concerning the relation between thinking
and existing; however, to import them into Meditation II
is a mistake. For example, in the Principles we are told
that "there is a contradiction in conceiving that what
thinks does not at the same time as it thinks, exist,"[16]
that "in order to think we must be" is incapable of being
doubted,[17] and "that he who thinks must exist while he
thinks" is an eternal truth.[18] Quite apart from the question
of the need for a divine guarantee for the law of
contradiction, the reason such indubitable major premises
are inappropriate (even as part of an enthymematic inference)
is because of the idiosyncratic, purely personal, alogical
character and intent of the "I think," which precludes
a logicizing of the cogito. The force of ego sum, ego
existo is, paradoxically, its egocentric contingency.
It is likewise concerning the activity of thinking. The
copresence of these two contingencies produces the
indubitability of ego sum as a contingent necessity. Granted
the contingent fact of thinking, Descartes is simultaneously
assured of his existence. To think is to exist. To exist
is not, of course, necessarily to think. Yet such an
asymmetry does not weaken the intuitive link between thought
and existence. It merely shows that existence is inseparable
from thinking, not identical to it.

To interpret the Meditation II proposition as an
inference thus does violence to Descartes' insistence on
intuition as the foundation of the logic of discovery.
In line with the Cartesian architectonic, the Ego which
survives the doubt is the very same ego which turned to self-
instruction in Discourse II. The intuition of Meditation
II must therefore be understood as a uniquely first-person
certainty, a paradigm of the art of discovery begun in

the Regulae.[19]   In Regulae III, e.g., Descartes states
that "each individual can mentally have intuition of the
fact that he exists, and that he thinks."[20]   Given the
exemption of the simple natures from the doubt, I take
issue with Curley's appraisal of the relation between
Meditation II and the Regulae:

> the Regulae . . . is an early, immature
> work. . . . it reposes a naive
> confidence in . . . intuition. In
> his later, published works, Descartes
> seems to have lost confidence and to
> think that there may be good grounds
> for doubting even the things that seem
> most evident to us (AT VII, 21, 36;
> HRI, 147-148, 158-159). In the later
> writings the proposition "I exist"
> is normally presented in a way which
> makes it look like the conclusion of
> an argument, "I think, therefore I
> exist." The second Meditation is
> notoriously an exception, but even
> there Descartes speaks of his existence
> as following from the fact that he
> judges that the wax exists.[21]

Meditation II repeats the Regulae not only in the way in
which the existence of the ego is shown. The Cartesian
epistemic-ontic correlation will also be at work in the
res cogitans and wax arguments.

CRITIQUE OF ARISTOTELIAN SOUL

The Aristotelian soul was understood as the single
principle of the unity of man by being the ground of two
diverse and comprehensive classes of functions--all modes
of awareness from perception to contemplation and all modes
of self-motion from metabolism to purposive bodily action.
Descartes' critique of Aristotle occurs in the inference
from ego sum to sum res cogitans. The identification of
soul with mind means that the living body is animate for
purely mechanical reasons. The soul drops out as a life
principle, but with this avoidance of the great mistake
of the ancients man becomes bifurcated.
The inquiry into the nature of the "I" is prefaced
by a brief foray into the realm of Descartes' supposedly
predoubt, precogito, and prescience opinion about what
he was. But this survey is undertaken only to show the
need to consider the soul in abstraction from the body
in order to know its nature. This abstraction from body,
plus the certainty of the existence of the "I" independently
from the question of mode, indicates, as Descartes will
explain, that in Meditation II epistemology has priority
over ontology. The key to both the critique of Aristotle
and the priority of epistemology is the elimination of
self-motion from the soul via the presumptive nonexistence
of body. The corollary to this is that the bodily-dependent
faculties cannot be attributed to the soul and are likewise

epistemologically defective in yielding knowledge of the
soul.   The Aristotelian notion of levels of soul (from
vegetative, through sentient, to rational) is thus
methodologically precluded from the start.

Descartes opens with a rhetorical refutation of
Aristotle. Concerning his nature he asks:

> What then did I formerly believe myself
> to be? Undoubtedly I believed myself
> to be a man. But what is a man? Shall
> I say a reasonable animal? Certainly
> not; for then I should have to inquire
> what an animal is, and what is
> reasonable; and thus from a single
> question I should insensibly fall into
> an infinitude of others more difficult.[22]

In this way an explicit discussion and critique of Aristotle
is avoided. Just as with the critique of sensation in
Meditation I, the jump is made from particulars to underlying
principles. The underlying principle of sensation was
reliance upon the imagination. The underlying principle
of man as rational animal, which Descartes wishes to
circumvent, is the existence of the animate body. This
initial rejection of Aristotle is apparently
methodological--as Descartes says, for the sake of economy.
The notion of "rational animal" is not shown to be false;
rather, it is abandoned because it prompts an interminable
analysis. A confrontation is avoided (as Descartes had
suggested to Regius) in order that the overthrow of Aristotle
(as Descartes had told Mersenne) emerge as the consequence
of the acceptance of the truth of Descartes' principles.

The analysis of "rational animal" confronts the problem
of soul-body relation. Consequently, if Descartes can
find a way to think about soul without having to think
about body, the notion of "rational animal" can be
superseded. The method used to show the fruitlessness
of grasping the nature of the embodied soul is the generation
of what seems an insuperable aporia involved in Descartes'
former (predoubt, precogito, prescience) opinion concerning
his nature. What follows is presumably an account of himself
in the natural attitude:

> In the first place, then, I considered
> myself as having a face, hands, arms,
> and all that system of members composed
> of bones and flesh as seen in a corpse
> which I designated by the name of body.
> In addition to this I considered that
> I was nourished, that I walked, that
> I felt, and that I thought, and I
> referred all these actions to the soul:
> but I did not stop to consider what
> the soul was, or if I did stop, I
> imagined that it was something extremely
> rare and subtle like a wind, a flame,
> or an ether, which was spread throughout
> my grosser parts. As to body I had
> no manner of doubt about its nature,
> but thought I had a very clear knowledge

of it; and if I had desired to explain
it according to the notions that I
had then formed of it, I should have
described it thus: By the body I
understand all that which can be defined
by a certain figure: something which
can be confined in a certain place,
and which can fill a given space in
such a way that every other body will
be excluded from it; which can be
perceived either by touch or by sight,
or by hearing, or by taste, or by smell:
which can be moved in many ways not,
in truth, by itself, but by something
which is foreign to it, by which it
is touched [and from which it receives
impressions]: for to have the power
of self-movement, as also of feeling
or of thinking, I did not consider
to appertain to the nature of body:
on the contrary, I was rather astonished
to find that faculties similar to them
existed in some bodies.[23]

Reflecting upon himself in an "unprejudiced" way, Descartes
believed he had a body, but which was a "system of members
composed of bones and flesh as seen in a corpse." Descartes
thought he had bodily equipment, but such equipment
considered by itself was sterile. The body as body was
considered lifeless. But in addition to a sterile body
he noticed that he engaged in metabolism, locomotion,
feeling, and thinking, and he ascribed these activities
to the soul. It would seem that Descartes was originally
an Aristotelian--the soul is the incorporeal, animate,
sentient, and thinking power of the body qua body which
is sterile. But not really. For when he considered this
soul by itself he believed it to be material, "something
extremely rare and subtle like a wind, a flame, or an ether,
which was spread throughout my grosser parts." Descartes,
then, was perhaps originally an atomist. An atomistic
soul could move the body because it was itself highly mobile
matter. But now occurs the _aporia_ of embodiment, since
Descartes describes his original conception of body as
inorganic and static, containing all and only those
attributes implied in the notion of figure (shape, place,
volume, solidity, perceptibility). This is the account
of body contained in the clear and distinct perception
of Cartesian science, the account of body presumably
nonexistent during, and in need of validation by, the
argument of the _Meditations_. Descartes misleadingly presents
all bodies as belonging to a single class--nonthinking
and nonmoving. That some are found conjoined with minds
makes no difference. For this reason the atomist or material
notion of the soul generates the _aporia_.

The denial of thinking and self-motion to the body
poses the following dilemma. If we accept Descartes'
recollection as history, originally the body was considered
to be sterile, such that thinking and self-motion were
referred to the soul. However, the soul was thought to

be bodily, and since body cannot think and move we reach
the paradoxical (if not contradictory) result that certain
bodies are seen to manifest characteristics which have
been precluded from appearing. Nonliving and nonconscious
bodies (bodies understood by Cartesian science) manifest
life and consciousness. As Descartes remarks, "I was rather
astonished to find that faculties similar to them existed
in some bodies". Granted the premises, the aporetic
conclusion must follow. The bare bones of the argument
are as follows:

1. Body qua body is sterile.
2. Thinking and self-motion are attributed to
   the soul.
3. Soul is bodily.
4. Reiteration of the sterility of body.
5. Some bodies manifest thinking and self-motion.
6. Ergo, perplexity ("astonishment").

What is revealed by Descartes' astonishment is that
the true premise of the argument has been misrepresented
and thereby misrepresents the true aporia--the functions
of motion and thought on a Cartesian, materialistic base.
Descartes' "prescientific" opinion concerning his nature
temporarily revives that portion of the doubt argument
concerning atheistic materialism as the "origin of my being."
In the regression from the Aristotelian notion of sterile
body, through the atomist soul, to the Cartesian notion
of body can therefore be detected a theoretical prejudice.
Predoubt Cartesian science rather than prescientific opinion
generates the aporia concerning the soul-body composite.[24]
The aporia is resolved only by the tacit acceptance of
organic automatism, which is the real Cartesian argument
for sum res cogitans.[25] Descartes conceals this
presupposition by allowing his astonishment to go unresolved.
He refrains from pursuing either of the two ways out
of the perplexity: 1) bodies move of their own accord
(automatism), the vital principle of the body being
mechanical rather than the action of an incorporeal soul,
such that Aristotle is wrong, or 2) an incorporeal soul
is needed to supply all of the powers not possessed by
the sterile body. While the account in the Passions of
the difference between a living and dead body suggests
Descartes' solution to be the former, since the soul departs
the body when the body dies a "natural death," rather than
the death or absence of the soul causing the death of the
body, here in Meditation II a resolution of perplexity
gives way to a methodological irresolution analogous to
that concerning the waking-dreaming problem in Meditation
I. As in Meditation I, the purpose is to divert the inquiry
into a preferred or more promising direction. The issue
of organic automatism versus animating soul is thus left
hanging, and after legitimating this paralysis concerning
the possibility of a bodily soul by remembering that the
deceiver is still at work rendering bodies dubious, Descartes
can proceed to a discussion of the soul in dual abstraction
from the body since bodily doubt puts questions of genesis
and embodiment to one side.

SUM RES COGITANS

The lingering doubt of body is the lever to move from
ego sum to sum res cogitans, and in the process the
elimination of the Aristotelian soul as life principle.
The automatism of the body machine is made to appear as
a consequence rather than a premise of sum res cogitans.
The key is the combination of presumptive bodily nonexistence
plus a working knowledge of the essence of body conceived
along Cartesian lines. Thus our initial question: Does
the res cogitans legitimately result from the existence
of thinking and the nonexistence of body, such that bodily
doubt is truly necessary and productive, or does the doubt
merely serve to suppress the existence of body whose nature
as Cartesian mechanicism covertly determines the analysis
of the soul as nonmoving in addition to nonbodily? Since
the hypothetical nonexistence of body does not render
inoperative the nature of body as nonthinking and seemingly
nonmoving extension, the doubt of body is deceptive. And
if, as was suggested, materialism is synonymous with
automatism, bodily doubt is doubly deceptive.

The suppression of body makes the transition to res
cogitans seemingly unproblematic. The aporia resulting
from Descartes' predoubt conception of himself has shown
that the inference from existence to mode of existence
requires an abstraction from our body-related faculties
of sense and imagination. As a result the attributes of
nutrition, motion, and feeling are quickly dismissed because
they involve the body. The epistemic regress concerning
the nature of the self quickly comes to a halt with the
following question:

> What of thinking? I find here that
> thought is an attribute that belongs
> to me; it alone cannot be separated
> from me. . . . But what then am I?
> A thing which thinks. What is a thing
> which thinks? It is a thing which
> doubts, understands, [conceives],
> affirms, denies, wills, refuses, which
> also imagines and feels.[26]

The threat of bodily intrusion into the res cogitans due
to the presence of imagining and perceiving (sensing) is
avoided by Descartes' methodic bifurcation of sense and
imagination. As the cause of perceptions they must involve
the body; as the effect of such bodily action, as reflections
into consciousness, they refer exclusively to mind. The
hyperbolic doubt of body makes this bifurcation plausible
since, as a continuation of the dream metaphor, it allows
from the possibility of conscious events in the absence
of their causal corporeal counterparts. Descartes thus
accomplishes discursively in Meditation II what was done
intuitively in the Regulae--the heterogeneity between
thinking and body which has become the basis of the modern
notion of the res cogitans as an Archimedian first principle.

As we have seen, the meaning of this result depends
upon the meaning of the access through bodily doubt. The
doubt of body performs an abstraction from body. And since

it is illegitimate to conclude that the soul is exclusively consciousness and not also the motive force of the body solely on the basis of the indubitability of consciousness and the dubitability of body, the abstraction from body falls short of establishing the soul as nonbodily. The denial of motive power to the soul is thus premature. (This is quite apart from the question concerning the substantiality of the res cogitans, which will be treated below.) Since the Aristotelian notion of the soul as an unmoved mover cannot logically be dismissed at this point, Descartes' rejection of such a conception (on the grounds of its being an occult quality) is simply the reverse side of his theory of automatism rather than a fortuitous consequence of the route to the soul as res cogitans through hyperbolic doubt. The critique takes its bearings from a conceptual difficulty in the Aristotelian account, namely, how a unitary incorporeal soul could possibly perform such disparate functions as thought and bodily motion and still retain its unity. Descartes' beginning is to assign separate causes to separate classes of functions. What makes such a separation initially plausible, despite its subsequent problems concerning the unity of man, is the intuitive heterogeneity between thinking and vital processes. The road to sum res cogitans through hyperbolic doubt thus gets its true direction from a prior commitment to dualism.

Since the soul must be conceived as embodied to exhibit itself as a cause of motion, its abstraction from the body merely renders this power literally invisible. That is, since the res cogitans is deprived of such power, the entire mind-body complex, the "true man," would have to be understood as an automaton which somehow possesses consciousness, but whose consciousness is powerless to produce bodily motion. Caton cites the following passage from the Treatise on Man in support of this interpretation. Speaking of the human body as a machine, Descartes says:

> I wish you to consider, finally, that all the functions which I attribute to this machine, such as digestion . . . nutrition . . . respiration, waking and sleeping; the reception of light, sounds, odors; the impression of ideas in the organ of the sensus communis and imagination; the retention of these ideas in the memory; the interior movements of the appetites and passions; and finally the movements of all the external members. . . . I desire, I say, that you consider that these functions occur naturally in this machine solely by the disposition of its organs, not less than the movements of a clock or other automaton. . . . . Thus it is not necessary to conceive that it has a nutritive soul, or sensitive soul, or any other principle of motion and life except its blood and spirits . . . which have no other nature than [that] found in inanimate bodies.[27]

The claim here is that organic automatism renders the Aristotelian soul superfluous as life principle. The single exception to such an automatism in the Meditations and again in the Principles is the will, which Descartes claims is capable of freely initiating bodily action. But as the Passions explains, the will suffers the same bifurcation as do sense and imagination in Meditation II. As a passion its source is the body; as a voluntary cause of bodily action we have only the testimony of ordinary experience, the "teaching of nature" of the Meditations.

The problem involved in going from ego sum to sum res cogitans can be summarized as follows. In the interest of scientific foundations (and also religious apologetics, if one takes seriously the rhetoric of the Letter to the Sorbonne), Descartes wants to assert as characteristic of the soul what he denies to the body. The hyperbolic doubt of body thus seems the perfect method. But if the body so doubted is truly as described according to Descartes' predoubt conception (nonthinking and also nonmoving), why ascribe only thought, rather than thought plus motive power, to the soul?[28] The notion in Meditation II that all bodies form a single class suppresses the distinction between inorganic bodies and organic bodies, which in turn means that the truly natural predoubt starting point (the living mind-body complex) is precluded from the outset. Descartes exchanges the prejudice of the "natural attitude" for the theoretical prejudice concerning the sterility of body as such. Strictly speaking, the only logical inference about the soul from such a conception of the body is the Aristotelian one of the soul as cause of both life and mind. Why, then, does Descartes make the logically erroneous inference to the soul as exclusively mind? Two explanations suggest themselves. Either Descartes' predoubt picture of body is correct, such that he simply commits an illogical inference to res cogitans and the desired automatism happily results by default, or the predoubt presentation is insincere, such that, as Descartes states in the Treatise on Man, the body is an automaton and the illegitimate inference is grounded not in faulty logic but in a prior commitment to bodily automatism. Deciding this question is made difficult by Descartes. On the one hand, there is presumably an abstention from ontology via hyperbolic bodily doubt. At the same time, the manifest argument oscillates between res cogitans and res extensa, neither of which is said to be the cause of motion or life. As was indicated above, to escape the aporia of embodiment resulting from the predoubt sterility of the bodily soul, Descartes must either revise the notion of the human body to include self-motion (automatism) so that the subsequent equation of soul with mind becomes plausible, or conclude that the soul is Aristotelian on penalty of making an illegitimate inference. Considering the remarks to Mersenne and Regius concerning the strategy for overthrowing Aristotle, and the open avowal of automatism in the Treatise on Man and the Passions, the charge of concealed automatism rather than faulty logic is the more appropriate explanation of Meditation II.

Given the goals of scientific foundations and religious apologetics-both of which require a distinction between mind/soul and body--the problem of embodiment remains

suspended pending a fuller elaboration of the res cogitans.
More specifically, in what sense is the res cogitans an
Archimedian first principle? And in what sense is the
res cogitans a thing?

Res Cogitans as First Principle

The sense in which the res cogitans is to be a first
principle is the sense in which it satisfies the requirement
of order.   Although Descartes warns against reading the
Principles as a commentary on the Meditations (in fact
he claims that the proper order is the reverse),[29] it is
justified in the case of the concept of order since the
Principles makes explicit what is meant in the Meditations.
However, when it comes to the question of the substantiality
of the res cogitans Descartes' advice must be followed
because the two works diverge.
In the Principles, Part I, 7, 8, we are told that
"this conclusion, I think, therefore I am, is the first
and most certain of all that occurs to one who philosophizes
in an orderly way," and that "this, then, is the best way
to discover the nature of mind and the distinction between
it and the body."[30] (It is through what we have seen as
the conflation of the res cogitans and the ego sum that
the meaning of the res cogitans as first principle is in
fact arrived at.) We have drawn the distinction between
the ordo cognoscendi and the ordo essendi.   Descartes
explicitly joins the res cogitans as "principle" to its
being first in the ordo cognoscendi in a letter to Claude
Clerselier in which he distinguishes two senses of
"principle."   In contrast to "principle" in the sense of
a "common notion" or logical truth (having universality
but no existential reference), the res cogitans is a
principle in the following sense: "a being whose existence
is known to us better than any other, so that it can serve
as a principle to discover them."[31] The res cogitans is
thus first in the order of knowing via abstraction from
its relation to body, which is the way Descartes presents
it in Meditation II:

> But perhaps it is true that these same
> things which I supposed were non-existent
> because they were unknown to me are
> really not different from the self
> which I know. I am not sure about
> this, I shall not dispute about it
> now; I can only give judgment on things
> that are known to me.[32]

This passage raises and postpones the ontological issue
by wondering about a possible synonymy between the thus
far dubitable body and the res cogitans. Perhaps either
neither is bodily (in which case bodies are perceptual
images of the res cogitans and perhaps caused by the hidden
faculty mentioned in Meditation VI), or both are bodily
(in which case the res cogitans is at best epiphenomenal).
But this discussion moves only on the level of knowing,
only on the level of method, and not on the level of being.

At this point, as the means by which subsequently to demonstrate the existence of body, the ego sum must be understood as res cogitans. What Descartes tells Mersenne dispells doubts about the distinction of the two orders as well as the overall Meditation II strategy:

> You should not find it strange, either, that I do not prove in my second Meditation that the soul is really distinct from the body, but merely show how to conceive it without the body. This is because I do not yet have, at this point, the premises needed for the conclusion. You find it later on, in the Sixth Meditation.
>
> It should be noted that in all my writing I do not follow the order of topics, but the order of arguments.[33]

The distinction between the soul and the body in Meditation II is thus methodological, or epistemological, rather than substantial, or ontological.

Ontological Indifference

Thinking is the indubitable attribute of the soul, the principal attribute of the soul, such that there is an identification between the soul and its principal (essential) attribute--"To speak accurately I am not more than a thing which thinks."[34] The equation of principal attribute with essence is treated in the Principles I, 52-53. In the context of a discussion of the nature and distinction between substances, we are told that attributes are the access to substance. Since "it is a common notion that nothing is possessed of no attributes, properties, or qualities . . . when we perceive any attribute, we therefore conclude that some existing thing or substance to which it may be attributed, is necessarily present."[35] Attributes exist in an order of dependence, the principal attribute being the sine qua non of the others, that is, the "nature and essence" of its substance. According to such an order of dependence, "imagination, feeling, and will, only exist in a thinking thing,"[36] such that thinking is synonymous with mental substance. Several recent commentators interpret the res cogitans of Meditation II along such lines;[37] however, such reasoning is not given in Meditation II. We have seen Descartes' recommendation concerning the Meditations as a prerequisite for the Principles. Unlike the textbook character of the Principles, written in the traditional terminology of substance, attribute, and so on, in the Meditations, which is said to be the more authoritative work, the substance ontology is not developed. This is not to suggest that the soul "conceived by itself" is not characterized by thinking, but to stress the purely epistemic status of the soul in Meditation II. Descartes' account of res cogitans shows this to be the case.

The nonsubstantiality of the res cogitans is indicated by two of Descartes' characterizations. They concern the relation between the res cogitans and time, and the res cogitans and its modes. What is shown is a modal as well as temporal fragmentation within the res cogitans. The two characterizations are:

> 1. What of thinking? I find here that thought is an attribute that belongs to me; it alone cannot be separated from me. I am, I exist, that is certain. But how often? Just when I think; for it might possibly be the case if I ceased entirely to think, that I should likewise cease altogether to exist. I do not now admit anything which is not necessarily true.[38]
> 2. But what then am I? A thing which thinks. What is a thing which thinks? It is a thing which doubts, understands, [conceives], affirms, denies, wills, refuses, which also imagines and feels.[39]

Although Descartes does refer to thought as "an attribute that belongs to me" and to himself as a "thinking thing," neither of the above passages can be construed as traditional substance ontology. The obstacle in the first passage is temporal discontinuity, in the second dispersion into modes.[40] By itself the modal dispersion is not fatal to the substantiality of the res cogitans, just as dispersing res extensa into its modes does not destroy substantiality. What robs res cogitans of substantiality is the consequence of the radical instantaneity of ego sum, ego existo, namely, that res cogitans cannot be conceived as a continuant, and consequently dissolves into a heap of temporally fragmented instants. There thus results a two-layered fragmentation of the res cogitans--division into modes, each of which is understood as a collection of temporally discrete acts. Res cogitans cannot be a substance without being a continuant, a one. Contrary to Kenny and others (see note 37), the radical instantaneity of the ego sum, ego existo necessitates nonsubstantiality. Since Descartes' existence is compressed into the awareness of his existence, and since such awareness is intermittent, fragmented existence is unavoidable. As Descartes stresses, "I do not now admit anything which is not necessarily true." The continued existence of res cogitans is ruled out in two ways by this criterion of indubitability. On the one hand, to claim existence when not thinking that existence is to make an inference beyond any possible available data. On the other hand, as we have seen, when thinking, one's existence is inevitably cointuited. Given the radical temporality of the res cogitans, any unity to be ascribed to it can be but synthetic. Since the mind is nothing beyond its modes, and each mode is nothing beyond its acts, the "I" is exhausted in each such episode. At the level of the experience of consciousness, the only identity ascribable to res cogitans is the essential reference to the self

which necessarily forms part of every mental episode (a
kind of de facto Kantian "I think"). Descartes thus steers
clear of the problem confronting those who try to define
the identity of the self in terms of substance, bundle,
or fastener of properties. It is precisely this avoidance
that constitutes the ontic indifference of the res cogitans
argument. In addition to its dispersion into temporally
discrete modal appearances, the distinction between the
two orders means that the hypothesis of the corporeality
of the res cogitans is still a live, though dormant, option.
That is, Descartes cannot rule out the possibility that
res cogitans may be a mode of body. (Given the gaps at
the level of consciousness, it would appear that the only
way to claim a nonsynthetic, unitary, identical res cogitans
is to reduce thoughts to brain activity. To insist, as
Descartes does only when pressed, that there are levels
of consciousness, that is, the unconscious is, to repeat,
totally incompatible witN the Meditation II criterion of
evidence.) So long as the relation between soul and body
remains indeterminate, it is not possible to conceive the
soul as a substance, "a thing which so exists that it needs
no other thing in order to exist."[41] Since the "true man"
is the mind-body whole, perhaps we must conclude that the
soul is an attribute of the substantial "true man." This
is consistent with the definition of substance in the
Principles, but we must wait until the arguments of
Meditation VI are considered. At this point, all that
can be said is the following. Thinking (alone) pertains
to the abstracted res cogitans, but not in the traditional
essentialist or substantialist way. Res cogitans is an
epistemic first principle, but since the order of being
is in fact first, perhaps the res cogitans will be shown
to be dependent upon a prior first principle--God or nature.

RES EXTENSA

     Part two of the demonstration that the human mind
is more easily known than the body is accomplished by part
two of the critique of Aristotle. The wax analysis shows
that body is res extensa versus substantial form, and that
mind is indubitable as the indispensable access to a world
which has become idea. The hyperbolic doubt temporarily
suspended for this purpose, with the existence of the wax
(and implicitly Descartes' own body) we return to the
purportedly prescientific perspective of Meditation I.
That is, what was accomplished by going from the teaching
of nature through hyperbole in Meditation I will be
accomplished by a presumably unprejudiced critique of
prescientific experience in Meditation II. In fact, both
procedures are the same in the decisive respect, the presence
of an epistemic-ontic regression leading to the pair res
cogitans-res extensa. What looks like an argument from
hyperbolic dream analysis in Meditation I and what looks
like a phenomenological critique of ordinary perceptual
consciousness in Meditation II produce the same result
because both are in reality two sides of the same argument.
In each case the dual role of the imagination is decisive,
and in each case Cartesian science is the lever of the
argument.

Descartes introduces the wax, the ideal object for his purpose, with a somewhat deceptive remark. We should not deal with "bodies in general, for these general ideas are usually a little more confused, but let us consider one body in particular."[42] Since he considers "one body in particular" to show how "bodies in general" can be known, we are again reminded of Meditation I, the advantage in Meditation II being that the wax represents generality without (apparently) going beyond the empirical, without having to suspend existence. What is uniquely appropriate about the piece of wax for Descartes is its lack of specificity as to nature. Although each piece of wax is not as every other, given their differing sensory properties, since wax as wax has an inexhaustible range of properties at the level of sense and image, wax as a type is uniquely nonspecific. In analyzing the piece of wax, Descartes is thus analyzing a "general particular."[43] Granted that, as Williams observes, the wax analysis is a thought experiment (see note 43), what is important is how the thought experiment is to be understood. The dream assumption in Meditation I was a thought experiment for the purpose of severing images from sensations. The quasi-experience of the perception of the wax is for the purpose of going from the teaching of nature to res extensa. Consequently quasi-existence must be granted so that sense and imagination appear to get their due rather than being methodologically precluded as in Meditation I. Unlike the a priori ontology of Meditation I, the ontology of Meditation II is made to appear firmly anchored in experience, as a nonscientific confirmation of Meditation I. But this is not so since, to repeat, each analysis is conducted on the basis of the same scientific presuppositions.

The analysis begins with a stress on the particularity of the "general particular" when conceived statically. Descartes lists its sensible qualities and concludes that "all the things which are requisite to cause us to distinctly recognize a body, are met with in it."[44] That is, in terms of the order of knowing we apprehend the wax no differently than any other concrete individual thing, any other particular representative of a type. From the static perspective wax appears like any body—it has all the required sensory properties and it is numerically individuated. Each piece of wax appears to have a perceptual nature of its own, without which the analysis could not get started. However, since the piece of wax behaves like no other kind of thing when it is induced to change its properties, its ambiguity concerning form becomes manifest.

Descartes rather quickly concludes that res extensa is the answer to the question of the wax's sameness through change. Upon being heated the wax changes all of its sensory properties, yet everyone judges it to remain the same wax. The judgment of identity, what is taken as homogeneous against the heterogeneity of sensations, is initially a judgment of common sense ("no one would judge otherwise"). This concession to the teaching of nature (sense-based prejudice) is for the purpose of subsequently showing the inability of the natural attitude to account for its own true judgment. Because the wax is judged the same and its sensory qualities have changed, sensory properties are not the basis of such a judgment and, correlatively, it is not our senses which make such a judgment. The sensory qualities are like clothing, underneath which is an "extended thing which is flexible and movable." Further, since such extension is capable of an infinity of shapes, it cannot be by our imagination that we grasp the sameness of the wax. Since the ground of the sameness of the wax is not sensible or imageable, the empirical and a priori imaginations are apparently both ruled out. It is as though we must conclude (almost by a process of elimination, or by default) that we know the sameness of such extension by a pure intuition of the mind. That the conclusion is really the ground of the argument and that the intention is to reject Aristotle can be seen by retracing its epistemic-ontic regression.

Sensation

Descartes' critique of sensation is scientific rather than phenomenological since he misrepresents the nature of the relation between change and identity in the perception of the wax. Descartes' rejection of sensation abstracts from the experienced sensory and temporal continuity that constitutes the perception of the changing wax. In this way the identity of the wax becomes an intellectual judgment rather than the phenomenological datum it is. The reason that wax is ideally suited for the analysis is precisely its combination of what seems to be complete sensory and shape change while retaining its identity. But such identity is discovered through the senses once we concentrate on the complete perceptual experience rather than its endpoints. Descartes introduces a discontinuity at the level of sensation by comparing sets of temporally distinct sensations, such that identity must be judged, and necessarily not on the basis (but rather in spite of) sensation. However, if it were not for the sensory and temporal continuity of the shift from sense qualities to other sense qualities, there would be no basis for the identity judgment since there would be no way to connect the two sensory sets to the same object. Such continuity of time, sensation, and spatiality is phenomenologically a feature of both sensation and imagination. In fact it is because the wax can assume an infinity of shapes (precisely the feature which presumably disqualifies the imagination as the judge of identity) that such sensed continuity is experienced in the wax. (The limit, of course, would be vaporization.) The introduction of sensory gaps is due to the opposition between sensory testimony and the essence of body posited by Cartesian science, not the defective nature of sensation. A static analysis could come to the same conclusion, but because the static analysis abstracts from sensation from the start, the argument could not be portrayed as a passage from the natural attitude to a vindication of science.[45]

Imagination

The argument from sensation to the pure image is through

a process of abstraction, whereby what is really abstracted from is the Aristotelian notion of body as an instance of substantial form. Descartes begins by distinguishing between a body and its appearances:

> Perhaps it was what I now think, viz. that this wax was not that sweetness of honey, nor that agreeable scent of flowers, nor that particular whiteness, nor that figure, nor that sound, but simply a body which a little while before appeared to me as perceptible under these forms, and which is now perceptible under others.[46]

In other words, and this is the explanation for the earlier dynamic versus static analysis, we are gradually approaching the particular in its generality by first showing the superficiality of sensory characteristics as indicators of what something is. Wax has an identity, but its identity cannot be understood as either sensory or substantial form. The above passage eliminates sensory form for the seemingly simple reason that wax cannot have an enduring sameness at the level of sense since the wax is judged to be the same in opposition to its sensory change. What Descartes says next dispels any illusions about grounding sameness in something like substantial form (e.g., waxness as opposed to woodness). Descartes does not draw the Aristotelian conclusion about the nature of the substrate. The wax is just as amorphous (and perhaps more so) as its shifting sensory properties:

> But what, precisely, is it that I imagine when I form such conceptions? Let us attentively consider this, and, abstracting from all that does not belong to the wax, let us see what remains. Certainly nothing remains excepting a certain extended thing which is flexible and movable.[47]

Descartes here parts company with common sense concerning the sameness of the wax. The wax remains the same through potentially infinite variation; however, it has become a sensory and formal chameleon. For this reason the abstraction to the essence of wax must pass beyond the visible. No image, sensed or constructed, can grasp wax as wax. Each such attempt is but a frozen moment, and hence an inaccurate picture. Hence the uniqueness of wax as a "general particular": "for as to wax in general it is yet clearer,"[48] which means, since wax in general represents bodies in general, that we have just been given the analysis of body as such. What began as a phenomenology concerning the identity of a particular has become a theory of abstraction concerning the essence of body.·

But can we really apply the wax analysis to any sensed object? Granted that sense and imagination are indispensable, are there not limits (though difficult to specify) to the preservation of sameness throughout sensory

and especially figural change?   Kenneth Dorter points
to what appears as an inconsistency in the _Meditations_
concerning identity and figural change:

> Had he chosen the human body as an
> example and, after rearranging its
> parts, asked whether the same body
> remains, he could scarcely have replied,
> 'no one denies it, no one judges
> otherwise'. As he himself states in
> the synopsis of this same meditation,
> 'the human body becomes a different
> entity from the mere fact that the
> shape of some of its parts has been
> changed'.   But this is contradicted
> by what he demonstrates in the meditation
> itself: with regard to all external
> things (i.e., bodies), they remain
> the same as long as their constituent
> matter remains the same. Descartes
> may have contradicted this deliberately,
> in the hope of covering his tracks
> by paying lip service to the hallowed
> principle his argument implicitly denies;
> or he may have done so inadvertently,
> as a result of the lingering effects
> of his Thomist training.[49]

I have tried to show that the first hypothesis is the more
likely. Characteristic of many of Descartes' contradictions,
they can be resolved when one connects a doctrine with
its context, that is, its audience and intention. The
context of the claim about the figure of the human body
is the apologetic intention addressed to the Sorbonne.
In the sequel Descartes concludes, "From this it follows
that the human body may indeed easily enough perish, but
the mind [or soul of man (I make no distinction between
them)] is owing to its nature immortal."[50] This anticipates
the dualism argument in _Meditation_ VI based on the extended,
hence divisible, hence perishable, body, and the nonextended,
hence indivisible, hence immortal, soul. These arguments
are not the same, yet they both rely on the changeable
character of body compared to the immutability of soul.
This "inconsistency" concerning the relation of change
and identity of body is representative of the overall tension
within the _Meditations_ between scientific and theological
aims.
     The _Meditation_ II context is purely epistemic--the
knowledge of the mind as _res_ _cogitans_ as the correlate
of a knowledge of body as pure extension. Concerning what
it is about bodies that allows us to know them, the
imagination is overcome by the potential infinite flexibility
of wax. At the same time, each of the infinite forms is
imageable. Although it is true, as Descartes explains
in _Meditation_ VI, that one cannot clearly and distinctly
imagine a chiliagon or distinguish between a chiliagon
and a myriagon, it is still the case that one can perceive
any such shape as spatially delineated, that is, as a figure
against a background. The fuzzier the perception because
of the increasing number of sides, the more nearly the

body appears as "pure extension." The elimination of the
imagination is thus paradoxical. Since it is true that
every single shape of the wax can be imaged (at least
clearly, if not distinctly), the problem faced by the
imagination in knowing body as body is its inability to
produce an image of their totality. We can only think
such a totality. Since body is not to be understood as
a sum of appearances but rather as their ground, the wax
cannot be known through the imagination. It would appear
that Descartes all along has been operating on the basis
of a nonimaged notion of body as intelligible extension,
whereby body has become the idea of body.

Intellect

The analysis has moved from sense to imagination to
intellectual abstraction. Wax qua body is knowable,
Descartes says, only by "an intuition of the mind."
Meditation II is consequently epistemological in two
respects. In addition to the abstraction from embodiment
in favor of res cogitans, corporeal existence is abstracted
from in favor of wax as intelligible extension. In the
process the ontological significance of the imagination
is suppressed by implying that imaginative awareness of
identity and essence requires an image of an infinite
totality. We learned in Regulae XII that what is incapable
of being imaged is an ens rationis, that whatever can exist
must be an imageable particular. Given the definition
of the imagination earlier in Meditation II ("to imagine
is nothing else than to contemplate the figure or image
of a corporeal thing"), the intellectual abstraction
concerning the knowledge of the essence of body should
not be taken to deflect from the ontological import of
the involvement of the imagination in the perception of
particular bodies. All particular bodies are differentiated
by change of geometric shape--the one universal "form."
The difference between types is on the same plane as that
between particulars. For Descartes, since extension is
the one "substantial form" the Aristotelian classification
of natural kinds is but a distinction of reason. Sensory
heterogeneity is preserved, but given the ultimate object
homogeneity, such heterogeneity is redefined as subjective
response. The nature of this subjectivity is the last
proof of res cogitans.
A dualistic theory of perception is offered to explicate
the meaning of knowing the wax through intellectual
intuition. Comparing the perception of the wax to the
perception of men:

> when looking from a window and saying
> I see men who pass in the street, I
> really do not see them, but infer that
> what I see is men, just as I say that
> I see wax. And yet what do I see from
> the window but hats and coats which
> may cover automatic machines? Yet
> I judge these to be men. And similarly
> solely by the faculty of judgment which

rests in my mind, I comprehend that
which I believed I saw with my eyes.[51]

Perception is a mediated process involving an intellectual
judgment of sensory data. Naive realism is loose talk.
Strictly speaking, what we sense are hats and coats, which
must be transformed into perceptions. We do likewise with
the wax. But the analogy is problematic in several respects.
First, the relation between men and their clothing is unlike
that between wax and its sensory qualities. Men and their
clothing are both on the same cognitive level since each
can be sensed. (This is also true of naked men, for which
there is no wax perceptual equivalent.) The judgment "men
versus automata" involves not an intellectual abstraction
from sense but prior sensory experience. Second, assuming
a judgment in each case, the criterion for the judgment
concerning the wax cannot be grounded phenomenologically
once sense and image have been disposed of. And since
prior experience is unavailable, we are left with the
self-validating pure intuition of Regulae XII.
    Granted that the analogy is poor, it is faithful to
the epistemic schema Descartes wishes to propose. The
reduction of body to the concept of body implies res cogitans
as their locus of mediation, since, whether true or false,
perception of the wax shows consciousness as the indubitable
access to any possible manner of object. As Descartes
says, in a phenomenologically sounding reminder of the
evil genius doubt, now that the presumptive existence of
body has served its purpose:

> For it may be that what I see is not
> really wax, it may also be that I do
> not possess eyes with which to see
> anything; but it cannot be that when
> I see, or (for I no longer take account
> of the distinction) when I think I
> see, that I myself who think am nought.
> . . . And what I have here remarked
> of wax may be applied to all other
> things which are external to me [and
> which are met with outside of me].[52]

Descartes concludes Meditation II by inferring sum
res cogitans from the understanding of body as res extensa.
The following inference is immune from the evil genius
since bodily existence is not at issue:

> But finally . . . since it is now
> manifest to me that even bodies are
> not properly speaking known by the
> senses or by the faculty of imagination,
> but by the understanding only . . .
> I see clearly that there is nothing
> which is easier for me to know than
> my mind.[53]

The indubitability of the res cogitans and the dubitability
of body mean that, as far as Descartes knows, worldly objects
may be no more than modifications of res cogitans. To

perceive the world is to think its conception once sense
and image are discredited. There results an encapsulated
consciousness on the model of reflection. In the place
of the object and its properties as the immediate object
of perception is the dyad of immanent idea plus judgment.
The world as idea (in the mode of clear and distinct
cognition) and consciousness as its locus (in the manner
of res cogitans) are the desired foundations of Cartesian
science. Abstracting from the need to resolve the dream
induced by the evil genius (that we have certainty concerning
a possibly nonexistent world) and the need to theologically
validate reason, in Meditation II Descartes has accomplished
quite a trick if we can take him at his word concerning
the absence of scientific doctrine--namely, an unprejudiced
analysis of the essence of mind and body producing the
precise conception of each required for the foundations
of science. But as we have seen throughout Meditation
II, there are several indications that the doubt of body
is not as neutral as it is presented, that the denial of
body does not preclude an influence by the Cartesian science
of body.

The incursion of science into the doctrine of
subjectivity in Meditation II can be summarized by the
way in which it affects the arguments concerning the res
cogitans as first principle. The transition from ego sum
to sum res cogitans respects the ordo cognoscendi-ordo
essendi distinction and at the same time overthrows the
Aristotelian soul. But, as we have seen, what appears
as the anthropological consequence of sum res cogitans
was in fact the first premise in the argument--Cartesian
bodily automatism. This premise is methodologically screened
by the presumptive nonexistence of body. What is likewise
screened is the perhaps ontic dependence of mind upon body,
since the res cogitans is as much an abstraction from the
mind-body whole as is res extensa an abstraction from sense
and imagination. The illogic of the argument for res
cogitans from bodily doubt (the denial of the soul as res
movens) is not mitigated by the restriction of Meditation
II to epistemology. Bodily denial in Meditation II merely
postpones an investigation of the soul's possible dependence
upon the body.

In the second half of Meditation II we find a similar
combination of Cartesian nature and a nature-free cogito.
The wax analysis eliminates sense and image from our
knowledge of body. The wax argument is presented as a
corroboration of the certainty of res cogitans as the
correlate of concluding that body is res extensa on the
basis of a critique of prescientific experience. Concerning
the nature of the wax itself, the discontinuity in the
argument from perception to abstraction to pure intuition
in revealing the wax as noetic extension forces us to see
the epistemic-ontic correlation of Regulae XII as the ground
of the analysis. As in Meditation I, in Meditation II
the analysis is according to the epistemic order stated
in Regulae VIII--senses, imagination, intellect.[54] To repeat,
the ground of this order is the Cartesian conception of
body, the cognitive faculties being the way in which body
is apprehended by the mind-body whole. Body as res extensa
can be grasped only by mind conceived as res cogitans.
Any other understanding on the basis of any other faculty

falls short of clear and distinct cognition. The res cogitans is thus the epistemic complement of the epistemic res extensa. The ontic basis of this complementarity is the mutually exclusive simple natures of thought and extension of the Regulae. However, in the light of the latent physiology of perception in Meditation II we begin to suspect an epistemology of body by body. The cognitive purity of the res cogitans was accomplished by a methodic abstraction from body. But the abstraction from the wax to res extensa shows that the pure intellect which so judges is indirectly tied to the body because abstraction requires sensation and imagination. Though the wax is considered as an existent for the purpose of the analysis, the bifurcation of the senses and imagination tends to conceal this relation. The twin poles of Cartesian science--res cogitans and res extensa--are in fact both products of abstraction, the former from bodily automatism and the latter from the sensory based ordinary understanding of body. The result, an epistemology containing subject and object as products of method, is perfectly consistent with the ontological limitation imposed upon Meditation II, but suggests that Descartes' concrete ontology may give more of a role to body than is generally conceded. As the Meditation VI proof of the existence of body shows, the senses and imagination must to some extent be vindicated. In Meditation II their role is as prerequisites for the knowledge of body as res extensa. To repeat, the wax must be presumed to exist since abstraction requires the mind-body whole in order to provide the corporeal imagination, upon which abstraction is made, with its impression. In this way the intellect, even in its most rarefied mode, is ultimately dependent upon the body. In this sense the Meditation II admission of body tacitly corrects the Meditation I procedure.

To solve the problem of the existence of body is perhaps to solve the problem of its essence in the sense that on the basis of the former is performed the abstraction to res extensa. Beck, for example, in discussing Regulae XIV points out that physiology is involved in the process of intuition and deduction, but does not apply this to the wax analysis of Meditation II.[55] Descartes says in the Regulae (XII-XIV) that reason alone cannot discover a new kind of being. This would appear to conflict with the account of "innate" in the Meditations. However, as he explains in the Replies to the Second Objections, "innate" means "the capacity for constructing such an idea."[56] And in the Notes Against a Program he refers to "innate" as a "certain disposition or propensity."[57] Innateness as functional rather than static suggests that innate ideas are abstractions rather than entities intuited by a nonbodily-related intellect. Contrary to the Meditations' claim about the psychological innateness of mathematics,[58] Descartes, it appears, is much more of an empiricist than generally acknowledged.

Given such indications about the fundamentality of the Cartesian understanding of body--be it body known as res extensa or functioning as automatism--it is clear that the notion of the res cogitans as first principle must be taken in the limited Cartesian sense of "a being whose existence is known to us better than any other, so that

it can serve as a principle to discover them."[59] As we
have seen, the res cogitans plays this role as a consequence
of a prior dualism concerning pure intellect as the access
to pure body. Since res cogitans may turn out to be a
mode of body, and given the fact that Meditation II denies
it the status of substance, it is even misleading to regard
it as a "being" (as opposed to a function) unless the term
be given the widest latitude.

The implications of the covert role of body in
Meditation II have been drawn by Norman Kemp-Smith, who
ties the theory of perception to the organism as automation.
Such automatism means that ideas are ultimately corporeal.
Since the mind receives corporeal motions in the brain,
it is thus in direct contact with external bodies, such
that "though Descartes' teaching is still that in all cases
our perception of external objects (i.e., of bodies external
to the animal organism) is indirect and to that extent
'representational', the 'representations' are, he declares,
physical, not mental."[60] Kemp-Smith bases this conclusion
on generalizing the theory of vision in the Dioptrics.
Caton subscribes to the same view of Descartes' account
of knowledge of body, which he refers to as the "true
Cartesian circle."[61] If Kemp-Smith and Caton are correct
(and in what follows I attempt to show, on the basis of
the anthropology of Meditation VI, that they are) then
the epistemic-ontic link, the ground floor of the Cartesian
metaphysic, is the mediation by "corporeal ideas,"
simultaneously first in the orders of being and knowing.
Despite the reduction of the world to idea, the epistemic
task for Descartes is not one of bridging the gulf between
immanent idea and transcendent thing, but rather one of
explaining the way in which things quite literally enter
into our subjectivity. Because of the dual function of
the imagination, as corporeal and ideational, the image
becomes the material upon which judgments are made concerning
both existence and essence. It is in this sense that the
development of the argument through Meditation II is true
to the advice forming the core of the Cartesian
architectonic--be guided solely by one's own thoughts.

4
THEODICY

It is universally recognized that the relation between Cartesian science and theology is the key to Cartesian rationalism. Although the status of Descartes' theological metaphysics continues to be debated, what has emerged as the consensus of contemporary interpretation regards Descartes' theology as indeed the core of his metaphysics, to which his rationalism is subordinate. Beck can be cited as representative. Connecting Descartes' theology to the mediating conception of consciousness presented at the start of Meditation III, the relation between epistemology and metaphysics is claimed by Beck to be the following:

> The argument of the Meditations is that when we know the nature of God, any doubts we may have are legitimately set at rest. For then we shall learn that God, who has created nature and controlled it by His laws, has also created our minds and implanted in them ideas, or ways of thinking, in conformity to the laws of nature. It is the knowledge of this harmony between the nature of things and the clear and distinct contents of our thinking and perceiving which converts the psychological fact, that we cannot help thinking that x and y, the two elements of an intuitus, are connected, into the logically justified convinction that x necessarily involves y. The persuasio and assensio are justifiably one. The knowledge of the harmony follows at once from, and is the expression of, a knowledge of God. This knowledge of God is the apex of all the Cartesian metaphysics and any attempt to interpret this metaphysics without the essential theology is a complete travesty of his views. Metaphysics is about God.[1]

Such a solution, argues Beck, assumes the legitimacy of the res cogitans as an Archimedian point of psychological, hence epistemic, self-enclosure:

> Descartes was forced . . . into his theory by his efforts to grapple with the doubt imposed by his own method. He was enclosed in his egocentric circle by the very nature of the doubt and he was methodologically obliged to escape from this circle, if possible without derogating from the exigencies of the doubt. For Descartes the idea, as a mode of cogitatio, is an aspect of reality. But its further representative function is uncertain and undecided. On our right to affirm the existence of what our ideas refer to, depends our escape from the threat of solipsism induced by the hyperbolical doubt.[2]

Curley and Williams also believe that Descartes sincerely attempts (but fails) to ground reason upon God. However, their versions of Descartes' sincerity are ambivalent in different ways. According to Curley:

> The Meditations will appeal . . . to the possibility of deception by a superior being, even in those things which seem most evident. Our ancient belief in God becomes a ground for doubting everything, so long as we do not know that God is not a deceiver. And this, as Descartes notes in the Principles, is the most important ground for doubting the truths of mathematics (AT VIII-1, 6, HR I, 220). . . . though the defense of reason does fail in the end, it fails because Descartes' arguments for God's existence are not good enough, not because the project is inescapably circular. . . . There is no difficulty in principle about Descartes' procedure in the Meditations . . . . If Descartes' arguments for the existence of God fail, then his system fails as a system.[3]

At the same time:

> That Descartes engaged--to some extent--in dissimulation cannot be denied.[4]

Curley even gives some evidence for dissimulation, but does not rebut it or attempt to explain the significance of "to some extent." Instead he undercuts the severity of the contest between reason and God. After stating that the doctrine of the divine creation of the eternal truths is fundamental to Cartesian metaphysics, he says "in the

Meditations Descartes is careful not to invoke that extravagant conception of omnipotence, and we would do him no service by bringing it in."[5] But Descartes has already done so, since God threatens mathematics and logic in Meditation III. Curley's retraction of omnipotence not only muffles the reason-God encounter, but in so doing precludes a proper evaluation of the Cartesian theodicy since the problem of the inscrutability of the divine will is not accorded its proper significance.

Williams' ambivalence concerns Descartes' relation to scholasticism. His appraisal alternates between a sociology of knowledge and a suspicion of insincerity, concluding with the former. Concerning Descartes' initial proof of God:

> This is a piece of scholastic metaphysics; and it is one of the most striking indications of the historical gap that exists between Descartes' thought and our own, despite the modern reality of much else that he writes, that he can unblinkingly accept this unintuitive and barely comprehensible principle as self-evident in the light of reason. The doctrine of degrees of reality or being is a part of the medieval intellectual order which more than any other succumbed to the seventeenth century movement of ideas to which Descartes' himself powerfully contributed.[6]

On the other hand, "there are important ways in which the scholastic notions are put to very different uses by Descartes. . . . Descartes is adapting scholastic terms to his own uses."[7] Williams writes concerning the treatment of God's will in Meditation IV:

> God's purposes are inscrutable, and it would be both impious and pointless for his finite mind to try to fathom them. In general . . . it is improper to look for final causes--that is to say, explanations in terms of purposes--in philosophy or science . . . it always involves the impiety of trying to discover more than God has revealed. At this point Descartes is looking forward, and with some ingenuity (and also, perhaps, some disingenuity) is using the claims of piety against the ecclesiastics who opposed the mechanistic outlook of the new science.[8]

Williams nonetheless concludes that:

> If Descartes' system is to work, then of course it does have to be true that

> there is a totally irresistable
> demonstration of the existence of a
> benevolent God, which will inevitably
> convince anyone who in good faith has
> tried as hard to understand it as any
> conscientious thinker can try. This
> is necessary for Descartes' vindication
> of knowledge, and also sufficient,
> but it is also not true. The trouble
> with Descartes' system is not that
> it is circular. . . . The trouble
> is that the proofs of God are invalid.
> . . . Descartes took these hopeless
> arguments for the existence of God
> to be self-evidently valid, conditioned
> in this by historical (perhaps also
> by temperamental) factors.[9]

The trouble with Williams' sociology of knowledge is that it totally ignores the teaching of the Cartesian architectonic concerning rational autonomy vis-a-vis history, environment, and temperament. As we have seen, it is such a personal code of honor that was a prerequisite for the doubt enterprise in <u>Meditation</u> I as the first step in rational self-legislation.

The minority view, challenging Descartes' sincerity, insists that Cartesian science is autonomous and that the theology is an elaborate exercise in prudence. Felix Grayeff concludes that "<u>God's existence is Descartes' symbol for existence as such</u>. . . . By re-shaping the concept of God . . . Descartes made certainty independent of revelation and the Church of his time and placed science above theology."[10] Caton concludes from an examination of the "Notes Against a Programme" that Descartes' considered opinion is "that when an author confronts his readers with a contradiction between the laws of nature and Scripture, it may be inferred that he does not believe Scripture. . . . the basis of this inference rule is Descartes' belief that in the event of a clash between reason and faith, it is impossible not to give precedence to reason."[11] As a result, "The Cartesian circle thus appears to be the legerdemain by which things in no need of proof are made to depend on things not susceptible of proof."[12] The sincerity and insincerity views agree that peaceful coexistence between them is not possible; supremacy must be granted to either the rationalism or the theology.

A third view sees Descartes attempting such a peaceful coexistence. In "Descartes on the Creation of the Eternal Truths,"[13] Frankfurt argues that despite its absence from Descartes' publications the doctrine of the divine creation of the eternal truths is indispensable to Descartes' metaphysics, and that Descartes consistently held to both his rationalism and his theology because there is in fact

no conflict--reason and revelation apply to separate and
discontinuous realms. Frankfurt claims that the theology
of the creation of the eternal truths testifies to a
threefold bifurcation within Cartesian philosophy: 1)
science and metaphysics concern distinct realms of truth,
2) reason and revelation are their equally legitimate
respective modes of access, and 3) Descartes' epistemic
conception of truth is one of coherence versus
correspondence, that is, logical consistency rather than
absolute certainty. In this way Frankfurt seems to effect
a compromise between the either-or of sincerity and
insincerity. In "Descartes on the Consistency of Reason,"[14]
Frankfurt modifies his position somewhat by shifting from
the dualism of coherence versus correspondence to one of
"certainty versus truth." His primary justification for
such an interpretation is Descartes' Reply to the Second
Objections:

> What is it to us, though perchance
> some one feigns that that, of the truth
> of which we are so firmly persuaded,
> appears false to God or to an Angel,
> and hence is, absolutely speaking,
> false? What heed do we pay to that
> absolute falsity, when we by no means
> believe that it exists or even suspect
> its existence? We have assumed a
> conviction so strong that nothing can
> remove it, and this persuasion is clearly
> the same as perfect certitude.[15]

According to Frankfurt, "In this passage, Descartes
explicitly acknowledges the possibility that what is certain
may not be true 'speaking absolutely', and he makes it
clear that certainty takes priority over absolute truth
in his conception of the goals of inquiry."[16] In what
follows I hope to show that Frankfurt's analysis, in either
version of the bifurcation between epistemology and
metaphysics, is unfaithful to Descartes' intentions, that
is, that the issue indeed comes down to rationalism versus
theology and that in such a clash revelation gives way
to reason.

THE THEOLOGICAL PROBLEM

     In Meditation I Descartes linked the foundations of
the sciences and mathematics to a theodicy. God is
simultaneously the gravest threat to, as well as the most
secure guarantor of, the truths of reason. If God is evil,
reason is untrustworthy; if God is good, reason can be
trusted:

> how do I know that I am not deceived
> every time that I add two and three,
> or count the sides of a square, or
> judge of things yet simpler, if anything
> simpler can be imagined? But possibly
> God has not desired that I should be
> thus deceived, for He is said to be
> supremely good. If, however, it is
> contrary to His goodness to have made
> me such that I constantly deceive myself,
> it would also appear to be contrary
> to His goodness to permit me to be
> sometimes deceived, and nevertheless
> I cannot doubt that He does permit
> this.[17]

Since divine omnipotence does not guarantee divine
beneficence, reason is dubitable if God's power is in the
service of an evil will. Since God's goodness does not
follow analytically from the concept of God, separate proofs
must be given for existence and goodness. As Descartes
says in Meditation III, "without a knowledge of these two
truths I do not see that I can ever be certain of
anything."[18] It is significant that the lists of God's
attributes in both the Discourse and Meditations omit
goodness. The central theological problem is thus the
reconciliation of divine power and goodness, such that
the surface project of the Meditations assumes the form
of a theodicy--Cartesian science must be vindicated by
God's veracity.

According to Frankfurt the Meditations is concerned
with combatting skepticism. Frankfurt has consistently
maintained this position. In Demons, Dreamers, and Madmen
he writes that "The substance of . . . 'metaphysical doubt'
concerning clear and distinct perception . . . is the
fear that judgments based on clear and distinct perceptions
may be mutually inconsistent."[19] In "Descartes on the
Consistency of Reason" he writes, "The question . . . about
reason is . . . whether it is possible that one clear and
distinct perception contradict another in the way that
one sensory perception may contradict another. . . . The
problem . . . was to rebut the skeptical contention that
reliance upon reason may give rise to inconsistencies which
reason cannot resolve, in the same way that reliance upon
the senses may lead to inconsistencies which cannot be
resolved by sensory testimony."[20] As we have seen earlier,
this is not Descartes' understanding of his project. The
primary target of Descartes' argument is not skepticism
but Aristotelianism. A reminder of Descartes' remarks
to Mersenne is in order:

> And I may tell you, between ourselves,
> that these six Meditations contain

> all the foundations of my Physics.
> But please do not tell people, for
> that might make it harder for supporters
> of Aristotle to approve them. I hope
> that readers will gradually get used
> to my principles, and recognize their
> truth, before they notice that they
> destroy the principles of Aristotle.[21]

The replacement of Aristotle is to be complete, which means that both the Aristotelian metaphysics and physics must be superseded by their Cartesian counterparts. The inseparability of physics and metaphysics is as real for Descartes as for Aristotle. (Frankfurt's thesis of the separability of science and certainty from metaphysics and absolute truth will be discussed below.) The manifest plan of the Meditations is thus not an attack upon the skeptics in order to salvage rational consistency, but a replacement of Aristotle through a sanction by a providential God of Cartesian rationality, whose expression is the application of the eternal truths (metaphysics, absolute truth) to the study of nature (physics, rational certainty). The crux of this theodicy is divine goodness, which is questioned in Meditation I and grappled with in the remainder of the work, rather than divine power, which is never questioned per se. When Frankfurt deals with God it is in terms of the extent of God's power vis-a-vis human reason (judging divine omnipotence as incoherent) or the relation of God's intellect to His will in creating the eternal truths, while dismissing the notion of an evil God as inconceivable.

      As we have seen, the issue of God's power, when taken alone, tends to misrepresent the heart of the contest between rationalism and theology.[22] This concerned the apparent victory of the cogito, whose certainty is the paradigm of clarity and distinctness, over an omnipotent God at the beginning of Meditation II. The supremacy of the cogito over omnipotent deception would render all controversies about divine malevolence superfluous. This would demonstrate a triumph of rationalism over theology and the subsequent theodicy could be summarily dismissed as Cartesian insincerity. In what follows I try to show that this judgment, while ultimately sound, is premature if based on the rivalry between the cogito and God's power in Meditations II and III.

      To repeat, the issue does appear as rationalism versus skepticism if the question is narrowed to that concerning God's power. Prior to the demand for proofs of God's existence and goodness in Meditation III, Descartes brings the theological problem sharply into focus. On the one hand:

it seems to me that already I can
establish as a general rule that all
things which I perceive very clearly
and very distinctly are true. . . .
But every time that this preconceived
opinion of the sovereign power of a
God presents itself to my thought,
I am constrained to confess that it
is easy to Him, if He wishes it, to
cause me to err, even in matters in
which I believe myself to have the
best evidence. And, on the other hand,
always when I direct my attention to
things which I believe myself to perceive
very clearly, I am so persuaded of
their truth that I let myself break
out into words such as these: Let
who will deceive me, He can never cause
me to be nothing while I think that
I am, or some day cause it to be true
to say that I have never been, it being
true now to say that I am, or that
two and three make more or less than
five, or any such thing in which I
see a manifest contradiction. [23]

Stated more succinctly in _Meditation_ VI:

For there is no doubt that God possesses
the power to produce everything that
I am capable of perceiving with
distinctness, and I have never deemed
that anything was impossible for Him,
unless I found a contradiction in
attempting to conceive it clearly. [24]

Taken in isolation these passages suggest an either-or
of skepticism (omnipotent deception about one's existence,
mathematics, and logic) or rationalism (defiance of such
omnipotence by human reason).

Dorter reads the passage from _Meditation_ III as
asserting rationalism. He states:

The doctrines are thus wholly
incompatible--one making certitude
possible, the other making it
impossible--and there seems to be no
way of resolving the dilemma without
simply rejecting one of the premisses.
. . . Had the theological premiss
been preferred, the result could only
have been skepticism. . . . reason

must be given precedence . . . if
skepticism is to be avoided.[25]

Descartes explains in the sequel that what is needed is
a theodicy so that reliance upon reason is not in defiance
of divine power but in accord with divine goodness. Dorter's
judgment thus requires confirmation by a demonstration
of the failure of such a theodicy. While Dorter and others
locate this demonstration in the perpetually debated
circularity, I intend to show this through God's
inscrutability, the divine attribute which Frankfurt uses
to justify the distinction between certainty and absolute
truth.

Unperturbed by the problem posed by divine
inscrutability concerning the formation of a clear and
distinct idea of God and therefore the existence proof,
as well as the difficulty of understanding the combination
of a good yet inscrutable divine will, Frankfurt adopts
his compatibilist position by arguing that the notion of
an omnipotent deceiver is "incoherent," that it exceeds
the bounds of rationality, thereby leaving reason intact
and immune from skepticism:

> Descartes takes his task to be precisely
> to show that the skeptic's reductio
> argument cannot be generated. He
> attempts this by offering a proof that
> there is an omnipotent deity who is
> not a deceiver and whose existence
> entails that reason is reliable . .
> . that there are no good reasons for
> believing that reason is unreliable--that
> the mistrust of reason is not supported
> by reason and that it is accordingly
> irrational.[26]

And this is because the evil genius, whose power and deceit
Frankfurt equates with those of God, is an unintelligible
notion:

> Descartes comes to recognize, moreover,
> that the demon hypothesis is not itself
> coherent. Infinite power entails
> infinite goodness, he observes, and
> the notion of an omnipotent being who
> is evil is not an intelligible one.
> The demon hypothesis turns out to be
> self-contradictory and thus it cannot
> serve as a good reason for skepticism.[27]

We can ask at this point that if divine omnipotence entails
divine goodness, why does Frankfurt not conclude that human
reason is in accord with divinely created absolute truth.

Frankfurt resorts to God's inscrutability to separate certainty from absolute truth, but in what does divine inscrutability consist if not recalcitrance to human reason, i.e., a questionable, if not malevolent, will in creating truths inaccessible to human reason? Can certainty escape God's malevolence? What does God's goodness mean if not a divinely willed harmony between such truths and human reason? Divine goodness and inscrutability cannot be simultaneously maintained, though Frankfurt takes this to be Descartes' position. I try to show in what follows that because divine inscrutability fails to vindicate God from possible malevolence, rather than being the capstone of His omnipotence, Descartes' position is that reason renders faith superfluous and that unassisted human reason is able to grasp absolute truth.

The surface argument of the _Meditations_ provides for a good God who justifies human reason (whose hallmark is the law of noncontradiction) by guaranteeing that what human reason cannot help but regard as true is in fact true. The validation concerns the rational faculty rather than the truths themselves since the doctrine of the divine creation of the eternal truths does not appear. Its logical place would appear to be _Meditation_ I, in the context of God's possible malevolence in creating truths contradictory to human reason. Or perhaps it should appear in _Meditation_ III following a proof of God's goodness. Its absence from the _Meditations_ suggests that God's benevolence is the problem. It was only by separating inscrutability from possible malevolence that Frankfurt maintained the centrality of the divine creation of the eternal truths to Descartes' metaphysics and the distinction between certainty and absolute truth.

ANTHROPOLOGY OF ERROR

Following upon the theology of _Meditation_ III, at the start of _Meditation_ IV Descartes connects theology, metaphysics, and physics:

> And it seems to me that I now have before me a road which will lead us from the contemplation of a true God (in whom all the treasures of science and wisdom are contained) to the knowledge of the other objects of the universe.[28]

In what follows I argue that the Cartesian road is other than it appears, not because, as Frankfurt claims, the regions of certainty and absolute truth are heterogeneous for Descartes due to God's mysterious (though presumably benevolent) will, but because revelation gives way to reason.

The theoretical problem is apparently solved with the divine imprimatur on the truth of clear and distinct ideas, yet a doubt remains:

> And no doubt respecting this matter could remain, if it were not that the consequence would seem to follow that I can thus never be deceived; for if I hold all that I possess from God, and if He has not placed in me the capacity for error, it seems as though I could never fall into error . . . yet . . . experience shows me that I am nevertheless subject to an infinitude of errors.[29]

The need to continue the theodicy indicates that the proofs of God's benevolence in Meditation III must be supplemented by a demonstration of the way in which the anthropology of error can free its perfect creator from the charge of malice. Since, as Descartes states at the start of Meditation IV, the problem is not one of establishing a criterion for truth, the form taken by the theodicy centers upon the will. Man's will, his similitude to God, is the faculty to be examined, and in such a way that God's will is to be exonerated. Most recent commentators would agree with the interpretation of the anthropology of error given by Williams:

> the existence of a faculty of judgement which, correctly used, will not lead to error, is sufficient to dispose of the fear of a malicious demon who is a universal cause of error. . . . though Descartes said he did not intend to enquire into the inscrutable purposes of God, there is nevertheless a sense in which God is justified after all. . . . The situation with error, then, is exactly the same as that with moral wrongdoing--the operation of the will is the same, whether one is concerned with reasons of 'the true' or of 'the good'. Descartes' account of the possibility of intellectual error in the face of God is straightforwardly an application of traditional Christian doctrine about man's relation to God in moral matters: God has provided us, as a special gift, with a free will that can be misused.[30]

An initial reading of Meditation IV appears to confirm Williams. Descartes' first candidate theodicy is in terms of traditional Christian metaphysics. Since "I am in a sense something intermediate between God and nought . . . between supreme Being and non-being . . . there is in truth nothing in me that can lead to error so far as a sovereign Being has formed me."[31] To be finite is to be

susceptible to error.   To be error-free is to stretch the
likeness between man and God beyond its limit.   But such
an ontology of error is rejected because of an uncertainty
about God's will:

> Nevertheless this does not quite satisfy
> me; for error is not a pure negation
> [i.e. is not the simple defect or want
> of some perfection which ought to be
> mine], but it is a lack of some knowledge
> which it seems I ought to possess.
> . . . And certainly there is no doubt
> that God could have created me so that
> I could never have been subject to
> error; it is also certain that He ever
> wills what is best; is it then better
> that I should be subject to err than
> that I should not?[32]

Since error is not lack of omniscience or mere finitude,
our status as creatures cannot totally explain it.   We
need an explanation which allows for the commission of
false judgment consonant with the divine will.   We must
ask why God did not choose to create us error-free since
He had the power to do so.   Apparently the corrigibility
of the human will is the vindication of God's will.   I
will discuss below whether such a vindication is adequate
given Descartes' insistence upon God's incomprehensibility
in the sequel: "I should not be astonished if my
intelligence is not capable of comprehending why God acts
as He does."[33] If God is incomprehensible can we ever claim
to know why we are created prone to error, why we are not
granted "a faculty . . . perfect in its kind?"   God's
incomprehensibility also precludes Descartes from explaining
error as a perhaps necessary imperfection in what is but
a part of the divinely created whole, that "the same thing
which might possibly seem very imperfect with some semblance
of reason if regarded by itself, is found to be very perfect
if regarded as part of the whole universe."[34] Despite God's
mysteriousness, this same explanation is inserted at the
end of Meditation IV and claimed to be indubitable.[35]

   Turning to the soul, Descartes offers a twofold cause
of error--the understanding as faculty of knowledge and
the will as faculty of choice.   This is quickly amended
in favor of a finite, blameless understanding and an
infinite, culpable will.   The understanding is blameless,
says Descartes, since error resides in judging: "For by
the understanding alone I [neither assert nor deny anything,
but] apprehend the ideas of things as to which I can form
a judgment."[36]   God is blameless because the finite intellect
is not the similitude between man and God.   The will, "so
extended as to be subject to no limits", is for this reason
the cause of error.   Unlike God's infinite and creative
will, the human will, the primary sign of our likeness
to God, must operate within a finite horizon.   Nonetheless,
the will's choosing is totally free of external restraint:

> the faculty of will consists alone
> in our having the power of choosing

> to do a thing or choosing not to do
> it (that is, to affirm or deny, or
> pursue or to shun it), or rather it
> consists alone in the fact that in
> order to affirm or deny, pursue or
> shun those things placed before us
> by the understanding, we act so that
> we are unconscious that any outside
> force constrains us in doing so.[37]

The will is autonomous in its choosing; however, its options
are limited "for the light of nature teaches us that the
knowledge of the understanding should always precede the
determination of the will."[38]

The question concerning the will's fallibility becomes
one of establishing the proper relation between the will's
freedom and a criterion for judgment. On what basis should
the will decide, and to what extent is the will independent
of the intellect? The will is free with respect to the
intellect in one of two ways. The liberty of spontaneity,
rather than the liberty of indifference, is the greater
degree of freedom and likewise explains the criterion of
judgment:

> For in order that I should be free
> it is not necessary that I should be
> indifferent as to the choice of one
> or the other of two contraries; but
> contrariwise the more I lean to the
> one--whether I recognize clearly that
> the reasons of the good and true are
> to be found in it, or whether God so
> disposes my inward thought--the more
> freely do I choose and embrace it.
> And undoubtedly both divine grace and
> natural knowledge, far from diminishing
> my liberty, rather increase and
> strengthen it.[39]

Whereas an obscure or confused presentation leaves the
will indifferent, a negative type of freedom, "from great
clearness in my mind there followed a great inclination
of my will; and I believed this with so much the greater
freedom or spontaneity as I possessed the less indifference
towards it."[40] We now know the cause of error. It consists
in judging from freedom of indifference. God's goodness
is not impugned since our faculties are perfect in their
kind. Consequently it is consistent with God's goodness
that the will "easily falls into error and sin, and chooses
the evil for the good, or the false for the true."[41] The
linkage of error and sin places the discussion within the
traditional framework of the divinely donated human will
solely responsible for its free choices. As Descartes
says, "Privation . . . is found in the act, insofar as
it proceeds from me, but it is not found in the faculty
which I have received from God, nor even in the act insofar
as it depends on Him."[42] Error can be avoided if the will
resolves to affirm clear and distinct ideas and suspend
judgment in all other cases.

Contra Williams, in what follows I argue that the Christian theological anthropology of error is Christian only in appearance. Theoretical error is not assimilated to moral error and requiring a critique of the free choice of the will. Moral error is instead assimilated to theoretical error, whereby sin becomes ignorance as the correlate of virtue as clear and distinct cognition. The spontaneity of the will as a separate faculty of the mind (contradicted by the later anthropology of the Meditations) is the way in which the dissimulation in Meditation IV serves to cloak rationalism rather than adhere to Christian voluntarism.

THE INTELLECT AND THE WILL

To decide the extents of voluntarism and rationalism in Descartes' theory of error the relation between intellect and will must be reexamined. The nature, scope, and dignity of the will are indicated by Descartes in many ways. As we have seen, the entire Meditations is launched by a willful resolve to doubt. Willful resolve figured preeminently in the Discourse as the basis for following one's own reason and in the provisional morals. In Meditation IV we seem to find two aspects of the will--as faculty of choice and attitude of resolve--the latter as the corrective for the vagaries of the former in judging in the absence of clear and distinct perception.

In the Principles Descartes gives more autonomy to the will, which is distinguished as a separate faculty from the intellect. In Part One, VI, the freedom of the will is said to resist God. Unlike the intellect, whose clear and distinct perception could be jeopardized by an omnipotent evil God:

> whoever turns out to have created us,
> and even should he prove to be
> all-powerful and deceitful, we still
> experience a freedom through which
> we may abstain from accepting as true
> and indisputable those things of which
> we have not certain knowledge, and
> thus obviate our ever being deceived.[43]

What frees the will from God's deception is also what prevents it from being a source of truth--its lack of content. Nonetheless a case can be made for a strong voluntarist element in Descartes since clear and distinct perception requires affirmation by the autonomous will. As he explains in Part One, XXXVII:

> the principal perfection of man is
> to have the power of acting freely
> or by will . . . this is what renders
> him deserving of either praise or blame.
> . . . And for the same reason when
> we choose what is true, much more credit
> is due to us when the choice is made
> freely, than when it is made of
> necessity.[44]

But is such a freedom a genuine autonomy in the doctrine of the <u>Meditations</u>? Concerning the relation between intellect and will, to speak meaningfully (and morally) about error and its avoidance would seem to require a legitimate latitude on the part of the will. Necessary choices eliminate the problem of error as involving a critique of the will. It would seem that an adequate account of the freedom of the will must provide for error as well as its corrigibility. In <u>Meditation</u> IV this ostensibly requires a separate and free faculty of will. The will's autonomy, however, is an empty autonomy without supplementation by the content in the intellect. And no sooner does it receive a content then it becomes enslaved to it when the content is perceived to be clear and distinct. That is, though the will is free from external or causal necessity, it may not be free from rational necessity. Descartes' method of reconciling willful autonomy and rational necessity is to distinguish between two types of freedom of the will vis-a-vis the intellect--freedom of indifference and freedom of spontaneity. It is by means of the shift from indifference to spontaneity that rationalism masquerades as voluntarism.

The distinction between the two liberties is elaborated upon in the Correspondence. The most extensive treatment is in the letters to Denis Mesland [?] of May 1644 and February 1645. In the first letter, after indicating that indifference can result either from insufficient knowledge or insufficient reasons to choose one of a pair of options, Descartes reiterates the freedom of spontaneity as described in <u>Meditation</u> IV:

> For it seems to me that a great light in the intellect is followed by a strong inclination in the will; so that if we see very clearly that a thing is good for us it is very difficult--and, on my view, impossible, so long as one continues in the same thought--to stop the course of our desire.[45]

The will is determined to follow what the intellect presents as choiceworthy. Descartes claims that when the will is irresistably drawn it has "a real and positive power to determine oneself." To choose in this manner is to embrace the true and the good, the corollary of which is that to choose from indifference is to choose blindly and to be correct only by chance.

In this same letter, after telling Mesland that he abstained from speaking about the freedom to choose good or evil in the <u>Meditations</u> in order to avoid theological controversy, Descartes agrees with Mesland that "whoever sins, does so in ignorance" because "wherever there is occasion for sinning, there is indifference". Kenny, after referring to this remark, states that "In the <u>Meditations</u> Descartes did not explain how the will falls into sin as explicitly as he explained how the will falls into error."[46] Beck goes further. Taking Descartes' disclaimer in the synopsis seriously, he maintains that Descartes excludes moral error, wrongdoing, and sin from <u>Meditation</u> IV. Beck adds in a note:

> but one can guess how he would treat
> the problem from the phrase in the
> Fourth Meditation: 'Privatio autem,
> in qua sola ratio formalis falsitatis
> et culpae consistit, nullo Dei concursu
> indiget' (AT. VII. 60^{31}-61^2).[47]

But I must disagree with Kenny and Beck since Meditation
IV contains the same analysis as the passage from the Mesland
letter:

> if I always recognized clearly what
> was true and good, I should never have
> trouble in deliberating as to what
> judgment or choice I should make, and
> then I should be entirely free without
> ever being indifferent.[48]

In the sequel Descartes explicitly presents the correlatives
of virtue and knowledge, sin and ignorance as a consequence
of the freedom of indifference:

> Whence then come my errors? They come
> from the sole fact that since the will
> is much wider in its range and compass
> than the understanding, I do not restrain
> it within the same bounds, but extend
> it also to things which I do not
> understand: and as the will is of
> itself indifferent to these, it easily
> falls into error and sin, and chooses
> the evil for the good, or the false
> for the true.[49]

It is clear that the freedom of spontaneity--the compelled
affirmation of clear and distinct perception--has both
a theoretical and moral function when it is recalled that
the rational and moral autonomy of the Discourse was for
the purpose of curing the vacillation, inconstancy, and
irresolution of the indecisive. In each case the freedom
of spontaneity remedies the errors of the freedom of
indifference concerning the evil and the false.

   A fuller account of the will is given in the letter
of February 1645, which begins by distinguishing a negative
and positive freedom of indifference. Indifference as
neutrality is a negative or low degree of freedom, yet
Descartes does not quarrel with those who regard it as
a positive freedom. As a matter of fact, says Descartes,
the will possesses what we can call a truly absolute freedom,
absolute in the sense that it can override freedom of
spontaneity:

> Indeed, I think it has it not only
> with respect to those actions to which
> it is not pushed by any evident reasons
> on one side rather than on the other,
> but also with respect to all other
> actions; so that when a very evident
> reason moves us in one direction
> although, morally speaking, we can

> hardly move in the contrary direction,
> absolutely we can. For it is always
> open to us to hold back from pursuing
> a clearly known good, or from admitting
> a clearly perceived truth, provided
> we consider it a good thing to
> demonstrate the freedom of our will
> by so doing.[50]

Such absolute or existential freedom seems to jeopardize
the master-slave relation between clear and distinct
perception and the will. Kenny takes issue with the
existentialist interpretation (of Ferdinand Alquié) because
of its consequences for the validation of reason project
in the Meditations:

> To abandon the theory that clear and
> distinct perception necessitates the
> will is to call in question the whole
> validation of reason in which the
> Meditations culminates. . . . The
> doctrine of the Meditations, the
> Principles and the letters is all of
> a piece. I see no reason for thinking
> that at the age of forty-nine Descartes
> underwent a spectacular conversion
> from rationalism to existentialism.[51]

Kenny labels this absolute, existentialist freedom the
"freedom of perversity," the unique power of the will to
demonstrate its freedom by apparently forsaking the true
and the good. For the will to reject the true and the
good in the absence of reasons means, according to Kenny,
that the will acts capriciously. But this is not Descartes'
meaning. The text of the letter refutes the existentialist
position since what Descartes calls absolute freedom is
a unique, perhaps limiting case, of freedom of spontaneity.
The freedom of spontaneity compels the will to assent not
only to a perceived truth but also to a perceived good.
Absolute freedom is an instance of the latter. We may
deny clear and distinct perception "provided we consider
it a good thing to demonstrate the freedom of our will
by so doing." This is the explanation for the seeming
subversion of reason by the perverse self-affirmation of
the will.
    In the remainder of the letter Descartes reinstates
the freedom of spontaneity by distinguishing the actions
of the will before and after they have been chosen. Prior
to choosing, the will experiences an absolute freedom since
either of two alternatives, as well as a rejection of both,
is logically possible. However, it does not experience
the freedom of indifference. We cannot "say that we are
freer to do those things which seem neither good nor evil,
or in which there are many reasons pro but as many reasons
contra, than in those in which we see much more good than
evil."[52] Freedom of spontaneity is reinstated because
freedom of indifference, although a logical possibility,
is a psychological impossibility. Freedom as autonomy
is inconsistent with choosing the worse while seeing the
better. Consequently at the moment a choice is made neither

variety of indifference is present when there are reasons
favoring one alternative. Because choosing from spontaneity
is easier and thus freer, "freedom, spontaneity, and
voluntariness are the same thing."[53] This is the doctrine
of Meditation IV, and it is reiterated several times in
Meditation V that the will necessarily affirms clear and
distinct perception. That is, we are most free when we
are most rational. We are most prone to error and sin
when the will detaches itself from the norm of clarity
and distinctness. While abstaining from drawing the
heretical consequence concerning the relation between faith
and reason implied by the subservience of will to reason,[54]
Descartes accomplishes by the liberty of spontaneity a
seeming voluntarism concerning truth as the complement
of a voluntarist theory of error. Rational and moral
necessity are made to appear as the free choice of the
God-given will.

However, when the liberty of spontaneity is properly
understood this voluntarism must be revised. As Caton
observes, Descartes' strategy was accurately exposed by
Etienne Gilson:

> In order to bring the problem of error
> within the scope of the theological
> argumentation about providence, Descartes
> construes error as sin; but since
> theology attributes sin to the will,
> the argumentative strategy conspires
> to generate an explanation of error
> that attributes it to the will. The
> mingling of the theological and
> philosophical points of view produces
> the result that, as Etienne Gilson
> put it, 'the problem of sin is the
> theological form of the problem of
> error, and the problem of error is
> the philosophical form of the problem
> of sin'. [La Liberte chez Descartes
> et la Theologie (Paris: Alcan, 1913)
> p. 266] To satisfy these requirements,
> Descartes must identify judgment with
> choice and attribute it to the will.[55]

Kenny, who links the anthropology of Meditation IV to the
dualism in Aquinas between apprehension and assent, rejects
the above interpretation:

> The crucial objection to Gilson's thesis
> is that it was not necessary, for
> Descartes to be able to exploit Aquinas'
> arguments, that he should have made
> judgement an act of the will; it was
> sufficient for him to make it a voluntary
> act of the intellect.[56]

I am suggesting that this is precisely what Descartes does
do in Meditations IV and V. Kenny's critique of Descartes'
manifest argument (separation of faculties of intellect
and will) is thus well taken and, properly understood,
confirms the Gilson interpretation. He states:

> The problem . . . is that the object
> of the intellect is truth, and that
> of the will is goodness; that error
> is a matter of falsehood, and sin of
> badness.[57]

Though expressed in terms of the language of distinct
faculties of intellect and will, Descartes' message is
the self-determination of reason, the resolve of reason
to follow reason. The utter passivity of the will in the
face of clear and distinct perception cannot be interpreted
in any other way. The famous criticism of Spinoza (Ethics,
Part II, 49, Scholium) concerning the separation of intellect
and will in Descartes is likewise misdirected since Descartes
intends no such separation of the mind into faculties.
How distinct can the will be if it exercises liberty of
spontaneity? As we have seen, the freedom of spontaneity
subjects the will to an external force, which means that
the judgment of the will in no way contributes to the initial
awareness of the truth. The judgment of the will follows
the determination of the knowledge of truth by the intellect.
What the will is capable of generating is falsehood since,
by the liberty of indifference, it goes beyond the content
in the intellect. The will truly judges only when it errs,
such that Descartes' voluntarism pertains only to the account
of error and sin. When it comes to the true and the good,
clear and distinct perception is, in effect, self-certifying.

The covert nature of the rationalism in Meditations
IV and V becomes clearer when it is recognized that Descartes
does not subscribe to a faculty psychology. This in turn
eliminates the issue of when and why Descartes apparently
changed his doctrine of judgment from the Regulae to the
Meditations. Kenny writes that:

> When he wrote the Regulae, Descartes
> still held the orthodox Thomist view.
> . . . Some time, then, between 1628
> and 1640 Descartes changed his mind
> about the nature of judgement. It
> is not easy to discover when or why
> he did so.[58]

Kenny's suggestion concerning Descartes' move to judgment
as an act of will is in terms of R. M. Hare's
phrastic-neustic distinction. But this does not answer
the why question since Hare's distinction seems no more
than a modern translation of Descartes' presentation-judgment
distinction. As we saw, Kenny's criticism to the effect
that Descartes was unaware that truth concerns intellect
and that goodness concerns will only reinforces the suspicion
that their conflation in Meditation IV is motivated by
Descartes' desire to soften his antitraditional doctrine.

In Meditation IV what casts doubt on the faculty
psychology is, to repeat, the replacement of indifference
by spontaneity. The freedom of indifference suggests a
duality of faculties since the will must act independently
of the intellect if a judgment is to occur. However, the
freedom of spontaneity, as we have seen, weakens the case
for the will's independence. A will which necessarily

assents is a will in name only.

The difficulty of separating intellect and will is expressed in terms of activity-passivity in the letter of May 1641 to Regius:

> Finally, where you say 'willing and understanding differ only as different ways of acting in regard to different objects' I would prefer 'they differ only as the activity and passivity of one and the same substance'. For strictly, understanding is the passivity of the mind and willing its activity; but because we cannot will anything without understanding what we will, and we scarcely ever understand something without at the same time willing something, we do not easily distinguish in this matter passivity from activity.[59]

These distinctions are hard to maintain not only because understanding and willing overlap and penetrate each other such that, as we have seen, the understanding becomes willful and the will becomes rational, but because action and passion, and by implication will and intellect, are in fact not separate faculties at all, but rather modes of operation of a unitary res cogitans, as Descartes' reformulation of Regius suggests. If one still wishes to maintain separate faculties one would have to reverse this active-passive relation between intellect and will since the liberty of spontaneity, by making the will passive to the intellect, makes the intellect active in relation to the will. But such a revision becomes unnecessary when it is realized that a unitary res cogitans, simultaneously intellect and will, active and passive, is Descartes' authoritative doctrine in the Meditations.

That intellect and will are modes of operation rather than separate faculties can be demonstrated by tracing the articulation of the res cogitans as it progresses through the Meditations. In Meditation I, which does not mention the will, apart from the reference to the launching of the doubt as an act of resolution, we get a critique of the cognitive faculties of sensation, imagination, and intellect, even though, as their critique revealed, they are nonautonomous collaborators in rendering experience possible on the basis of the Cartesian ontology of body. The will makes its first explicit appearance in Meditation II as belonging to a nonsubstantial, metaphysically neutral res cogitans comprising every conceivable mode of thought. The res cogitans is not identified as a multiplicity of distinct faculties. It is simply "a thing which doubts, understands, [conceives], affirms, denies, wills, refuses, which also imagines and feels."[60] Following the mediated conception of consciousness concluding Meditation II, we get from Meditations III-V a seeming faculty conception, epitomized in Meditation IV by a passive intellect and an active, judging will. This latter faculty is said to be our similitude to God. The dichotomy of ideas and judgments, intellect and will, appears as Descartes' epistemic and moral psychic schema.

Prior to the <u>Meditations</u> there appears to be a faculty conception in <u>Regulae</u> I. However, in <u>Regulae</u> XII this is replaced by a multiplicity within the intellect itself which enables it to reflectively judge its contents. Combining this self-reflective intellect with the unmitigated rationalism it is meant to reinforce, Descartes writes:

> Thirdly we assert that all these simple natures are known per se and are wholly free from falsity. It will be easy to show this, provided we distinguish that faculty of our understanding by which it has an intuitive awareness of things and knows them, from that by which it judges, making use of affirmation and denial. For we may imagine ourselves to be ignorant of things which we really know, for example on such occasions as when we believe that in such things, over and above what we have present to us or attain to by thinking, there is something else hidden from us, and when this belief of ours is false. Whence it is evident that we are in error if we judge that any one of these simple natures is not completely known by us. For if our mind attains to the least acquaintance with it, as must be the case, since we are assumed to pass judgment on it, this fact alone makes us infer that we know it completely.[61]

What is made explicit here is latent in <u>Meditation</u> IV. In <u>Regulae</u> XII, just as in the conclusion of <u>Meditation</u> III and the beginning of <u>Meditation</u> IV, there is no doubt expressed about the criterion of truth. The absence of the theological issue, that is, the need to reconcile Cartesian science with faith, which necessitated the will as the arbiter of truth by cleansing itself from error and as the locus of virtue by equating sin with false judgment, allows the <u>Regulae</u> to present the relation between truth, intellect, and judgment more candidly. Contrary to Beck, Kenny, and Williams, the introduction of judging, as Descartes explains, is only to reinforce the necessity of the intellect to assert the truth of the simple natures it cannot but perceive as true. Since they are true in themselves and we can intuit them as such, to assert or judge them as true adds nothing to their truth status. The self-reflective judging capacity of the intellect, whereby it affirms what is perceived as true, precludes a voluntarism of the traditional type since a separate faculty of will is not involved. Despite the vocabulary of "that faculty of our understanding," to avoid the regress of faculties within faculties we must conclude that the <u>Regulae</u> does not ascribe judging to the will as a distinct faculty. It is ascribed to an enlarged notion of the

intellect. Modes within modes more accurately portrays
the multiplicity within unity which is the Cartesian res
cogitans. The Meditations continues this doctrine, the
faculty terminology from Meditations III-V necessitated
by prudential theodicy.

The overthrow of the faculty conception of the soul
begun in Meditation II is completed in Meditation VI.
When distinguishing the imagination from the intellect,
Descartes does not describe it as a separate faculty.
"I find that it is nothing but a certain application of
the faculty of knowledge to the body which is immediately
present to it."[62] Descartes goes on to say that the
difference between the imagination and the pure intellect
is not one of kind but one of effort, more of an effort
needed in the case of imagining figures than in simply
thinking them. The faculty conception of kinds thus gives
way to the notion of a single agency admitting of kinds
and degrees of application. This helps explain the apparent
tension in the analysis of the wax between the intellectual-
intuitive-pure grasp of the wax as extension and the approach
by means of the imaginative-abstractive-empirical route.

When Descartes distinguishes the mind from the body
he gives us an explicit statement of the unity that is
res cogitans:

> In order to begin this examination,
> then, I here say, in the first place,
> that there is a great difference between
> mind and body, inasmuch as body is
> by nature always divisible, and the
> mind is entirely indivisible. For,
> as a matter of fact, when I consider
> the mind, that is to say, myself inasmuch
> as I am only a thinking thing, I cannot
> distinguish in myself any parts, but
> apprehend myself to be clearly one
> and entire; and although the whole
> mind seems to be united to one whole
> body, yet if a foot, or an arm, or
> some other part, is separated from
> my body, I am aware that nothing has
> been taken away from my mind. And
> the faculties of willing, freely,
> conceiving, etc. cannot be properly
> speaking said to be its parts, for
> it is one and the same mind which employs
> itself in will and in feeling and in
> understanding.[63]

Although the move from extensive indivisibility to psychic
unity may appear unwarranted since faculties as well as
modes would not require extensive divisibility, Descartes
uses it to assert a unitary res cogitans comprising all
manner of thinking. This is consistent with what he writes
to Mersenne just prior to the publication of the Discourse:

> You argue that if the nature of man
> is simply to think, then he has no

> will. I do not see that this follows;
> because willing, understanding,
> imagining, sensing, and so on, are
> just different ways of thinking, and
> all belong to the soul.[64]

The nature of the mind is exhausted in the various modal
applications of the one cognitive power. The most
straightforward denial of faculties is in the Passions,
Descartes' true anthropology:

> For there is within us but one soul,
> and this soul has not in itself any
> diversity of parts; the same part that
> is subject to sense impressions is
> rational, and all the soul's appetites
> are acts of will.[65]

The reason for different accounts of the soul in
different parts of the Meditations is, as we have seen,
because of the specific problem under consideration. It
is likewise with God. In the Meditations the absence of
the doctrine of the divine creation of the eternal truths
is coupled with a faculty conception so that God's will
can be isolated as a threat to reason handled along
traditional theodicy lines. In the Correspondence the
divine creation of the eternal truths is coupled with a
unitary divine nature. Accounting for this shift will
reveal the relation between Descartes' theological
metaphysics and nontheological physics.

THEOLOGY AND RATIONALISM

The Divine Nature

The unitary character of God's nature is asserted
in the context of the divine creation of the eternal truths.
To Mersenne in May 1630 Descartes explains that "In God,
willing, understanding and creating are all the same thing
without the one being prior to the other even
conceptually."[66] Concerning the relation between God's
nature and the nature of the human soul, Frankfurt
articulates the generally accepted view:

> Descartes does not explain just why
> it is a mistake to distinguish God's
> understanding and His will. The
> following general line of argument
> would have been available to him,
> however, given his views on the relevant
> subjects: in humans, the understanding
> is a passive faculty; but since it
> is inadmissable to ascribe any passivity
> to God, the divine understanding must
> be construed as active; and this means
> supposing that, like the divine will,

> it necessarily has an effect upon its
> object. It is plausible to conjecture
> that Descartes came to this theory
> through his association . . . with
> the Oratory of Cardinal Berulle. The
> central feature of Berulle's theory
> was its particular emphasis upon the
> unity and simplicity of God's nature.[67]

It is true that Descartes' unification of God's attributes
is the doctrine of the Oratory; however, its rationale
is not an interest in distinguishing the divine from the
human soul but, as Descartes explains to Mersenne, the
intention of "adapting theology to my style of philosophy."[68]
Moreover, given the likewise unitary res cogitans, perhaps
this is the real similitude between man and God--a nature
which is at once reason and will, that is, what Descartes
calls resolution--thereby effecting an apotheosis of the
human soul as the reverse side of divine inscrutability.
The very gulf between man and God, consistent with the
tradition of a finite human understanding, is thus a threat
to this tradition since God's mysteriousness is what prevents
a convincing proof of his goodness so necessary for theodicy
(not to mention the difficulty of coming up with a clear
and distinct idea of God). In the place of a demonstration
of such goodness, Descartes shrouds the divine nature by
drawing a conclusion concerning physics from the abyss
separating human and divine capacities:

> Knowing that my nature is extremely
> feeble and limited, and that the nature
> of God is on the contrary immense,
> incomprehensible, and infinite, I have
> no further difficulty in recognizing
> that there is an infinitude of matters
> in His power, the causes of which
> transcend my knowledge; and this reason
> suffices to convince me that the species
> of cause termed final, finds no useful
> employment in physical [or natural]
> things; for it does not appear to me
> that I can without temerity seek to
> investigate the [inscrutable] ends
> of God.[69]

In the name of piety, says Descartes, we must remain ignorant
of God's purposes since His will is unintelligible to human
reason. From this we must draw the conclusion that if
God's will is unintelligible to human reason we can no
longer confidently demonstrate God's goodness. Beck and
Grayeff resist such a conclusion. Beck writes:

> It is true, Descartes admitted, that
> the infinite is by nature
> incomprehensible to the finite
> understanding. . . . But 'the Infinite
> is shadowed forth in something finite',
> and our idea of God, though not
> exhaustive, is sufficiently clear and

distinct. . . . We know . . . that
everything which we can conceive as
positive, perfect, or real, is included
in God's nature. Our idea of God is
partial or incomplete, not in the sense
that it only grasps a part of Him:
it represents the total cause or whole,
though not exhaustively, as clearly
and distinctly as possible for the
idea belonging to a finite mind to
represent what is infinite or absolutely
complete. . . . 'it is enough to
conceive God as a thing confined by
no limits'. The limitations of finite
knowledge do not prevent us from
attaining to a clear understanding
of the general nature of God, of the
principal attributes of His being.[70]

More recently, Grayeff writes:

Descartes has been accused of
contradicting himself by saying that
we do not comprehend God yet we are
sure that he is no deceiver. But this
is no just charge. We may be sure
of one aspect of God without
understanding him fully. All that
Descartes says is that while we can
be certain of God's veracity we neither
comprehend his purpose nor all that
is embraced by infinity; or--expressed
in modern terms--that (a) teleological
studies of nature lead us nowhere;
(b) we shall never be able to grasp
the cosmos in its entirety.[71]

Descartes' insistence on the unitary nature of God's
attributes renders such a partial knowledge of God difficult
to understand. Given Descartes' notion of clarity and
distinctness, knowledge of God's nature appears to be an
all-or-none affair. Further, judging God to be good in
the absence of reasons (i.e., judging from faith or piety)
is in flagrant violation of the norm expressed by the liberty
of spontaneity, the willful resolve to follow one's reason
(clear and distinct ideas) in all matters.
What Descartes responds to Johannes Caterus appears
to justify the view of Beck and Grayeff:

I admit along with all theologians
that God cannot be comprehended by
the human mind . . .at once in His
entirety. . . . But those who try to
attend to His perfections singly, and
intend not so much to comprehend them
as to admire them and to employ all
the power of their mind in contemplating
them, will assuredly find in Him a
much ampler and readier supply of the

> material for clear and distinct cognition
> than in any created things.[72]

That this is not possible concerning God's goodness should
be evident, since Descartes in _Meditation_ IV explicitly
lists God's will among the unintelligibles. Reason and
faith are thus not only separate but mutually exclusive,
because from the epistemic and anthropological points of
view the cognitive and psychological imperatives of the
liberty of spontaneity leave no room for faith. And since
faith defers to human reason we must confirm the suspicion
that the theodicy of the _Meditations_ is insincere. This
is also borne out by the way in which Cartesian mechanicism
replaces teleology.

Mechanicism vs. Teleology

The elimination of final cause from nature, that is,
the critique of Aristotelian physics, is accomplished by
extracting a nontraditional conclusion from traditional
premises. Since nature is not _causa sui_, if there are
to be any purposes in nature they must have their source
in the divine mind, God's intentions at the time of creation.
Since these intentions are unknowable we cannot impute
final cause to nature. Cartesian nature thus appears as
the consequence of the theological postulate of an
incomprehensible Creator. This permits Descartes to separate
the world into the nonhuman (nontelic) and the human by
regarding final cause as nothing more than an anthropomorphic
projection. He robs nature of ends and locates them in
mind, but since it is the divine rather than the human
mind, mechanicism emerges as a theologically derived
consequence rather than from a rational argument on purely
scientific grounds (as is done in _The World_ and the
Principles, Part Four). We are led to believe that the
hiddenness of God's aims testifies simultaneously to a
science of nature comprising only efficient causes and
Cartesian piety. The two are apparently not in conflict
since "we must trust to this natural light only so long
as nothing contrary to it is revealed by God Himself."[73]
Presumably what God does reveal is not final cause, which
would force revisions within mechanicism, but a vindication
of efficient cause by the coincidence of the primary notions
of Cartesian science and the eternal truths He created.
Whether Descartes intends an either-or relation to exist
between mechanicism (reason) and teleology (faith) thus
depends on the interpretation of Descartes' negative
theology.

Descartes cautiously appears to avoid this either-or
relation since he restricts mechanicism to the human account
of nature rather than the inner workings of nature, which
is the exclusive province of the divine mind. He seems
to opt for a proto-Kantian dualism of outward mechanicism
(appearance) and inner teleology (thing-in-itself). This
is the early view of Frankfurt, who bases his reading not
only upon the epistemological implication of the negative
theology but also upon the reconciliation of science and
religion that this permits Descartes to effect with respect

to the Galileo controversy which Descartes tried in vain
to avoid. Frankfurt writes:

> Descartes adopts neither the position
> of the Church nor that of Galileo.
> His alternative neatly avoids the point
> of contention between them and makes
> it unnecessary for him to deny the
> autonomy either of science or of
> revelation. Galileo and the Church
> fought because each claimed special
> access to the nature of things. . .
> . Descartes, on the other hand, leaves
> God's truth to God and claims for science
> only a truth sufficient for man. .
> . . His solution . . . has a Kantian
> flavor: men may content themselves
> with certainty about phenomena and
> leave the noumenon to God.[74]

Frankfurt adds that he does not wish to press this analogy
any further; however, he uses it to support what might
after all turn out to be the distinction on which his
interpretation depends--the distinction between physics
as the human account of nature and metaphysics as the divine
understanding. We must therefore question the analogy,
for whereas it is clear that for Kant the science
(lawfulness) of nature is limited to the phenomenal realm,
this is not the case for Descartes. For Descartes the
laws of nature are at the same time the eternal truths,
such that their certainty stands or falls together. If
we cannot be sure of God's creation of truth we cannot
be sure of its corporeality as mechanics--but Descartes
insists that we are. Thus we either accept an unintelligible
metaphysics and physics or ground them both in human reason
minus a divine guarantee. Descartes' strategy is revealed
in what he writes to Mersenne in reference to the fate
of Galileo: "I desire to live in peace and to continue
the life I have begun under the motto that to live well
you must live unseen."[75]

Frankfurt's more recent position is a shift to the
distinction between certainty and truth. God's transcendence
produces

> a decisive and ineradicable uncertainty
> concerning the relation between the
> class of judgments that correctly
> describe the inherent nature of reality
> . . . . Descartes' vision . . . is
> that the world may be inherently absurd
> . . . there may be a discontinuity
> in principle between what we can
> understand and what God knows.
> Rationality may be nothing more than
> a convenient collective form of lunacy,
> which enables those who suffer from
> it to communicate with each other,
> but which isolates them all from what
> is ultimately real. . . . the assertion

> that reality as it is in itself may
> be in principle unintelligible to us
> exempts reason from having to regard
> itself as a competitor of transrational
> modes of access to truth. . . .
> Descartes' doctrine . . . renders human
> reason and divine reason discontinuous.[76]

We are asked to believe that Descartes' epistemology is
not also a metaphysics since the certainty of the former
is discontinuous with the truth of the latter. But this
goes against Descartes' explicit statements concerning
the relation between God, mathematics, and physics in
Meditations V and VI. Since physics is intimately tied
to metaphysics because the eternal truths are the essence
of body, Descartes' physics would be open to ultimate
skepticism if "human reason and divine reason [are]
discontinuous." We would be forced to conclude from an
inscrutable God an equally inscrutable metaphysics and
physics since, as Descartes explains to Mersenne concerning
"the mathematical truths which you call eternal . . . it
is God who has laid down these laws of nature."[77] Pure
mathematics, ambiguously distinguished from the sciences
concerning existence in Meditation I, is in fact the essence
of body. With respect to God, then, we must inquire not
into the possibility that He can create essences which
would be alien to our science, but why He would choose
to do so. An inscrutable metaphysics renders physics
erroneous, i.e., simply wrong, no matter how certain it
may appear to be. This does not reflect well on God's
veracity and benevolence. It should also be remembered
that the practical side of physics--technology--would be
difficult to legitimate if nature operated at some level
in accordance with God-given purposes. Technology requires
the detheologizing of nature in order to make it morally
amenable to "mastery and possession."

In the Meditations Descartes follows the advice he
has given to Regius concerning the comprehensiveness of
mechanicism as the replacement for substantial forms.
While the traditional terminology is retained, in that
final cause is not said to be a fiction but merely "finds
no useful employment in physical [or natural] things,"[78]
Descartes pours new wine into these old bottles by allowing
the force of the argument to demolish the traditional
doctrine by implying that the nonuse of final cause derives
from its nonexistence. This ploy of "adapting theology
to my style of philosophy" was seen very clearly by Leibniz,
who expresses the relation between Cartesian theology and
science as follows:

> I am told that Descartes established
> so well the existence of God and the
> immortality of the soul. I fear that
> we are deceived by such beautiful words.
> For the God or perfect being of Descartes
> is not a God such as one imagines,
> and as one would wish, that is to say,
> just and wise, doing all things for
> the good of the creatures so far as

is possible, but rather he is something
approaching the God of Spinoza, that
is to say, the principle of things,
and a certain sovereign power called
primitive, which puts all in action,
and does all that can be done; which
has no will nor understanding, since
according to Descartes he does not
have the good for the object of his
will, nor the true for the object of
his understanding. For he does not
wish that his God act according to
some end, and it is for that reason
that he excluded from philosophy the
quest for final causes, under this
clever pretext that we are not capable
of knowing the purposes of God.[79]

In agreement with Leibniz, we can say that Cartesian nature
has become detheologized by its dependence upon a God which
has become naturalized, the inscrutability of God's will
being the personification of nonteleological nature. As
we have seen from the architectonic of the Discourse,
Descartes' theology was composed subsequent to his physics,
such that the rejection of final cause was independent
of theological considerations from the start.

The shift from nature to God in order to discuss final
cause was necessary because a mechanical physics precludes
a discovery of teleology by an inspection or investigation
of nature itself. In fact it would be difficult to prove
in the first place that God existed as a wise and beneficent
creator by reflecting upon a nature showing no signs of
such wisdom and goodness. While in Meditation IV Descartes
proceeds immediately to the divine nature and from there
back to nature, the difficulties of going from nature to
God are mentioned in the Correspondence. To Mersenne
Descartes wrote, in a somewhat equivocal manner, that "the
number and orderly arrangement of the nerves, bones, and
other parts of an animal do not show that nature is
insufficient to form them, provided you suppose that in
everything nature acts in exact accord with the laws of
mechanics, and that these laws have been imposed on it
by God," so much so that "I have found nothing whose
formation seems inexplicable by natural causes."[80] The
inner teleology and functional wholeness of living things,
regarded by the Aristotelian tradition as the paradigm
of natural purposiveness, is demoted to the status of the
effect of natural, mechanical action. The insertion of
God as the source of this mechanics falls short of
reinstating nature as purposeful and thereby becoming a
sign of the intentions of God, because God is said to create
mechanics and not substantial forms, which at best are
mere surface phenomena. Organic, functional wholeness
is replaced by a mechanical disposition of parts, a genesis
of structures as opposed to the actualization of form.
Why God should create teleology through the medium of a
self-sufficient mechanics truly points to the inscrutability
of God's will.

The nonorganic realm likewise offers no guide to God.
In spite of the seemingly beneficent nature of God as

revealed in his creation of such things as the sun, Descartes writes to Hyperaspistes that "it would be childish and absurd for a metaphysician to assert that God, like some vainglorious human being, had no other purpose in making the universe than to win men's praise; or that the sun, which is many times larger than the earth, was created for no other purpose than to give light to man, who occupies a very small part of the earth."[81] Manifest teleology is at best a partial, perspectival view of reality. In truth it is an interpretation stemming from anthropocentric bias rather than the detached metaphysical attitude. Since God's larger aims are not revealed in His creation, the problem raised as early as Meditation I of resolving the question concerning God's goodness from the anthropocentric perspective, either pro (via nature's provisions) or con (via the fact of deception), is now undercut and with it the theological objection that God's goodness sometimes requires human deception. God's inscrutability is pushed to such an extreme as to render either alternative undecidable. From the standpoint of human reason, God's nature becomes unintelligible to the point of nonrelevance.

The conclusion from the rejection of teleology about the relation of nature, God, and reason is the following. By not revealing God's intentions, nature does not point to the existence and nature of God. The proof of God depends solely upon the logical implications of the idea of Him found within the res cogitans, which proof (irrespective of its validity) is in fact an exercise of rational autonomy. It appears that the order of creation has been reversed, since the proof of God's existence depends upon the res cogitans, the only content of nature capable of transcendence. And the divine nature is likewise in accord with such a natural origin by becoming the personification of mechanics. Such a God is consistent with the overall plan of the mastery and possession of nature, which would be impossible if nature were understood to be the instantiation of divine order and goodness. That the absurd nature of God's transcendence culminates in a theology of irrelevance when it comes to the question of truth based in faith in God or grounded in rational autonomy is seen finally in the doctrine of the divine creation of the eternal truths and the reason for its exclusion from the Meditations.

Divine Creation of the Eternal Truths

That the truths of logic and mathematics are created by God is stated by Descartes only in the Correspondence and the Replies to the Fifth and Sixth Sets of Objections. The doctrine's inclusion in the Meditations would, as I have mentioned, appear logically to belong in Meditation I where the doubt concerning reason pertained to the questionable correspondence between human rationality and divinely created truth. Or, with His reappearance in Meditation III as a threat to reason, we would expect to find the doctrine accompanying the proofs of God's goodness. But we are disappointed again. That the divine creation of the eternal truths appears nowhere in the Meditations (Descartes' chief metaphysical work) must therefore be explained in terms of the doctrine itself--the theology

upon which it is based and its import for the emancipation
of reason from God.

In 1630 Descartes communicates the doctrine to Mersenne
in a series of letters. The mathematical-eternal truths
are said to depend upon God as His willful creations.
To conceive of such truths as valid independently of God
would be "to talk of Him as if He were Jupiter or Saturn
and to subject Him to the Styx and the Fates."[82] In the
name of preserving God's unlimited power an intellectualism
of independently valid truth is denied. Such truths exist
neither apart from God nor exclusively in God's intellect.
Their existence and validity depend upon God willing them
into being. Since God's will cannot change, even though
it is initially free (which is explained by the
incomprehensibility of His power and the perfection and
immutability of His nature, which eliminate potentiality
and hence change), these willed truths remain eternally
the same. The extent of God's power is such that "we can
assert that God can do everything that we can comprehend
but not that he cannot do what we cannot comprehend."[83]
God's creative power is simply limitless. In the letter
of May 27 Descartes tells Mersenne:

> You ask what necessitated God to create
> these truths; and I reply that just
> as He was free not to create the world,
> so He was no less free to make it untrue
> that all the lines drawn from the centre
> of a circle to its circumference are
> equal. And it is certain that these
> truths are no more necessarily attached
> to his essence than other creatures
> are.[84]

While the truths selected are eternally the same because
of God's immutability, which truths are initially created
still depends upon God's discretion, so that what is regarded
as necessary and noncontradictory by human reason may not
be so regarded and decreed by God, their changelessness
notwithstanding.

The problem concerning the relation between God's
nature and the rational truths is not the immutability
of His will, but rather its manner of choosing ex nihilo.
The significant passage at the beginning of Meditation
VI brings the issue of the relation between God, the eternal
truths, and human reason sharply into focus:

> For there is no doubt that God possesses
> the power to produce everything that
> I am capable of perceiving with
> distinctness, and I have never deemed
> that anything was impossible for Him,
> unless I found a contradiction in
> attempting to conceive it clearly.[85]

Taken by itself this passage subordinates God's creative
power to the law of contradiction as understood by human
reason. However, when seen in its theodicy context it
can perhaps be rendered consistent with the reliance of
logic upon God. Coming after the apparent demonstration

of God's goodness in <u>Meditations</u> III-V, the creative power
of God in the service of a benevolent will is what is
responsible for the noncreation of the noncontradictory
rather than His conformity to norms apprehended as valid
apart from and hence binding upon God. As we have seen,
Descartes claims that God's intellect and will cannot be
separated. The coincidence between what God may create
and what human reason perceives as necessary attests not
to the supremacy of human reason or an uncreated logic
binding upon God and man but rather, it would appear, to
the harmony of power and goodness in God. Consequently,
to show that Descartes does in fact place the autonomy
of reason above divine decrees we would have to show that
God's will cannot in fact be known to be good. We revert
to the divine inscrutability, shown by the relation between
intellect and will. If God's will is uncertain His power
cannot be known to be limited by His goodness. The choice
then becomes either an all-powerful but incomprehensible
(and therefore perhaps evil) God, which renders human reason
uncertain, or an incomprehensible God who therefore becomes
irrelevant to truth and must by default be replaced by
an unsupported human reason.

   Descartes handles the traditional problem of the
supremacy of God's will or intellect by adapting the theology
of the unity of God's faculties to his purposes. The amalgam
of voluntarism and intellectualism, in which priority is
given to neither intellect nor will, does justice to the
theologians while straddling the issue. If neither will
nor intellect is prior, God's decrees can be neither wholly
arbitrary nor wholly necessary. But yet they are claimed
to be freely chosen and eternally binding. This combination
of creativity and immutability is attributed to God's liberty
of indifference in creating <u>ex</u> <u>nihilo</u>. Descartes explains
to Mesland[?]:

> And even if God has willed that some
> truths should be necessary, this does
> not mean that he willed them necessarily;
> for it is one thing to will that they
> be necessary, and quite another to
> will them necessarily, or to be
> necessitated to will them.[86]

In the sequel Descartes reiterates that what we distinguish
as intellect and will cannot be so distinguished in God
because in Him they are the same thing. He quotes St.
Augustine (<u>Confessions</u> XIII. 30): "They are so because
you see them to be so; because in God seeing and willing
are one and the same thing."[87] The freedom of spontaneity
is denied to God because it would subject Him to fate (i.e.,
rational necessity concerning the true and the good).
God's freedom is that of indifference, which enables
Descartes to claim that the true and the good emanate from
God and in a nontyrannical or wholly arbitrary way because
of the oneness of His intellect and will. However, despite
the insistence upon the nonseparateness and nonprecedence
of the will over intellect in God, the stress does fall
on God's will since, due to freedom of indifference, whereby
God's intellect does not necessitate the will, the emphasis
placed upon the eternal truths is their status as created

rather than understood. For God, to create is to will.
As Descartes explains God's freedom (in terms of
distinguishable faculties) in the Replies to the Sixth
Objection:

> As to the freedom of the will, a very
> different account must be given of
> it as it exists in God and as it exists
> in us. For it is self-contradictory
> that the will of God should not have
> been from eternity indifferent to all
> that has come to pass or that ever
> will occur, because we can form no
> conception of anything good or true,
> of anything to be believed or to be
> performed or to be omitted, the idea
> of which existed in the divine
> understanding before God's will
> determined Him so to act as to bring
> it to pass. . . . Thus that supreme
> indifference in God is the supreme
> proof of his omnipotence.[88]

While Frankfurt concludes from this unlimited power of
God that there remains an inevitable discrepancy between
certainty and truth, since "a person may be justified in
asserting that a proposition is self-contradictory without
being justified in asserting that it is false,"[89] the
voluntaristic emphasis and its devastating consequences
for the true and the good were again seen by Leibniz:

> Also, by saying that things are not
> good by any rule of goodness but by
> God's will alone, it seems to me that
> one unthinkingly destroys all love
> of God and all His glory. For why
> praise Him for what He has done, if
> He would be equally praiseworthy in
> doing just the contrary? Where then
> will be His justice and His wisdom,
> if there only remains a certain despotic
> power, if will takes the place of reason,
> and if, according to the definition
> of tyrants, what pleases the most
> powerful is just by that alone?[90]

Leibniz grasps Descartes' intention well in judging the
doctrine of the divine creation of the eternal truths to
be autonomous rationalism rather than a divine support
of it:

> I cannot even imagine that M. Descartes
> can have been quite seriously of this
> option. . . . It was apparently one
> of his tricks, one of his philosophic
> feints . . . I suspect that he had
> in mind here another extraordinary
> manner of speaking, of his own invention,
> which was to say that affirmations

and negations, and acts of inner judgment
in general, are operations of the will.
Through this artifice the eternal
verities, which until the time of
Descartes had been named an object
of the divine understanding, suddenly
became an object of God's will. Now
the acts of his will are free, therefore
God is the free cause of the verities.
. . . But if the affirmations of
necessary truths were actions of the
will of the most perfect mind, these
actions would be anything but free,
for there is nothing to choose. It
seems that M. Descartes did not declare
himself sufficiently on the nature
of freedom, and that his conception
of it was somewhat unusual: for he
extended it so far that he even held
the affirmations of necessary truths
to be free in God. That was preserving
only the name of freedom.[91]

Descartes presents God's creative freedom in such a way
that it ends in unintelligibility. To free God from rational
necessity the freedom of spontaneity is exchanged for the
freedom of indifference. But unlike in the human soul,
in which indifference liberates the will from the intellect,
in God's indifference they are said to coalesce. This
has the effect of perhaps mitigating God's caprice, but
at the price of an unintelligible indifference. Due to
the unity of intellect and will the divine indifference
is neither spontaneity nor indifference. A case for pure
indifference can perhaps be based upon Descartes' statement
in the Reply to the Sixth Objections to the effect that
the divine intellect has no content prior to the action
of the will. However, as Leibniz observes, in such a case
there is nothing for the will to choose. God's nature
is not only an unfathomable unification of intellect and
will, but the stress on creativity renders it incompatible
with God's perfection. Descartes cannot simultaneously
insist on divine immutability as the ground of the eternal
sameness of truth and on an indifference which gives God
creative options. God's perfection, which involves the
denial of unactualized potentiality, implies that He has
no options but acts invariably and once and for all. Why
God "chooses" one set of truths rather than another thus
appears unintelligible as an activity and capricious
concerning content. Choosing as such introduces too much
latitude into the divine perfection and the impenetrable
character of God's will makes its actions exceed the scope
of rationality. Contra Frankfurt we must conclude with
Leibniz, and more recently Caton,[92] that the doctrine of
the divine creation of the eternal truths is a "philosophic
feint," and one whose absence from the Meditations is
explained by the inscrutability of the theology in which
it is couched. The limitless freedom accorded to God casts
an irremediable doubt on His veracity. As a result the
limitation of God's power by His goodness cannot be

demonstrated, the corollary of which is the self-grounding
of human reason in the absence of a meaningful transrational
norm.

Descartes' perhaps most candid statement on the
supremacy of reason over faith was made in the Notes Against
a Programme:

> For as we were born men before we became
> Christians, it is beyond belief that
> any man should seriously embrace opinions
> which he thinks contrary to that right
> reason that constitutes a man, in order
> that he may cling to the faith through
> which he is a Christian.[93]

Meditation V expresses the same conviction when Descartes
writes that "whatever proof or argument I avail myself
of, we must always return to the point that it is only
those things which we conceive clearly and distinctly that
have the power of persuading me entirely."[94] Such remarks
can be consonant with faith only if God guarantees reason.
But because God is unintelligible to reason there cannot
be such a guarantee. The attempts to found reason on God,
and in the process extricate Descartes from the circularity
involved in God's validation of and dependence upon clear
and distinct ideas, cannot succeed.[95] Kenny, for example,
tries to save Descartes from the charge of circularity
by distinguishing between particular clear and distinct
ideas, which as such do not require God's guarantee, and
the general rule, which does. However, since God can violate
the law of contradiction, it is difficult to see how the
former can really stand on their own in light of the
perpetual dubiety of the latter. Once the law of
contradiction becomes suspect, even the simple natures
of the Regulae become threatened.[96]

More recently, Charles Larmore has tried to free
Descartes from the circle by stressing the "psychologistic
theory of assent."[97] The context is Descartes' famous
statement in the Reply to the Second Objection:

> What is it to us, though perchance
> someone feigns that that, of the truth
> of which we are so firmly persuaded,
> appears false to God or to an Angel,
> and hence is, absolutely speaking,
> false? What heed do we pay to that
> absolute falsity, when we by no means
> believe that it exists or even suspect
> its existence? We have assumed a
> conviction so strong that nothing can
> remove it, and this persuasion is clearly
> the same as perfect certitude.[98]

As we have seen, according to Frankfurt "In this passage,
Descartes explicitly acknowledges the possibility that
what is certain may not be true 'speaking absolutely',
and he makes it clear that certainty takes priority over
absolute truth in his conception of the goals of inquiry."[99]
Concerning Descartes' remark, Larmore writes:

It cannot be right to claim that, in view of this passage, Descartes was not concerned with this possibility of absolute falsity, since that possibility, as described here, is identical to the one he treats seriously enough in the Third Meditation to attempt to prove the existence of a benevolent God. . . . In neither case should we overlook who is claiming that he finds the truth of certain propositions indubitable. It is someone who is "directing his attention" to the proposition in question and who does not "even suspect" that it could be false.[100]

Larmore rejects the charge of circularity by taking issue with Frankfurt's certainty-truth distinction:

Descartes has not begged the question by assuming the truth of the premises when it is their truth, and not just their certainty, which is at issue. Our very ability to conceive of them as possibly not being true and thus to ask whether their truth is being illegitimately assumed depends, in virtue of his psychologistic theory of assent, on our not attending to what makes them evident. When attending to the soundness of the proof we are just not in a position to distinguish between the certainty and the truth of either the premises or the conclusion. It was thus his psychologistic theory of assent which rescued Descartes' proof from the twin dangers of circularity and ineffectuality. It enabled him to show, from within the constraints imposed by the nature of our mind, that we must believe in the ability of our mind to arrive at the truth.[101]

Larmore's seems to be an adequate response to Frankfurt in that it closes the certainty-truth gap. However, it confronts the same difficulty as Kenny's since the "nature of our mind" is psychologically but not epistemically compelled since, so long as God's benevolence is not known, psychological compulsion cannot be equated with truth. Larmore does not think that Meditation III permits a Frankfurt-type duality, that is, that it is conceivable that an unattended to, presumably sound proof can produce a certain but not true conclusion. This is because Meditation IV, according to Larmore, resolves all such hyperbolic doubts by supplying the criterion of truth--a divinely guaranteed liberty of spontaneity.[102]

It appears that we must pick from the following three interpretations of Descartes' position concerning reason, theology, certainty, and truth. Frankfurt maintains that certainty and truth must be kept distinct because we cannot know God's mind, yet the divine creation of the eternal truths is to be taken as sincere. Larmore closes the Frankfurt gap by claiming that Descartes' psychologistic theory of assent provides a noncircular proof of God and thereby a vindication of reason. Caton's response to the passage from the Replies to the Second Objections is as follows:

> The thought that subjective persuasion may be "absolutely false" is idle because it cannot be consummated as a reasonable doubt and if it were, it could not be redeemed. It follows, therefore, that the refutation of this doubt by the veracious God, with its assurance of an absolute truth to guarantee subjective persuasion, is equally idle. The Cartesian circle thus appears to be the legerdemain by which things in no need of proof are made to depend on things not susceptible of proof.[103]

In Meditations I and II Descartes raises but postpones the threat to the reliability of reason by an omnipotent and possibly evil God. Meditations III to V are to contain the required theodicy. However, if it is as I have suggested, that Descartes' god is a god whose will is not bound by the good and whose intellect is not bound by the true, then the only guarantee that reason can have is its own self-evidence. The Frankfurt distinction, as Descartes himself says in the Reply to the Second Objections, is beyond the limit of conceivability. Larmore's response falls prey to the difficulties confronting Descartes' theodicy discussed in the present chapter. In agreement with Caton, whether one regards the challenge to clear and distinct perception as reasonable or hyperbolic, I think it must be concluded that Descartes has constructed his theodicy in such a way that piety and reason are not only irreconcilable but that piety gives way to reason.

FROM METAPHYSICS TO SCIENCE?

According to Caton the lesson to be learned from the Meditations is of decisive historical import. With the threat of the deceiving god permanently banished, science is free to construct an account of the whole which renders any future metaphysics redundant:

> To grasp the maxim that clear and distinct ideas are true is to understand that metaphysics is useless. For it says, as Spinoza points out, that truth is known by its own sign; hence, it requires no "justification" or "validation". The Meditations is a

satiric reductio of metaphysics showing
the delinquency of the idea that
conceptual analysis can remedy any
shortage of certainty from which science
might suffer. The lesson of the
Meditations is therefore contemporary.
Although positivists wished to eliminate
metaphysics, they unawares embraced
the hydra when they set out to "justify"
science. They failed, of course, but
they did convince many that science
needed justification. . . . Meanwhile
scientists, unaware that philosophers
had allowed their certificate of
rectitude to lapse whilst handing them
over to Cardinal Bellarmine, moved
as usual from one splendid discovery
to another. As a matter of fact,
progress in the biological sciences
during the past two decades has brought
to fruition the most splendid discovery
of all: the first stage of an
experimental science of man. We are
now in the midst of an intellectual
revolution as far-reaching as the
revolution of the spirit inaugurated
in the Seventeenth Century. Whig history
has always pitched its tent in this
camp, and enrolled under the banner,
"The deus deceptor is slain; long live
clarite". And so it will be in the
future.[104]

I take Caton's claim that science makes metaphysics
superfluous to mean that science has become the true
metaphysics. In what follows I attempt to challenge Caton's
claim by discussing the following two issues which his
claim raises. The issues are the extent to which an appeal
beyond the world to God can be repudiated, and the extent
to which scientific rationality can produce an intelligible
and comprehensive account of the whole.
    Caton's excellent book on Descartes concludes with
a Socratic response to the "incommensurables" contained
within Descartes' project for a universal science. As
Caton explains, the fundamental tensions within Cartesian
philosophy arise from the conflict between the desire for
an indubitable mathesis universalis and the recalcitrance
of the subject matter. Descartes' attempt to mediate the
order of knowing (the immutability of reason and its intuited
first principles) and the order of being (nature in its
perceptual concreteness) results in circularity:

        The foundational endeavor is meant
        to establish that reason is immutable
        and its principles irrevisable. .
        . . The theory of simple natures
        permanently fixes the order of cognition
        and the order of nature. The problem
        of science is to surmount the confused

thought of prejudice. For this reason
he found it plausible to argue that
the science could be placed on an
unshakable foundation by demonstrating
that there is a point of
intersection--corporeal ideas--between
the two orders. The argument is of
course circular--the true Cartesian
circle--since it purports to show that
thought and extension exhaust reality
by first assuming these principles.
But the circle actually reflects the
basic dilemma of the foundational search
for certainty, for the circle provides
a certain coherence and completeness
to a system whose foundation otherwise
rests exclusively upon intuition. .
. . Cartesian consciousness therefore
cannot be said to be one thing; it
oscillates between philosophical
selfconsciousness aware of its mediation,
and scientific empirical consciousness
that tends, in Descartes' expositions,
to degenerate to the immediacy of
prephilosophical consciousness.[105]

The failure to coordinate reason and observation shows
Descartes' inadequate account of the positive function
of perception in his theory of science. His commitment
to truth as intuition and the inviolability of its principles
of cognition prevented Descartes from moving toward what
has become a dominant contemporary position concerning
scientific method. On the assumption of a heterogeneity
between the order of knowing (be it pure reason or "the
natural attitude") and the order of nature, the order of
nature can and must be discovered progressively. At the
same time, the possibility of recalcitrant perceptual data
renders all theories tentative, inherently revisable.
What blocks a Cartesian mediation between theory and data
is Descartes' assumption of an ultimate homogeneity between
reason and nature.[106] As Caton explains, there is in fact
a tension in Descartes between a concession to the role
of hypothesis and experiment and an insistence on the
inviolability of reason:

he recognized the inductive hiatus
created by the introduction of
hypothetical causes, since deduced
effects do not prove the hypothesis.
His last word on the subject combines
this acknowledgment with an attempt
to escape its consequences: while
we cannot infer the truth of isolated
hypotheses, still, when one considers
that so many effects are deduced with
mathematical rigor, we can only deem
God a deceiver if they are not true.
[Prin. IV, #206] The suggestion is
that we substitute one breathtaking

>   leap   for   many   isolated   inductions.
>   Just here, where he should have doubted,
>   his assurance of the coincidence of
>   certainty and truth asserts itself.[107]

The issue for Descartes is not the justification for positing
as certain what can never be known to be false due to the
presence of an omnipotent deceiving God, but rather whether
he is justified in his conviction concerning the immutability
of reason. The mutability of reason means the mutability,
the historicity, of reason's first principles. In spite
of the empirical scientific work of others, as well as
his own experimental studies, Descartes was not prepared
to grant the contingent status of the basic principles
of science.

Descartes remained an Aristotelian in the sense that
science aims to know things as they are in themselves;
however, the unresolved tension in Cartesian science between
intuition and sensation suggests a Kantian interpretation
along Frankfurtian lines--science pursues subjective
certainty rather than objective truth. Caton correctly
rejects such a distinction as an account of Descartes'
intentions. What separates Caton and Frankfurt, as we
have seen, are their interpretations of the relation between
reason and theodicy. According to Frankfurt, God's
limitless, inscrutable, creative will necessitates a limit
to human knowledge. According to Caton, "Descartes
associates the creating God with the anti-science of the
biblical God, both of which are incompatible with the
veracious God."[108] It would appear that Caton is prepared
to accept the plausibility of the Frankfurt distinction
on nontheological grounds, on the basis of the tension
between truth as conceptual and access to nature as
perceptual: "It is nevertheless true that the ambiguities
of the Cartesian foundation are truly such as to lead to
the transformation of the veracious God or creating God
into an unknowable Ding an Sich and the associated
distinction between phenomenon and noumenon."[109] But Caton
adopts a Socratic rather than Kantian position:

>   Everywhere we find the objectivity
>   of science in collision with the
>   subjectivity of thinking. . . . the
>   greatness of Descartes' philosophy
>   is due less to the problems it solves
>   or to the certainties it produces than
>   to the depth of its contradictions.
>   Their depth may be appreciated by
>   observing that although nearly every
>   significant thinker of the past century
>   was a critic of dualism, none surmounted
>   it. So long as our concept of nature
>   is mechanical, it is improbable that
>   it can be surmounted. Dualism seems
>   to be both necessary and impossible:
>   a skeptical predicament. But there
>   is no bar to conceiving the predicament
>   in the Socratic manner, as an occasion
>   to philosophize.[110]

Caton's current position is post-Socratic and post-Kantian. Is his praise of science as metaphysics based on a belief that the Cartesian "incommensurables" have been overcome? The difficulties surrounding the post-Cartesian attempt at something like a <u>mathesis universalis</u> suggest that such a belief is more properly a wish,[111] more of a dreamt than an actual metaphysics. This is due to science's increasing transformation (reminiscent of the dream doubt of <u>Meditation</u> I) of pretheoretical experience into a conceptual structure in conformity with the norms of mathematical intelligibility. The distinction between a philosophical and a fictional account presupposes the distinction between conceptual construction and natural experience. To the extent to which a science of the world is grounded in mathematics and mathematically inspired methodology, the difference between a philosophical and a dreamt account of the whole tends to disappear. The content of ordinary experience, however, cannot be translated out of existence, since no conceptualization can be judged to be adequate prior to a comparison between the conceptual and the experiential. Unless prescientific experience is seen as the beginning and end of scientific conceptualization, such conceptualization is, to repeat, indistinguishable from a coherent dream.

One could try to mediate scientific conceptualization and experience by subjecting every hypothesis and every theory to empirical and experimental validation or refutation. However, to adopt what amounts to a revisionist view of truth is, to repeat, to concede that at bottom metaphysics and history are perhaps indistinguishable, unless something like an ultimate consensus (the end of history) is envisioned. In the absence of such a consensus, to posit perpetual progress as an infinite goal means consigning oneself to perpetual frustration.

The more comprehensive the mathematization of experience, the more one transforms reason from the receiver of a pregiven order to the giver of an order. The more one imposes an order, the more one runs the risk of a theoretical estrangement from that which one seeks to understand. To some extent, an alienation from the being of the world is inevitable since human knowledge must conceptually mediate experience. A certain form of psychologism is thus unavoidable and legitimate. However, in the case of mathematization there has been the tendency to substitute the product of a sophisticated conceptualization for the reality on the basis of which it arose. According to Stanley Rosen, "Kant articulates the major discovery of the modern epoch (as dramatized by the Cartesian <u>cogito</u>) that the most certain sense of 'to be' is 'to think.' Modern philosophy is then, at least since Descartes, a recapitulation, at a higher level of logical explicitness, of Eleaticism. . . . Philosophy is the conceptualization of the world."[112]

The epistemological emancipation of reason's intrinsic norms from God or nature is one thing. A rational metaphysics along the lines of clear and distinct ideas, whose essential connection with the world is in need of demonstration, is something else. The metaphysical status of mathematics is therefore of crucial importance in assessing the viability of modern science as metaphysics.[113] To posit a thoroughgoing mathematization is to assume an ultimate homogeneity of being. But the _prima_ _facie_ recalcitrance of various parts of the whole to such mathematization suggests that Aristotle was perhaps correct in maintaining that being is heterogeneous. In such a circumstance the attempt to place a mathematical account on the whole might more properly be termed science fiction rather than scientific metaphysics.

Caton refers to the marvelous practical achievements of scientific methodology. But we must ask whether such progress attests to the truth of its mathematical dream. Although the scientist can master nature, whereas the dreamer merely conceptualizes, science as mastery is in the service of the will to power rather than the will to know of the scientist. Nature manipulated (perhaps violated) cannot be equated with nature understood. The metaphysical question is therefore not decided by a reference to progress in technology, since such progress does not establish an equivalence between the nature of nature and scientific cognition.

Science has given us countless examples of the mathematical lawfulness of nature, but can nature itself be understood as the source of such lawfulness? If, as Galileo claimed, the language of natural phenomena is mathematics, must one not have a prior knowledge of such a language in order to so understand nature? Mathematics would appear to be as transnatural as the conceptualizing intellect. That is to say, the accessibility of mathematical truth to reason seems to be independent of any relation to natural beings and phenomena. At the same time, the scientist reminds us that bodies qua extended and events qua spacial and temporal are quite amenable to mathematization. The geometrical features of bodies and the rates of acceleration of bodies appear to be natural features. But does such applicability really rest on an identity between such bodies and motions and mathematical structure? The disparity between the degree of precision of pure mathematics and the mathematization of natural phenomena suggests that the assumption of an ultimate sameness between mathematics and nature is questionable.

Given the modern rejection of Platonism as a viable account of mathematics, we return to autonomous reason. And to assert the autonomy of reason is to deny the world as encountered as a source for norms of scientific cognition. The only ways to avoid such a situation are to regard ourselves as the makers of the world or to appeal to a transcendent creator god. Science rejects both possibilities. The world must be understood on its own terms, yet human reason rather than the world is the source of principles of intelligibility.

The liberation of reason from God, however, would appear to be premature. For as Rosen observes, "It is not the case that the world clearly shows us its eternity, or that it was not created by God, or that there is no God. The world, eternal or created, shows us nothing but itself."[114] Unless and until modern science can give an account of the whole in the sense of _physis_--nature as

the explanation of both its cause and being--the elimination
of the theological is dogmatism.

Even if the claim of the redundancy of metaphysics
is taken in a more restricted sense--scientific methodology
concerning the nature, if not the origin, of worldly
beings--it is difficult to support. Given the assimilation
of all forms of cognition to the monolithic methodology
which has characterized modern science, it would appear
that what Caton announces as the replacement of metaphysics
by science is in fact the metaphysical neutrality of science.
In the words of Kennington:

> Epistemically speaking what is "first
> to us" can be identified with what
> is "first in itself" if what is "first
> to us" is method, and not what "comes
> to sight" of itself, through sensation
> and opinion. The awareness of our
> ignorance of what is first simply,
> or eternal, which is the original sting
> that gives rise to philosophy, now
> becomes a matter of indifference.[115]

Scientific progress is perfectly consistent with such
metaphysical blinders, whereas science as metaphysics is
not. Science must remain aware of the perhaps permanent
tension between mind as philosophical self-consciousness
and as empirical consciousness. The realm in which this
tension shows itself most conspicuously is that of man.
It appears that the increase in scientific understanding
has been accompanied by a lack of human self-understanding.
Can a science which defines knowledge as mathematical
precision deal successfully with such issues as the relation
between science and justice? Can the human soul be
intelligibly bifurcated in the direction of either the
body machine or res cogitans? Descartes' own attempt at
reconciling the demands of method and experience can serve
as a lasting reminder of the aporetic character of the
attempt to incorporate the human within a mathesis
universalis.

5
MIND AND BODY

Descartes' architectonic is a composite of theory and
practice, in which the primacy of the practical is the
rationale for the attainment of a sphere of theoretical
purity. In anthropological terms, this necessitates
distinguishing between two souls. The prephilosophical
soul is guided by passion and equates the good with the
pleasant; however, it lacks the knowledge needed to implement
its hedonism. The philosophical soul is methodologically
liberated from the bodily in order to pursue knowledge;
however, because of such a separation it is incapable of
action. The prephilosophical soul posits the end but is
ignorant of means. The philosophical soul knows the means
but is neutral to ends. The union of thought and action
thus requires a conception of the mind-body composite as
a genuine whole. Such a whole is the "true man" of Discourse
V. Descartes' argument in Discourse V can thus serve as
a valuable index for an understanding of the anthropology
of Meditation VI.

THE TRUE MAN

In Discourse V Descartes prudentially presents an
ambiguous account of genesis. He compares the Cartesian
origin of the universe (a progression from the inanimate
to the animate and finally to man, that is, an atheistic,
materialistic genesis) to the Christian genesis. On the
one hand:

> I did not at the same time wish to
> infer from all these facts that this
> world has been created in the manner
> which I described [in The World, i.e.,
> an atheistic, materialistic genesis];
> for it is much more probable that at
> the beginning that God made it such
> as it should be. . . . [Yet,] their
> nature is much easier to understand
> when we see them coming to pass little
> by little in this manner, than were

we to consider them as all complete
to begin with.[1]

This disjunction between the probable and the understandable
is the one between faith and reason we saw in the
Meditations' theodicy. If my conclusion about the
replacement of faith by reason is correct, the Christian
account of genesis becomes a prejudice since it lacks clarity
and distinctness. The "true man" spoken of in _Discourse_
V is a composite, but a composite of Cartesian science
and epistemology. The former accounts for the physiological
mechanics and the latter requires the _res cogitans_. The
issue of embodiment concerns the extent to which the _res
cogitans_ is nothing more than epiphenomenon. The discussion
of the difference between man and animal is instructive
in this regard.

The intention of the distinction between man and animal
is apologetic, an attempt to demonstrate that Cartesian
physics is compatible with Christian doctrine. Employing
arguments about speech and freedom, Descartes concludes
his summary of _The World_ by claiming to demonstrate the
absence of soul in animals, rendering them thoughtless
machines, and the presence of an immortal soul in man,
rendering him the lone image of God. He begins by stating
that in addition to the error involved in denying the
existence of God:

> There is none which is more effectual
> in leading feeble spirits from the
> straight path of virtue, than to imagine
> that the soul of the brute is of the
> same nature as our own, and that in
> consequence, after this life we have
> nothing to fear or to hope for, any
> more than the flies and ants.[2]

The motive, as we saw in the letter to the Sorbonne, is
to demonstrate the distinction for moral-religious reasons
since fear of the afterlife is the ground of virtue for
the weak and vacillating minds. But if it can be shown
that the distinction between man and animal is not as rigid
as it appears, i.e., that soul is perhaps not an
all-or-nothing affair and that man is earthly like the
animals, the "true man" may be closer to the animals than
the apologetic conclusion suggests. As we have seen, earthly
man would require earthly morals, some blend, according
to Descartes, of Stoicism and Epicureanism.

The distinction between man and brute is presented
as an extension of the distinction between man and artificial
automata. Even though machines may resemble men in
appearance and outward behavior, Descartes claims that
there are two crucial differences between automata and
men. Machines never speak or use other signs in order
to communicate and they act solely from the disposition
of their parts, thereby lacking intelligence. The
explanation of these differences shows that the decisive
criterion is linguistic and behavioral freedom. Although
a machine can be programmed to utter sentences, "it never
happens that it arranges its speech in various ways, in
order to reply appropriately to everything that may be

said in its presence, as even the lowest type of man can do."[3]   And although machines can do some things quite well or better than men, since "reason is a universal instrument which can serve for all contingencies, these organs have need of some special adaptation for every particular action."[4]   It is the handling of the appropriate and the contingent that manifests the freedom (as a mode of the universal rational instrument) that marks a man contrasted with the rigidity of behavior that characterizes a machine.

Descartes then extrapolates to the difference between man and animals. One difficulty here is that, as the Passions explains, since the soul does not move the body (in spite of the insistence on the uniqueness of man's will) the variety observed in human behavior (or even speech, considered as motions of speech organs) can be explained mechanically. Although there would still be a difference between man and animal since man manifests more complex and subtle behavior than that of animals, such a difference would not necessarily imply a soul exclusively in man. The difference between man and animal can be explained by attributing to man a somewhat paradoxical combination of rigid mechanicism (e.g., conditioned reflexes) and limitless freedom since such conditioning can take a variety of paths. That is, the difference between man and animal (at least as far as action is concerned) might be degree or subtlety of complexity coupled with the epiphenomenality of consciousness. This is why the extrapolation to animals is carried out primarily in terms of the speech criterion. As Descartes says to [the Marquess of Newcastle?]:

> In fact, none of our external actions can show anyone who examines them that our body is not just a self-moving machine but contains a soul with thoughts, with the exception of words, or other signs that are relevant to particular topics without expressing any passion.[5]

Descartes tries to show that speech (or sign language) is not a matter of degree but either-or, and that since speech indicates soul it is fully present in man and totally absent in animals. The motive is clearer than the argument since it is due to the apologetic interest that Descartes cannot content himself with a less than total distinction between man and animal. In the same letter Descartes remarks that if animals thought as we do they would also have immortal souls, but that this does not seem possible "because there is no reason to believe it of some animals without believing it of all, and many of them such as oysters and sponges are too imperfect for this to be credible."[6]   Soul is denied to oysters and sponges due to their "imperfection," and by the all-or-none rule this is extended to all animals. Whereas if humans lack an immortal soul they will fear the afterlife no more than the flies and ants, which is morally and religiously disastrous. We have seen that for Descartes the soul is without parts and that the Aristotelian levels of soul are not a live option. This seems to justify the all-or-none rule, but such a rule can cut both ways if soul cannot be denied to some animals.

Descartes admits in this same letter that some animals think:

> The most that one can say is that though
> the animals do not perform any action
> which shows us that they think, still,
> since the organs of their body are
> not very different from ours, it may
> be conjectured that there is attached
> to these organs some thoughts such
> as we experience in ourselves, but
> of a very much less perfect kind.[7]

Yet he concludes that such animals lack soul because, using the all-or-none rule, oysters and sponges lack soul because they are imperfect. Their imperfection is physiological; they lack the required organs. The implication of such a physiological grounding of soul is the atheistic materialistic "origin of my being," that is, that soul emerges along with, and its degree is correlated to, physiological complexity of a certain sort. Such a distribution of soul is not permitted in _Discourse_ V since it conflicts with the apologetic aim and would be theologically problematic. God's inscrutability would once again have to be called upon to explain the gift of soul to some animals and its denial to others. Even on the assumption of the absence of soul in all animals the divine inscrutability would have to be invoked to account for the creation of animals whose behavior (desire, pleasure, and pain) falsely suggests a self-awareness and self-concern.

The correlative to the absolutizing of the nonthinking of animals is the thinking, hence rationality, of man. Descartes claims that all men, "without even excepting idiots,"[8] can communicate by means of spoken or sign language. Though this is not the case (and thus introduces a radical discontinuity of reason-soul in man), even granting its truth introduces a more-or-less into the supposed full possession of soul in man because an idiot cannot communicate to the extent of others. The gradation of intellect was a dominant theme throughout the _Discourse_, beginning with the "proof" of equality in _Discourse_ I. The argument for equality on the basis of species form in _Discourse_ I is abandoned in _Discourse_ V as Descartes draws the following comparison:

> And when we notice the inequality that
> exists between animals of the same
> species, as well as between men, and
> observe that some are more capable
> of receiving instruction than others,
> it is not credible that a monkey or
> a parrot, selected as the most perfect
> of its species, would not in these
> matters equal the stupidest child to
> be found, or at least a child whose
> mind is clouded, unless in the case
> of the brute the soul were of an entirely
> different nature from ours.[9]

Combining this passage with the statement to the Marquess
of Newcastle concerning the less perfect kind of soul in
some animals, Descartes presents us with two overlapping
soul continua, the most intelligent animal equalling the
least intelligent child. Notwithstanding the tremendous
distance between the extremes, the presence of the overlap
means that the presence of soul is not an either-or between
man and animal. Some animals therefore have soul. Descartes
softens this conclusion by equivocating concerning the
nature of soul--humans and animals are said to have
qualitatively different souls. The animal soul is restricted
to the outward expression of passions and perceptions,
there being no accompanying self-awareness, but such a
restricted soul is a soul in name only. Also, to speak
about nonexperienced or nonconscious passions and perceptions
is difficult concerning animals since we cannot see into
them. This reveals the importance of the speech criterion
(unless, of course, human speech can be explained
mechanistically). Speech signifies thought in the fullest
sense. Descartes uses this to conclude that animals lack
soul in its entirety, from the barest sensation up to
explicit and vocal self-consciousness, on the premise that
partial implies total lack of the soul. That this is not
Descartes' view can be seen from the following.

As we have seen, the characterization of soul as an
all-or-none principle is retracted by the admission of
overlapping continua of intelligence in man and animal.
The possibility of thoughts in animals is also granted
in the _Passions_ I, 50. Attributing different kinds of
soul to animals destroys the univocal meaning of soul by
which it was originally granted to man and denied to animals.
The difficulty with Descartes' soul apologetics is thus
the following. On the basis of the univocal concept of
soul, if all men participate equally in soul, then some
animals do also because of the equality of man and animal
at the lower end of human rationality. However, if no
animal possesses a rational soul, then some men do not
because of this same lower level equality. In _Discourse_
V Descartes opts for neither alternative, yet he argues
that the meaning of soul is univocal. By falsifying the
range and equality of rationality in man and suggesting
rather than proving that some animals at least have a
qualitatively different type of soul, Descartes claims
that a rational and immortal soul exists in all men and
that all animals are nonthinking automata.

What for Descartes is really a matter of degree is
presented as a difference in kind, again, because of the
focus on speech in the service of apologetics. But speech
is not the whole of soul, which is why Descartes cannot
rule out animals. The analogy between animals and machines
is thus deceptive. Though in both cases a genuine inwardness
cannot perhaps be posited, animal behavior has features
denied to machines--passions and perceptions. To Mesland
Descartes even ascribes to them the freedom of
indifference.[10] Consequently their lack of speech, and
perhaps inwardness, does not disqualify animals from
possessing a degree of soul. Soul is therefore shared,
though unequally, by man and animal. Aristotle's levels,
or forms, of soul are still eliminated; however, the

correlation between organic development and degree of soul takes their place.

The continuity between man and animal suggests the following picture of the human composite. Contrary to the apologetic conclusion drawn from the summary of The World, Descartes' "true man" has become a mechanical man plus consciousness. Descartes concludes the summary of The World cosmogony as follows:

> I had described after this the rational soul and shown that it could not be in any way derived from the power of matter . . . but that it must be expressly created. I showed, too, that it is not sufficient that it should be lodged in the human body like a pilot in his ship, unless perhaps for the moving of its members, but that it is necessary that it should also be joined and united more closely to the body in order to have sensations and appetites similar to our own, and thus to form a true man. . . . As a matter of fact, when one comes to know how greatly they differ, we understand much better the reasons which go to prove that our soul is in its nature entirely independent of the body, and in consequence that it is not liable to die with it. And then, inasmuch as we observe no other causes capable of destroying it, we are naturally inclined to judge that it is immortal.[11]

The "true man" is one in whom the soul is related to the body in two ways. Soul is diffused throughout the body to make possible sensations and passions, and is localized in order to move the body. (Whether such a conception of diffusion and localization of the soul is an inconsistency on Descartes' part will be discussed below.) Descartes' apologetic position here in the Discourse is that, on top of the mechanical self-sufficiency of bodily motion and its corporeal soul, there is the rational soul. Its nature is not made determinate apart from its being superfluous to life, such that the death of the body does not entail the death of the rational soul. The tenuousness of such a dualism is suggested by Descartes' statement that this has not been a proof but rather a "natural inclination to judge." The denial of mind as "thinking matter" is also questionable given what Descartes says many times about the dependence of mind on the body for its improvement and what we saw as the correlation between the genesis of thought and physiological complexity. When the continuity of soul in man and animal is considered, this has the effect not of humanizing the animals but of animalizing man. Man is not different from the animals because of the possession of a uniquely rational and immortal soul but because of the vast superiority of human over animal

thoughts. Notwithstanding speech, man is primarily a
passionate animal possessing intellect (and which is perhaps
nothing but brain activity). His reason is the "universal
instrument" by which the objects of his passions are pursued,
which is indicated by the totally utilitarian account of
reason and speech in Discourse V and VI. The dualism of
the Discourse "true man" is thus more apparent than real.
The anthropology of the Passions, the true Cartesian
anthropology, is less ambiguous. There the physiological
automaton is nondualistic in the sense that mind-body
relationships, the priority of the body, are seen as
unproblematic. Turning now to Meditation VI, the unmasking
of Descartes' theodicy and apologetics puts us in a position
to evaluate the anthropology of the Meditations.

THE DISTINCTION BETWEEN MIND AND BODY

     The title of Meditation VI announces that the "real
distinction between the Soul and Body of Man" will be
explained. That Descartes does not say "substantial" or
"separation" indicates, and which is borne out by the text
of Meditation VI, that the soul-body problem is not a problem
about the interaction of mutually exclusive substances.
     The substantialist formulation is found in Kenny:

          On Descartes' principles it is difficult
          to see how an unextended thinking
          substance can cause motion in an extended
          unthinking substance and how the extended
          unthinking substance can cause sensations
          in the unextended thinking substance.
          The properties of the two kinds of
          substances seem to place them in such
          diverse categories that it is impossible
          for them to interact.[12]

Such a statement of the problem not only leads to an obvious
impasse, but it is based on the notion, contradicted by
Meditation II (and also Meditation VI), of an unambiguously
incorporeal thinking substance. Nonetheless, a dualism
of a certain sort is present, which might better be called
a dualism of ambiguity, a methodological dualism, in order
to do justice to what appear as material and immaterial
phenomena. Though Descartes' intentions, evident from
the Passions, were to produce a thoroughgoing physiological
psychology, a methodological dualism remains in order to
do justice to phenomena difficult to comprehend in purely
mentalist or physicalist terms. What must be reconciled
is the coexistence in one nature of what appear to be
heterogeneous kinds of union--how the soul can relate (or
not relate) to the body in the form of sensations and
passions, and as the res cogitans of Meditation II which
contemplates peculiarly mental data. The ambiguity in
the soul was unproblematic in Meditation II because of
the methodological suspension of body. Res cogitans was
therefore a substantially neutral compendium of all modes
of thought. Sensation and imagination did not cause a
problem since the suspension of body permitted the

distinction between sensations and images as conscious
effects and the body as their cause. Granted the existence
of body in _Meditation_ VI, what must be accomplished is
a conception of soul which can account for the obvious
dependence of the soul on the body (perception and passion)
as well as its seeming independence (thought, reason).
Posing the problem of the unity of man as a combination
of incompatible substances is not only unfaithful to
Descartes' perception of the problem but is contradicted
by the presentation of the mind-body dualism of ambiguity,
that is, the methodological distinction between mind and
body begun in _Meditation_ II and persisting throughout
Meditation VI.

The approach to the mind-body relation in _Meditation_
VI begins by demonstrating the existence of body by reversing
the epistemic-ontic progression from sense to intellect
which earlier had established the essence of body as pure
extension. The imagination and senses are now interrogated
in order to discover the cause of their contents.
Imagination proves only probable bodily existence, whereas
bodily existence can be demonstrated by a combination of
the contents of sensation, the nature of mind-body
interaction, and the divine veracity. This last item is
said to be indispensable. However, in order to appreciate
the nature of the argument in _Meditation_ VI, I propose
that the following hermeneutic be followed. Following
from the dismantling of Descartes' theodicy, the role of
God in _Meditation_ VI must be read as a dissimulation for
Cartesian nature. This allows us to see the way such a
nature poses and tries to resolve the problems of embodiment.

Continuing the theme of the previous _Meditation_,
Descartes opens _Meditation_ VI by observing that material
things are possible existents because they are perceived
clearly and distinctly qua objects of pure mathematics.
The imagination extends the status of bodies from possible
to probable existents. But first the imagination must
be defined and distinguished from the intellect. Descartes
defines imagination as "nothing but a certain application
of the faculty of knowledge to the body which is immediately
present to it, and which therefore, exists."[13] The existence
of body, i.e., one's own, seems contained analytically
within the concept of imagination, which repeats the
definition of imagination given in _Meditation_ II. In
addition to the reference to body, by calling the imagination
"nothing but a certain application of the faculty of
knowledge," Descartes indicates a nonfaculty conception
of the mind. This becomes clearer in the distinction between
imagination and pure intellect. Since a triangle can be
thought and imaged, but a chiliagon can be thought but
not imaged, it would appear that the difference between
intellect and imagination resides in the bodily independence
of the former and bodily dependence of the latter. That
is, they appear to be distinct faculties because they
differently relate to bodily existence. But this is not
the case. What differentiates intellect and imagination
is not a difference in their objects, nor a difference
in their embodiment. As Descartes explains:

> And thus I clearly recognize that I
> have need of a particular effort of
> mind in order to effect the act of
> imagination, such as I do not require
> in order to understand, and this
> particular effort of mind clearly
> manifests the difference which exists
> between imagination and pure
> intellection.[14]

Meditation VI recapitulates the Regulae. Imagination and
intellect are not separate faculties cognizing objects
of different ontic status. They are two of the ways in
which the one cognitive power takes cognizance of body.

    According to Wilson the distinction between imagination
and intellect signals the beginning of the dualism of
Meditation VI. She writes:

> The significance of this distinction
> between imagination and understanding
> for Descartes' dualism is brought out
> well in the Fifth Replies, where
> Descartes responds to Gassendi's
> 'materialist' objections.
> Descartes answers:
> 'I have . . . often distinctly showed
> that the mind can operate independently
> of the brain; for certainly the brain
> can be of no use to pure understanding,
> but only to imagination or sensing.'
> According to Descartes, the mind may
> be distracted, impeded or limited in
> its operations by the condition of
> the body. But he seems to allow no
> connection at all between the mind's
> basic capacity for pure intellection
> or ratiocination and anything that
> does or could occur in the brain or
> other parts of the body.[15]

Wilson cites Regulae XII as confirmation, in which Descartes,
referring to "that power by which we are properly said
to know things," states that "if it acts alone it is said
to understand."[16] She concludes:

> the replies to Gassendi and other
> passages do require us to conclude
> that Descartes regarded his mind as
> essentially only intellect, and denied
> corporeal correlates of pure intellectual
> acts, capacities and powers. Bodily
> states are not only not merely not
> identical with mental states: they
> are not even relevant to a subclass
> of such states. . . . Pure understanding
> is carried on independently of all
> physical processes; any physiological
> study will necessarily be irrelevant
> to it.[17]

Wilson attributes Descartes' immaterialism to a problem with his science rather than to apologetic prudence. She claims that although Descartes desired that his views be accepted by the regnant religious and political powers:

> Yet it is impossible to believe that the enormous range and variety of Cartesian pronouncements concerning the independence of intellect from body . . . could have been dictated by this type of prudence or hypocrisy. Descartes' position as a scientist provides a much more plausible explanation for his insistence on the complete immateriality of the operations of the understanding. . . . A reason for his dualism may be found in his commitment to mechanistic explanation in physics, together with the perfectly credible belief that human intelligence could never be accounted for on the available mechanistic models.[18]

At this point the following responses can be made to Wilson. Descartes' response to Gassendi cannot be taken as an argument for immaterialism since his statement of an independence of mind from brain referred to a mode of operation rather than a mode of being. The statement is thus consistent with the doctrine of pure intellection as abstractive thinking, the apprehension of the schema of body but on the basis of data conveyed by sense and imagination. This is also true of the passage concerning the pure intellect from Regulae XII, which likewise concerns mode of operation rather than mode of being. This is not to suggest that Descartes satisfactorily explains the genesis of such abstractions in terms of a theory about the being of mind. It is to suggest that whatever explanation he gives cannot be said to be the positing of an incorporeal soul qua reason. While it is true, as the Passions reveals (despite treating the mind-body relation as unproblematic), that a complete reductionism cannot perhaps succeed, Descartes offers no justification for an immaterial rational soul in the Meditations. As I indicated at the outset, the issue is not the necessity of substantial dualism and the resultant aporia of embodiment. Descartes' problem is to come up with a unification of the mental and the physical which does justice to phenomena as diverse as intellection, blood circulation, and passion. The methodological dualism of the Meditations does not provide such an anthropology. It goes only so far as to set the stage for the attempt in the Passions by indicating the problem of unification. It is theologically motivated prudence which is responsible for the exaggerated claim of a nonbodily, immortal soul in the Meditations.

Prior to proving that bodies exist from an analysis of sense perception, Descartes progresses from the distinction between imagination and intellect to the "real distinction" between mind and body. Descartes' oscillation between the language of distinct psychic faculties and

nonseparable modes makes it difficult to grasp the purely
methodolgoical, i.e., nonsubstantival, character of the
distinction between mind and body. The initial difference
between imagination and intellect was stated as modal.
But then Descartes appears to relapse into a separatist
account when he says:

> this power of imagination which is
> in one, inasmuch as it differs from
> the power of understanding, is in no
> wise a necessary element in my nature,
> or in [my essence, that is to say,
> in] the essence of my mind; for although
> I did not possess it I should doubtless
> ever remain the same as I now am, from
> which it appears that we might conclude
> that it depends on something which
> differs from me.[19]

According to Wilson, Descartes regards the phenomenological
differences between intellection, imagination, and sensation
as sufficient grounds for denying that the body (the brain)
is in any way involved in pure understanding. Since pure
understanding is heterogeneous with both sensations and
corporeal images, "the brain (or body) is not at all involved
in pure thought. For what task would there be left for
it to perform?"[20] If Wilson means that pure thought as
the complement of sense and image in perception is nothing
more than beholding such images, I agree. I disagree that
an incorporeal intellectual substance is their beholder.
Such a faculty conception is contradicted by what Descartes
states in the sequel concerning the relation between
imagination, intellect, and body. Describing the
imagination:

> this mode of thinking differs from
> pure intellection only inasmuch as
> mind in its intellectual activity in
> some manner turns on itself, and
> considers some of the ideas which it
> possesses in itself; while in imagining
> it turns toward the body, and there
> beholds in it something conformable
> to the idea which it has either conceived
> of itself or perceived by the senses.[21]

The mind is a single power, equally imagination and
intellect. Its turning to the body permits it to function
in the imaginative mode. Its turning to itself permits
it to function in the mode of intellect. Since neither
activity can be construed as a separate faculty, Descartes
misleads when he says that only intellect is essential
to his nature as mind. The above passage must therefore
be understood as a reiteration of the res cogitans of
Meditation II and cannot be interpreted as implying
ontological distinctness. Consider the elusive statement
following the argument for dualism from clear and distinct
perception:

> I further find in myself faculties
> employing modes of thinking peculiar
> to themselves, to wit, the faculties
> of imagination and feeling, without
> which I can easily conceive myself
> clearly and distinctly as a complete
> being; while, on the other hand, they
> cannot be so conceived apart from me,
> that is without an intelligent substance
> in which they reside, for [in the notion
> we have of these faculties, or, to
> use the language of the Schools] in
> their formal concept, some kind of
> intellection is comprised, from which
> I infer that they are distinct from
> me as its modes are from a thing.[22]

Apart from the inauthentic use of Scholastic terminology,
what is claimed in the first part of the passage is undone
in the second part. The first part implies a separation
of the faculties of intellect, imagination, and sensation.
No mention is made of body. However (and this difficulty
also afflicts the argument for dualism based on clear and
distinct perception), the clear and distinct perception
of something as a complete being does not preclude an
ontological dependence upon body. The second part of the
passage undoes the faculty conception since it repeats
the res cogitans, in which imagination and feeling are
"distinct from me as its modes are from a thing." And
if imagination and feeling require body, then perhaps so
does the intellective mode, given the all-or-none nature
of res cogitans vis-a-vis its modes. As we have seen,
the intellect requires body because by intellect Descartes
understands the power to abstract pure images and numbers
from sensory data through the medium of the corporeal
imagination. Descartes does not explain the precise meaning
or nature of the intellect's turning to its own ideas,
but this does not preclude an ultimate assumption of a
form of mind-brain identity. Although at this point, given
the apparent incommensurability between images and body,
the way in which mind generates images by turning to body
appears inexplicable, the subsequent identification of
the imagination with the sensus communis (already begun
in Meditation II) explains the sense in which such images
are corporeal. As Caton points out, "This implies that
the 'body' to which the cognitive power turns when it
imagines is the image at the pineal gland. The theory
of the pure intellect and its relation to imagination turns
on this identification."[23] Descartes' most straightforward
repudiation of the faculty conception is by way of explaining
the indivisibility of mind compared to the divisibility
of body. "And the faculties of willing, feeling, conceiving,
etc. cannot be properly speaking be said to be its parts,
for it is one and the same mind which employs itself in
willing and in feeling and understanding."[24]

To the extent that Descartes argues for a mind-body
dualism it is in the famous epistemological argument whereby
the transition from the distinction in the order of knowing
is made to the distinction in the order of being in terms
of clear and distinct perception:

And first of all, because I know that
all things which I apprehend clearly
and distinctly can be created by God
as I apprehend them, it suffices that
I am able to apprehend one thing apart
from another clearly and distinctly
in order to be certain that the one
is different from the other, since
they may be made to exist in separation
at least by the omnipotence of God;
and it does not signify by what power
this separation is made in order to
compel me to judge them to be different:
and, therefore, just because I know
certainly that I exist, and that
meanwhile I do not remark that any
other thing necessarily pertains to
my nature or essence, excepting that
I am a thinking thing [or a substance
whose whole essence or nature is to
think]. And although possibly (or
rather certainly, as I shall say in
a moment) I possess a body with which
I am very intimately conjoined, yet
because on the one side, I have a clear
and distinct idea of myself inasmuch
as I am a thinking and unextended thing,
and as, on the other, I possess a
distinct idea of body, inasmuch as
it is only an extended and unthinking
thing, it is certain that this I [that
is to say, my soul by which I am what
I am], is entirely and absolutely
distinct from my body, and can exist
without it.[25]

Williams defends Descartes' argument against the charge
that it contains an illegitimate inference from knowing
to being by claiming that the issue is not whether such
a faulty inference is performed but rather what Descartes
can legitimately claim to intuit.[26] According to Williams:

To arrive at the Real Distinction,
it is necessary first that I can remain
uncertain about the existence of my
body, while certain of my existence
as a thinking thing, however carefully
and clear-headedly I consider the
situation: that is to say, in Descartes'
terminology, that I can clearly and
distinctly conceive of myself existing
without a body. . . . Descartes
certainly supposes that he can: though
assured of his own existence in the
cogito, he supposes that the most careful
scrutiny will not reveal anything in
the existence so disclosed which implies
that he must have a body.[27]

God's guarantee of the validity of clear and distinct ideas,
says Williams, provides the step to "objective
possibility."[28] Williams supports his interpretations by
importing the ontology of the Principles ("the whole system
of ideas substance-attribute-mode") into the Meditations.
Judging the concept of essence to be the "primary notion"
in Descartes' demonstration, he concludes:

> Attributes and their modes do not exist
> by themselves; they have to belong
> to substances. Descartes indeed takes
> the Real Distinction to distinguish
> two different substances (Princ. i
> 60), and regards the thinking thing
> whose essential attribute is thought
> as being one substance, a conclusion
> which is one of the most characteristic
> expressions of his dualism. The
> terminology of substance is not just
> an archaism in Descartes' system; the
> peculiar way he uses it embodies some
> of his most basic beliefs.[29]

Wilson concurs with Williams and takes Descartes to mean
that a) the concept of res cogitans involves no concept
of extension, and that b) this provides him with a clear
and distinct idea of himself as a "complete thing." As
a result mind and body are "distinctly conceived as being
separate from each other."[30] The function of the epistemic
argument, according to Wilson, is to show that the res
cogitans of Meditation II ("clearly and distinctly perceived
as a complete thing in virtue of having the property of
thought") provides a legitimate ground for the conclusion
that the mind is a distinct thing in reality. The validation
by God of clear and distinct ideas as trustworthy pointers
to reality is taken as an essential requirement for this
transition.[31] Wilson therefore endorses the epistemic
argument, claiming that:

> Descartes' position . . . is just that
> since he recognizes that thought is
> sufficient 'for me to subsist with
> it alone,' he thereby knows no other
> attribute is necessary. To claim that
> thought and extension are different,
> and that either is sufficient to
> determine a complete or true thing,
> is already to deny the possibility
> of some 'hidden' necessary dependence
> of a thinking thing on the attribute
> of extension. Thus a 'complete
> knowledge' in Descartes' originally
> intended sense is sufficient for the
> Epistemological Argument to go through.[32]

Wilson raises what I take to be a criticism of her
interpretation and that of Williams when she questions
the reliability of the clear and distinct conception of
mind qua mind. The reservations she has about clear and

distinct conception are identical to those expressed by
Descartes in Meditation II when he carefully restricted
the discussion of the res cogitans to what was
phenomenologically available. That this phenomenology
was a quasi-phenomenology because of the maintenance of
the doubt of body does not matter. Wilson asks how one
can be certain that one's clear and distinct concept of
what thought is, i.e., that it is free of any bodily
attributes, is not in fact ignorance of the nature of
thought. No matter how "'intimate' my apprehension of
thought seems to be," a mistake is always a possibility.[33]
Such a phenomenological limit, I suggest, must be seen
as the expression of the dubitability of what appears as
the ontic premise of the epistemic argument--that unless
mind and body did admit of a "real distinction" it could
not be possible to arrive at a clear and distinct perception
of mind apart from body. The phenomenological limitation
is necessary in the light of the truth Descartes claims
for his physiologically based psychology. On the one hand,
an argument for mind-body separation on the premise of
"real distinction" is circular. On the other hand, no
phenomenology can discover the dependence Descartes claims
for conscious experience on data below the level of
consciousness, e.g., the motions from sense organ to the
brain in Descartes' theory of perception. Descartes'
physiological psychology as a whole is responsible for
what Wilson raises as an ever-present phenomenological
limitation. The bifurcation of sense and imagination in
Meditation II in terms of bodily genesis and conscious
effect pointed in this direction. The summary of the
automaton theory of perception in the latter portions of
Meditation VI is its confirmation.

The claim that the "real distinction" justifies a
"substantial distinction" is even more tenuous. In the
first place there is the appeal to the divine veracity
as in some sense instrumental to the "real distinction",
as though Descartes were continuing the "origin of my being"
theme of Meditations I and III. Since we have seen that
God's creativity is bound by the law of contradiction,
the argument is really conducted in terms of human reason
alone. Descartes indicates this in the latter half of
the epistemological argument:

> because, on the one side, I have a
> clear and distinct idea of myself
> inasmuch as I am only a thinking and
> unextended thing, and as, on the other,
> I possess a distinct idea of body,
> inasmuch as it is only an extended
> and unthinking thing, it is certain
> that this I [that is to say, my soul
> by which I am what I am], is entirely
> and absolutely distinct from my body,
> and can exist without it.[34]

Descartes' removal of God in favor of clear and distinct
perception means that the argument for dualism is being
made solely on the basis of Cartesian principles--the
knowledge by res cogitans of the relation between res

cogitans and res extensa. We are still at the level of Meditation II--epistemic separation coupled with ontic indeterminacy. Concluding an ontic separation solely from an epistemic distinction commits (as Antoine Arnauld pointed out in the Fourth Objections) the unwarranted inference made in the Discourse and which was warned against by Descartes himself in the preface to the Meditations. Given the dual elimination of God from the argument for dualism (the prior removal via the apologetics of inscrutability, such that the theodicy of Meditation VI is really the question of the beneficence of Cartesian nature, and the explicit removal midway through the epistemic argument), the motive for a proof of a substantial and immortal soul is more understandable than its demonstration. As we have seen, the letter to the Sorbonne cited the existence of God and the immortality of the soul as indispensable in convincing the infidels of religion and perhaps also moral virtue. And since the proofs are defective by the standards of natural reason the true audience for such demonstrations is the faithful. As Descartes explains to Mersenne:

> I could not prove that God could not annihilate the soul but only that it is by nature entirely distinct from the body, and so that it is not bound by nature to die with it. This is all that is required as a foundation for religion, and is all that I had any intention of proving.[35]

Although the faithful can make the leap from knowing to being, the fact that the soul is united to the body makes such a leap difficult for the others. As Descartes wrote to Princess Elizabeth:

> There are two facts about the human soul on which depend all the things we can know of its nature. The first is that it thinks, the second is that it is united to the body and can act and be acted upon along with it. About the second I have said hardly anything; I have tried only to make the first well understood. For my principal aim was to prove the distinction between soul and body, and to this end only the first was useful, and the second might have been harmful.[36]

The question concerning the bodily aspect of the soul receives an inadequate response in the epistemic argument because, in addition to the unsoundness of the argument, the unity of mind and body has been methodologically abstracted from by attempting to prove the separability and immortality of the soul from the clear and distinct idea of soul and body conceived in isolation. Products of an abstraction are used to justify the claim that the abstraction represents the real. Even assuming that Descartes seriously tries to establish a separable and

perhaps immortal soul, this attempt remains premature pending
a thorough understanding of body. Descartes explains in
the synopsis of Meditation II that "the premises from which
the immortality of the soul may be deduced depend on an
elucidation of a complete system of Physics."[37] As he
says in the sequel, the issue concerns the corruptibility
of substances. Given the materialist account of man
summarized in Discourse V, which was completed prior to
Descartes' religious interest, it is difficult to see how
settling the question concerning the incorruptibility of
substances contributes to the proof of an immortal soul
(unless, perhaps, the brain as the seat of the soul is
incorruptible). In the Passions, where Descartes claims
to speak "not as a rhetorician, nor as a moralist, but
as a physicist,"[38] we get such a physics of the soul in
which nothing is said concerning immortality. Despite
Descartes' hopes for medical progress, the Stoic conclusion
of the Passions points in the direction of man's finitude
in both body and spirit.

The Passions contains but a hint that there is perhaps
a mind-body separability. To the extent that the soul
is said to depart the body when the latter dies from purely
"natural causes," there is a suggestion of separability.
But this is not clarified. Even conceding that something
like a soul substance survives the body, what proof is
there that such a substance remains intact permanently,
that is, that such a soul substance is incorruptible?
Immortality does not logically follow from the separability,
even survival, of the soul from bodily death. What Descartes
continually stresses is the soul's dependence on the body
since the presence or absence of soul is coterminous with
the presence or absence of organically determined life.
Since the soul is present only in a living body, there
must be a genuine soul-body union, yet the soul is powerless
to move such a body. Since the soul of a living body is
not responsible for life and yet there must be an intimate
union between soul and body, the likely sort of union,
the most intimate sort of union, is an epiphenomenalism
(to accommodate consciousness). "Soul or mind" may designate
nothing more than the living and thinking activities of
an appropriately evolved and structured organic body.
The argument for a substantial distinction between mind
and body cannot be made if the argument for the "real
distinction" cannot be made. As we have seen, the problem
of understanding the human composite is not one of resolving
the paradox of the interaction of two substances defined
in mutually exclusive terms, making any causal connection
unintelligible, but one of comprehending how a unitary
organism can manifest itself in such heterogeneous types
of activity as metabolic, passionate, perceptual, and
cognitive behavior.

The correspondence with Elizabeth sheds some light
on the apparent miracle of the two-as-one mind-body relation.
It likewise serves as an adumbration of the way in which
the problem is handled in the latter parts of Meditation
VI. The suspicion that the soul is material for Descartes
prompts Caton to dismiss the exchange with Elizabeth since
the corporeal ideas thesis renders the interaction problem
superfluous. According to Caton, "The correspondence with

Elizabeth, in which Descartes appears to commit himself
to the inexplicability of the interaction, must be evaluated
in light of Descartes' evident reluctance to discuss the
subject with her."[39] This is perhaps the case; however,
the correspondence is valuable for the way in which Descartes
indicates the dilemma inherent in his anthropology. He
simplifies to her what is presented in a more obscure way
in the second half of <u>Meditation</u> VI.

The irresolvable tensions within what <u>Meditation</u> VI
refers to as the various "senses of my nature" are
communicated in the letter of 28 June 1643, in which
Descartes writes:

> First of all I distinguished three
> kinds of primitive ideas or notions
> each of which is known in its own proper
> manner and not by comparison with any
> other: i.e., the notion of the soul,
> the notion of the body, and the notion
> of union between soul and body. .
> . . the soul can be conceived only
> by pure intellect; the body (i.e.,
> extension, shape and movement) can
> likewise be known by pure intellect,
> and finally what belongs to the union
> of the soul and the body can be known
> only obscurely by pure intellect or
> by the intellect aided by imagination,
> but it can be known very clearly by
> the senses.[40]

The notions of mind, body, and mind-body union are said
to be primitive, that is, equally fundamental and
irreducible. They differ, of course, in that the first
two represent the methodological perspective of <u>Meditation</u>
II. <u>Res cogitans</u> and <u>res extensa</u>, in other words, are
abstractions from the "true man" revealed by the senses.
<u>Res cogitans</u> and <u>res extensa</u> arise from scientific thinking
(they are simultaneously its cause and effect since, as
we have seen, pure intellect is what grasps body as <u>res
extensa</u> and <u>res extensa</u> is what is graspable by pure
intellect), whereas mind-body union can be known only
prescientifically, through the epistemically confused
experience of embodiment.

Descartes suggests that any attempt at reconciliation
is beyond human comprehension because it is involved in
contradiction. He explains in the same letter to Elizabeth:

> It does not seem to me that the human
> mind is capable of conceiving at the
> same time the distinction and the union
> between body and soul, because for
> this it is necessary to conceive them
> as a single thing and at the same time
> to conceive them as two things; and
> this is absurd.[41]

According to Wilson this statement betrays an inconsistency
in Descartes' own conception. Wilson interprets Descartes'
dualism as a dualism of potentiality, i.e., "that mind

and body are <u>potentially</u> separate." Consequently there
is no conceptual difficulty in regarding mind and body
as distinct substances and as combined "at present." This
statement to Elizabeth, argues Wilson, is thus to be taken
"as an overt admission on Descartes' part that his position
on the mind-body relation is selfcontradictory."[42] Wilson's
criticism would be well taken if Descartes' position were
in fact such a dualism of potentiality. What Descartes
warns against in the passage to Elizabeth concerns a
difficulty in our conception and not a contradiction in
being. The simultaneity referred to concerns not the
identity of two things and one thing but rather the
conflation of the senses in which mind and body must be
conceived as united and as distinct. Descartes in no way
suggests that two substances are one substance; this is
precisely what the passage is denying. The earlier of
the two passages to Elizabeth indicates Descartes'
problematic--how to account for the diverse human phenomena
by a satisfactory account of mind-body relation. The <u>aporia</u>
is real and perhaps irresolvable. However, it is not a
problem in the logic of substance, but rather a question
of synthesizing what may be ultimately irreconcilable
perspectives. The perspectives of science and prescientific
experience require Descartes to show "how it is possible
to conceive the soul as material (which is what it is to
conceive its union with the body), while still being able
to discover that it is separable from the body."[43] That
is to say, how can the soul be conceived of as natural
and as transnatural in order to engage in both thought
and action? Concerning action (motion), as the <u>Passions</u>
makes clear, to equate the soul with matter to account
for bodily motion is to posit the body as an automaton.
Concerning thought, the sense in which the soul can be
conceived as transnatural is as <u>res cogitans</u>. The
methodological abstraction of <u>Meditation</u> II is preserved
throughout <u>Meditation</u> VI. The argument for the "real
distinction" is patently inconclusive and the elaboration
of the nature of <u>res cogitans</u> is not in terms of a substance
ontology. If thought cannot be attributed to an incorporeal
substance, then perhaps it is a mode of the physiological,
perhaps some form of neurological self-consciousness.
I will discuss below the sense in which Descartes commits
himself to a mind-brain identity, that mind is matter and
that matter can think.

THE EXISTENCE OF BODY

      Prior to pursuing the problematics of mind-body
relatedness Descartes gives a proof of bodily existence
by retracing the epistemic-ontic regression which culminated
in the notion that, because they are perceived clearly
and distinctly as objects of pure mathematics, bodies are
possible existents. Bodily existence, and along with it
the question of the relation of similarity between bodies
and perceptions, was suspended by the methodological severing
of sense and imagination from the body as part of the <u>res
cogitans</u>. The bodily genesis of perception was replaced
by an immanentist conception of sensation and image which

transformed the perception of body into the contemplation of an idea of body. This is not to deny a form of idealism in Descartes (the nature which will be discussed below).

The first step in the reinstatement of body was the distinction between imagination and intellect, which, as we have seen, are not distinct faculties but modes of relating the one cognitive power to body. Given Descartes' definition of imagination as "nothing but a certain application of the faculty of knowledge to the body which is immediately present to it, and which therefore exists,"[44] the existence of body (i.e., one's own) is apparently unproblematic. It is the imagination qua res cogitans which disqualifies it as the certain access to external body, since, when imagining, the cognitive power "turns toward the body, and there beholds in it something conformable to the idea which it has either conceived of itself or perceived by the senses."[45] External body is doubtful because the contemplation of such data, though originally corporeal, is conceived along the lines of the epistemic schema concluding Meditation II--the image as an incorporeal, purely ideational content of the mind--which fosters the illusion of a pure or autonomous inner psychic realm. The apparent disparity between images so conceived and sensations means that such images cannot conclusively demonstrate external existence. According to Wilson, for whom this disparity is more real than apparent, Descartes saw "no contradiction in supposing that my phenomenal states of imagination occur although no body exists. And this means (I take it) that the experiences of imagination can be clearly and distinctly conceived in separation from anything physical."[46] For this reason, according to Wilson, Descartes rejected the argument from imagination to body as anything beyond probability. Wilson adds that such an immaterialist conception is much less plain in the case of sensation. My suggestion is that once the ambiguity in Descartes' discussion of imagination is appreciated, however, we come to realize that the situation is the same for sensation and imagination since it is only as imaged that bodies are readmitted. Though sensation and imagination are equally integral to the perception of bodies, the reason Descartes rejects the argument from imagination to body is in order to reject the relation of similarity between perception (immanent "incorporeal" idea) and body. This sets the stage for the proof of bodily existence from sensation, whereby existence is claimed without having to claim perceptual similarity, since motion rather than form is communicated by the physiological contact with body making perception possible.

The distinction between passive and active perceptual capacities is the way in which Descartes proves bodily existence from sensation. Since every step in the perceptual process involves body on body, the nature of the "hidden faculty" to which he refers is revealed as the corporeal imagination. The two perceptual capacities are correlative since the "passive faculty of perception, that is, of receiving and recognizing the ideas of sensible things" could not be of use "if there were not either in me or in some other thing another active faculty capable of forming and producing these ideas."[47] The question of Descartes'

materialism turns on the identification of the active
capacity. In accordance with the axiom of the
proportionality of cause and effect, Descartes is claiming
that that which is capable of producing material for the
passive capacity must be at least on the same ontic plane
as such material. Since the path from external body to
perception is to be explained mechanically, the active
faculty (i.e., the "hidden faculty") is synonymous with
one's physiology. As he says, "this active faculty cannot
exist in me [inasmuch as I am a thing that thinks] seeing
that it does not presuppose thought, and also that those
ideas are often produced in me without my contributing
in any way to the same, and often even against my will."[48]
The physiological system of sensory stimulation, animal
spirits, and corporeal imagination is distinct from res
cogitans, below conscious awareness, and involuntary, thus
satisfying Descartes' criteria for the active faculty.

In order that such sensory stimulation not be illusory,
Descartes claims to appeal to God's veracity once again.
But since God is the personification of Cartesian nature,
whose epistemic meaning is the distinction between clear
and distinct ideas concerning essence as opposed to the
confused ideas attesting likeness, we can charge Descartes'
appeal to God as the guarantor of existence with
inconsistency. As Kennington puts it:

> But if the divine guarantee can be
> invoked to salvage the existence thesis
> from its dubitability, we inevitably
> wonder why it could not also be invoked
> to save the similarity thesis as well.
> The answer would seem to be that
> Cartesian science requires the existence
> thesis to be a science of the world
> (or to avoid "idealism"), but is in
> irrevocable conflict with the similarity
> thesis.[49]

Descartes' theological founding of a science which can
provide knowledge of essence but, paradoxically, not
existence fails because of the inscrutability of God's
capricious will. The way through perception is the true
Cartesian proof of existence. The theory of perception
presented in Meditation VI exemplifies Cartesian science,
yet Descartes makes this difficult to see by misleadingly
continuing the bifurcation of sensation and imagination
of Meditation II. The dichotomy is misleading because
the distinction between the passive and active perceptual
capacities showed that, since the passive power of
contemplating ideas is directly responsive to the active
power of external bodies, the proof of the existence of
bodies involves imagination as well as sensation. This,
of course, is not to suggest that similarity between percept
and body is reestablished, since knowledge of body on the
basis of idea does not imply nor require knowledge of body
as similar to idea. The issue of similarity is resolved
by the disparity between body understood in the mode of
clear and distinct idea and body encountered in the mode
of physiological response to data of the corporeal

imagination. Since embodiment is the source of confused ideas, Descartes' judgment of the senses as guides to existence but not likeness is based neither on an unprejudiced critical phenomenology of perception nor on God's veracity. It follows from the fact that body is understood as res extensa by the pure intellect and as existent through the physiology of perception. In each case (intellect cognizing res extensa, senses contacting body) it is a question of like knowing like. The problems involved in relating like to other are encountered when Descartes tries to explain the relatedness of mind and body which can accommodate both the "true man" and what appears to be the heterogeneous dyad of res cogitans and res extensa.

THE RELATION BETWEEN MIND AND BODY

The epistemic argument for mind-body distinction left Descartes' anthropology at the methodological level of Meditation II--man is a composite of the mental and the physical, whose relation is as yet to be determined. The last half of Meditation VI is devoted to determining the mode of mind-body relatedness. Descartes' discussion is conducted not within the confines of the ontology of substance but in terms of what Kennington has aptly termed "a Cartesian 'antinomy' of mechanism and teleology" contained within what Descartes calls "my nature in particular."[50] By "my nature in particular" is meant the union of mind and body which "nature teaches me"--not res cogitans and its nonbodily truths, not res extensa and its purely material attributes, but an irreducible composite, i.e., the teleological "true man." The "antinomy" results because the teleological understanding of the "true man" has been invalidated by the scientific understanding's rejection of purposiveness. Following our hermeneutic concerning the Meditations' theodicy, this tension between the prescientific and scientific anthropologies represents the problem inherent in opting for Cartesian nature rather than God as the "origin of my being." From the prephilosophical, practical perspective, mind and body are inextricably united. From the philosophical, theoretical perspective we clearly and distinctly distinguish what belongs to mind from what belongs to body. The "natural teaching" introduced in Meditation III is as accurate from the practical perspective as it is incorrect from the theoretical perspective. This situation produces the three primitive notions mentioned to Elizabeth and their two truths. On the one hand, "the nature here described truly teaches me to flee from things which cause the sensation of pain, and seek after the things which communicate to me the sentiment of pleasure and so forth"; on the other hand, "it is mind alone, and not mind and body in conjunction, that is requisite to a knowledge of the truth in regard to such things."[51]

A somewhat different account of the problems confronting Descartes' anthropology is offered by Wilson. She argues that Descartes tried to maintain two incompatible notions of mind-body relation, what she calls the "Natural

Institution" and "Co-extension" theories. The Natural
Institution theory is "philosophically resourceful and
relatively intelligible":

> The connection between a particular
> type of mind state and a particular
> type of brain state is said to be
> arbitrary, or depend on divine
> institution, for, I imagine, the simple
> reason that Descartes could not see
> any way of establishing an <u>intrinsic</u>
> connection between the two.[52]

The subsequent move to the Co-extension theory is interpreted
as Descartes' attempt to better explain such sensations
as pain, etc. In the Co-extension theory the soul unites
with the entire body. Wilson cites the <u>Passions</u> I, 30
and 31, which, along with <u>Meditation</u> VI, are seen to involve
a "potential for contradiction." Descartes says the
following in the <u>Passions</u> I, 30 and 31:

> the soul is truly joined to the whole
> body, and one cannot properly say that
> it is in some one of [the body's] parts
> to the exclusion of others. . . .
> although the soul is joined to the
> whole body, there is nevertheless in
> the body a certain part in which the
> soul exercises its functions more
> particularly.[53]

This merely reiterates the part-whole relation stated in
<u>Meditation</u> VI, concerning which Wilson concludes that there
exists "the potential for contradiction" in the <u>Meditations'</u>
claim "that the mind is both restricted to a small part
of the brain and 'sort of intermingled' with the whole
body."[54] Concerning Descartes' statement that mind is
extended throughout the body, Wilson asks, "If it is in
some sense correct to say this, why should Descartes also
say that it exercises its functions directly only in the
pineal gland?"[55] The difficulty with Wilson's (and also
Williams' and Ruth Mattern's) analysis is its literalism.
It is incorrect to interpret what she calls "Natural
Institution" and "Co-extension" as competing theories,
such that Descartes ambivalently moved from the former
to the latter. If my account captures Descartes' meaning,
their resolution consists in seeing them as complementary.
The problem is not one of comprehending two competing
conceptions of mind-body union (which implies a prior
mind-body distinction, rejected by Descartes), as though
two equals one, but comprehending how the one form of union
(automatism plus nonsubstantial awareness) can handle the
"true man" phenomenology and the mechanical, scientific
anthropology. Descartes' two-in-one of the soul becomes
less incoherent when taken as positing the soul as both
the aliveness of the body as body as well as the awareness
of its motion in the form of brain states.
    The truth of the "natural attitude" is Descartes'
argument for mind-body intimacy. As he explains:

> But there is nothing which this nature
> teaches me more expressly [nor more
> sensibly] than that I have a body which
> is adversely affected when I feel pain.
> . . . nor can I doubt there being
> some truth in all this. Nature also
> teaches me by these sensations of pain,
> hunger, thirst, etc., that I am not
> only lodged in my body as a pilot in
> a vessel, but that I am very closely
> united to it, and so to speak so
> intermingled with it that I seem to
> compose with it one whole.[56]

What for Descartes is an indubitable union, an irreducible unity, is for Williams a phenomenology in search of an ontology. Williams interprets Descartes' anthropology as a problem in dualism, how to achieve union from separation. He puts what he takes to be Descartes' question as follows:

> I exist as a thinking thing. . . .
> If I, strictly speaking, am my soul
> (as Descartes, against St. Thomas,
> held) what is the relation of my soul
> to my body? . . . the entire content
> of Descartes' denial that he is a pilot
> in a ship is phenomenological--it is
> exclusively about what the experience
> of being embodied is like. Further
> argument is needed to connect that
> with any ontological claims. How do
> we know what is metaphysically necessary
> to make such an experience possible?

Descartes' answer, according to Williams, is "that he was tempted to read that phenomenological fact as a metaphysical one, in relation to his talk of a substantial union. Much the same occurs also with regard to the pineal gland."[57]

What Williams refers to as the problem of the relation between the phenomenological and the metaphysical arises on the basis of a mistaken dualist premise. Neither the phenomenological nor the metaphysical, for Descartes, is to be explained in terms of a dualism of substances. We must resist the "one from two" account of mind-body unity in favor of a primordial "two in one." It is not through substance ontology nor clear and distinct perception, but rather through our senses ("confused modes of thought") that we are convinced of mind-body wholeness. If such wholeness were not the case, adds Descartes, sensations such as hunger and thirst would be contemplated but not felt. Williams' dualistic premise arises from construing the methodological (res cogitans) rather than the phenomenological ("true man") as primordial.

Descartes' anthropological dilemma is the following: Confused modes of thought are pragmatically valid but theoretically false, whereas clear and distinct ideas are theoretically valid but pragmatically ineffectual because

of their divorce from eros. What the mind-body whole
naturally and truly regards as beneficial or harmful it
cannot theoretically comprehend. What res cogitans clearly
and distinctly understands it cannot judge in terms of
good or evil. As we have seen, this is because of the
characteristics of the passions. As the Passions explains,
"the principal effect of all the passions in men is that
they incite and dispose their soul to desire those things
for which they prepare their body."[58]   In other words,
there is a bodily based erotic intentionality. But as
Meditation VI concedes, such a cause and effect relation
is theoretically mysterious. Because there is no likeness
between feelings and their physiological origins, "when
I inquired, why, from some, I know not what, painful
sensation, there follows sadness of mind, and from the
pleasurable sensation there arises joy, or why this
mysterious pinching of the stomach which I call hunger
causes me to desire to eat, and dryness of throat causes
a desire to drink, and so on, I could give no reason
excepting that nature taught me so."[59] Just as the internal
either-or of man as a dualism of res cogitans and res extensa
or as an irreducible mind-body whole cannot be resolved
in favor of one conception or the other, the external
either-or of nature's teleological meaning for the "true
man" and mechanical indifference in itself cannot be resolved
without sacrificing the clear and distinct ideas of science
or the confused teleological ideas of practice. Since
the "true man" cannot be constructed from res cogitans
and res extensa, and since nothing in nature corresponds
to a whole composed of teleology and mechanics, the best
that Descartes offers is a tension between prescientific
and scientific perspectives. And since God has given way
to Cartesian nature, the question of God's goodness in
the face of erroneous practical judgments is Descartes'
admission of such a tension between Cartesian nature and
anthropology. As we have seen, it was such a tension which
prevented the finalization of the perfect moral science.

The remainder of the Meditations indicates the direction
the desired reconciliation would take. What Descartes
says about the soul when contrasting it with the body in
the final statement of the difference between mind and
body suggests the ontological dependence of mind upon body
which lurked behind the argument for res cogitans in
Meditation II. Meditation VI reaffirms Meditation II:

> When I consider the mind, that is to
> say, myself inasmuch as I am only a
> thinking thing, I cannot distinguish
> in myself any parts. . . . And the
> faculties of willing, feeling,
> conceiving, etc., cannot be properly
> speaking said to be its parts, for
> it is one and the same mind which employs
> itself in willing and in feeling and
> understanding.[60]

Since the various modes of thought do not inhere in a mental
substance, perhaps they inhere (in a way which is possibly

inexplicable) in body. Thoughts may be no more than an awareness of brain states. As Descartes explains:

> I further notice that the mind does
> not receive the impressions from all
> parts of the body immediately, but
> only from the brain, or perhaps even
> from one of its smallest parts, to
> wit, from that in which the common
> sense is said to reside, which, whenever
> it is disposed in the same particular
> way, conveys the same thing to the
> mind.61

The material side of Descartes' dualism becomes apparent when we recall that the process is not reversible. Soul as mind cannot cause motion in the body machine since

> functions occur naturally in this machine
> solely by the disposition of its organs,
> not less than the movements of a clock
> or other automaton. . . . Thus it
> is not necessary to conceive that it
> has a nutritive soul, or sensitive
> soul, or any other principle of motion
> and life except its blood and spirits
> . . . which have no other nature than
> [that] found in inanimate bodies.62

Thinking occurs, but it is bodily based and noncausal since mechanics explains why and how objects are either pursued or avoided. The experience of psychic causality (the teaching of nature) is thus epiphenomenal. It appears then, at least as far as human action is concerned, that Descartes' science views man as a conscious automaton. And since such consciousness cannot be dismissed as mere illusion, an irreducible stratum remains a part of Descartes' dualism due to the inability to embrace either a material or ideal monism. This is the case epistemically as well as anthropologically. Thinking occurs, such that to this extent Descartes is properly res cogitans, but since the immediate object of thought is physiological, res cogitans partakes of res extensa. Since the experiential content of such thought is ideational, there is the temptation to take such an experience as prior epistemically. What Descartes presents in Meditation II as methodological--the epistemic schema involving the priority of ideas--easily becomes, as the history of modern philosophy shows, a first principle in being. The world becomes the idea of the world and knowledge of the world becomes self-knowledge. For Descartes, despite the ideational character of one's conscious experience, the immediate object of such awareness is a brain state. Mind and its cognition are therefore simultaneously bodily and a reflection upon body. Descartes' dualism therefore oscillates between the extremes of the ontic priority of body and the methodic-epistemic, experiential priority of consciousness.
      According to Mattern, Descartes' discussion in Meditation VI is consistent with a dualism of causal

interaction, that is, of substances. With respect to such
Cartesian statements to the effect that mind is "very closely
united to body" (HR I, 192) or that mind "informs body"
(HR I, 289), she writes:

> mind-body union as portrayed at these
> points is really nothing more than
> certain special capacities of mind-body
> interaction. Here, nothing more than
> particular causal connections (especially
> the capacity of mind to be affected
> by internal sensations) distinguishes
> the intimate relation of the mind to
> its body from the less intimate relation
> of a sailor to his ship. Descartes
> avoids the suggestion of any union
> than interaction by intimating that
> a stronger relation is only apparent.
> For example, Meditation VI refers to
> 'the union and apparent intermingling
> of mind and body' (HR I, 192).63

Mattern assumes along with Kenny, Wilson, and Williams,
a prior mind-body separation, that the "real distinction"
has produced a substantial dualism. I have tried to show
that Descartes' intention was to conceive of mind as a
metaphysically neutral effect of physiological causality
rather than as the entity so affected. To interpret mind
and body as causally interacting is to introduce a false,
superfluous dichotomy of things. Descartes' dualism is
a dualism between nature and experience rather than between
mutually exclusive substances. By res cogitans is meant
nothing more than the awareness of the occurrence of
thoughts. And since such thoughts are at bottom brain
states, res cogitans participates in res extensa. Science
posits mind-brain identity; experience posits mind-body
heterogeneity because of the nonexperienced connection
between the source and result of sensations. The inability
to close or explain the quantum leap from sensus communis
to awareness of image or idea persists, but does not induce
Descartes to introduce an immaterial mind. As we have
seen concerning human action, he attempts to solve the
antinomy of mechanics and purpose by ascribing an
intentionality to the passions.
       As we have seen, Descartes solves the problem of the
existence of external bodies scientifically rather than
phenomenologically, on the basis of bodies as sensed rather
than as imaged. Descartes argues this on the basis of
the principle of the homogeneity of cause and effect.
It is thus a case of like knowing like, since what is
communicated from sense organ to brain is motion rather
than species form. There is in fact, says Descartes, a
one-to-one correlation between sensory stimulation and
resultant sensation, since "whenever [the sensus communis]
is disposed in the same particular way, [it] conveys the
same thing to the mind." Regulae XII had already conceived
of the relation between sense organ and stimulation in
the manner of wax and its impressions. Descartes stressed
there that this was no mere analogy. The argument by analogy

begins with the transition from sensus communis to mind
as pure intellect. The context of Regulae XII was the
epistemic-ontic progression from sensation to simple natures.
Analogy was necessary because, as with the other cognitive
powers, the nature of the intellect must correspond to
its objects. This seems to produce a mind-body split since
"that power by which we are properly said to know things,
is purely spiritual, and not less distinct from every part
of the body than blood from bone, or hand from eye."[64]
This "transnatural" intellect is described as follows:

> It is a single agency, whether it
> receives impressions from the common
> sense simultaneously with the fancy,
> or applies itself to those that are
> preserved in the memory, or forms new
> ones. . . . It is one and the same
> agency which, when applying itself
> along with the imagination to the common
> sense, is said to see, touch, etc.;
> if applying itself to the imagination
> alone in so far as that is endowed
> with diverse impressions, it is said
> to remember; if it turn to the
> imagination in order to create fresh
> impressions, it is said to imagine
> or conceive; finally if it act alone
> it is said to understand. How this
> latter function takes place I shall
> explain at greater length in the proper
> place.[65]

The proper place would appear to be the Meditations, but
the accounts in the two works are the same. What is
accomplished by abstracting from embodiment in the Regulae
is repeated at the methodological level as res cogitans
in the Meditations. In each case intellect is a mode of
mind, mind in turn inextricably bound to body. What is
"transnatural" is the experience rather than the being
of mind. The same duality occurs in the Passions. What
is accomplished at the methodological level in the
Meditations in order to free up the knowing intellect is
accomplished at the physiological level in the Passions
in order to produce the passion of resolve to doubt, etc.
The phenomenological chasm between physiology and conscious
experience (a mental image of an extended body is not itself
an extended thing) does not resolve the tension between
nature and experience in favor of mind-body separateness.
Descartes' one-to-one correlation between sensus communis
and mind is closer to the isomorphism between brain pattern
and conscious experience of Gestalt psychology than to
the various forms of dualism. The internal relation between
the mental and the corporeal is "resolved" by Descartes
in the direction of the corporeal.

The external relation between the teleological mind-body
composite and nonteleological nature is the final theme
of the Meditations. The earlier solution to the theoretical
problem of judgment leaves the practical problem intact
because, in spite of the identification of knowledge and

virtue with clear and distinct cognition in Meditation
IV, errors still occur with respect to the beneficial and
the harmful. Descartes ostensibly tries to handle the
problem of practical judgment by demonstrating that God's
goodness is manifest in the very mechanical physiology
which poses the problem. If we assume for the moment that
the theodicy of the Meditations is sincere, one thing is
apparent. That Descartes once again feels the need to
vindicate God implies that the earlier theodicy was not
quite convincing. It still appears that God is perhaps
to blame for creating beings who can be systematically
deceived, e.g., by eating poisoned food which they are
naturally inclined to eat because of its pleasant taste.
However, in line with our identification of God with
Cartesian nature, that God permits the sick (the dropsical)
to desire the harmful is not a continuation of the theodicy
problem but rather Descartes' way of presenting the tension
between the mastery and possession and the recalcitrance
of nature. Descartes concedes the problem in science
overcoming the dichotomy between mechanics and purpose
because the mind-body composite cannot be understood
mechanistically:

> But certainly although in regard to
> the dropsical body it is only so to
> speak to apply an extrinsic term when
> we say that its nature is corrupted
> . . . in regard to the composite
> whole, that is to say, to the mind
> or soul united to this body, it is
> not a purely verbal predicate, but
> a real error of nature, for it to have
> thirst when drinking would be hurtful
> to it. And thus it still remains to
> inquire how the goodness of God does
> not prevent the nature of man so regarded
> from being fallacious.[66]

The reconciliation of constitutional error and divine
goodness, that is, of practical judgment and morally neutral
mechanics, is accomplished not by a theology of the will
as in Meditation IV (not appropriate here since the problem
is what we are more so than what we choose), but by what
can be termed a fortuitous physiology.
    The beneficent nature of the machinery of practical
perception is explained by Descartes as follows. The mind
receives impressions only from the brain; similar motions
in the brain produce similar sensations in the mind. These
similar brain motions, however, do not require similar
motions toward the periphery. Conceiving the nerves as
cords, any stimulation along a particular pathway will
produce the same terminal condition in the brain, and hence
the same sensation, so long as the same type of motion
is produced in the appropriate brain location. A feeling
of itching in the toe (whether present or amputated) results
from a stimulation anywhere along the appropriate pathway
from the toe to the brain. The mind responds directly
to the brain motion but feels the itch as occurring in
the toe. Such a mechanical isomorphism between consciousness

and physiology is generally and for the most part, i.e.,
in nonpathological or nonexceptional cases, the arrangement
most conducive to the well being of the composite. On
the basis of such a regular connection a pleasure-pain
calculus becomes feasible. If any other arrangement were
to occur (for instance, feelings of pleasure generated
by harmful stimuli or the reverse, or an irregular relation
between stimulus and sensation, or sensations being felt
as occurring somewhere between the brain and the periphery)
the well-being of the composite would not result. Descartes'
fortuitous physiology is an attempt to solve the problem
of constitutionally based practical error by what Beck
refers to as a "statistical averaging."

Although critical of Descartes' attempt to "justify
God by a sort of statistical averaging", Beck relies on
the inscrutability of God's will to conclude that "The
Meditations suggest that it is a justified assumption that
God has done His best for creation and His creatures."[67]
However, Descartes' closing words of the Meditations are
an admission that the problem of the composite is intractible
to theodicy:

> But because the exigencies of action
> often oblige us to make up our minds
> before having leisure to examine matters
> carefully, we must confess that the
> life of man is very frequently subject
> to error in respect to individual
> objects, and we must in the end
> acknowledge the infirmity of our
> nature.[68]

According to Williams the reconciliation of practical error
and human nature entails a Platonic mind-body split:

> If there is an answer to this, it no
> doubt lies once more in the distinction
> between systematic and particular
> beliefs. That we should be misled
> in particular matters about the external
> world is not a frustration of our
> fundamental nature as rational minds:
> to be mistaken in systematic and
> philosophical beliefs, would be. In
> such an answer one could sense the
> Platonic presupposition that it is
> as pure rational intelligences that
> men have their real worth and purpose,
> and that although we find ourselves
> with bodies, we must recognize that
> fact as a limitation. Such a
> presupposition is highly characteristic
> of Descartes' metaphysics.[69]

Descartes' problem goes deeper than the contrast between
systematic and particular belief, temporality and the
exigencies of action. Williams' conception of a Platonic
Descartes not only goes contrary to the primacy of the
bodily as the core of the anthropology of the Cartesian

architectonic. It also falsifies the nature of the account
of the mind-body composite, i.e., of human action, with
which the Meditations ends. Even if practical judgments
were infallible the mechanics-purpose tension within
Descartes' anthropology persists because the analysis of
the action taken by the composite is in fact an analysis
of the automaton. Since the soul qua incorporeal cannot
move the body, the source of human action must be understood
physiologically. That certain stimuli are accompanied
by certain types of awareness, on the basis of which are
made judgments of pursuit and avoidance, is gratuitous
as an explanation of the cause (if not the meaning or
significance) of behavior. The fortuitous physiology is
analogous to the clock that happens to tell the correct
time although its modus operandi does not differ from that
of the clock which gives the incorrect time.

For the most part the fortuitous physiology prevails,
but its so doing is not a satisfactory resolution of the
science-experience conflict. The significance of human
action has become but an extrinsic characteristic of man
conceived as machine. Yet the "true man" is mysteriously
purposeful. Such is the Cartesian solution to the problem
of embodiment.

CONCLUSION

The Cartesian architectonic as presented in the Discourse
established the hermeneutic for the relation between science,
subjectivity, and theology in the Meditations. Discourse
I and II teach that the origin of Cartesian philosophizing
is the egocentric passion of self-concern. The
prephilosophical soul relates to the world as material
for its self-enhancement through "mastery and possession."
Cartesian science and its creator, the philosophical soul,
are in the service of such natural egoism since the practical
goal of utility grounded in certainty is the rationale
for the auto-emancipation of reason from the heteronomies
of the past, the teachings of others, and one's own
embodiment. This practical goal, not the desire for
knowledge as the perfection of a natural eros to know,
gives the ultimate sense of the doubt procedure of Discourse
IV and Meditation I. The Discourse evolution of
philosophical reason from the natural attitude to the
methodological .is the source of the natural light with
which the Regulae begins and of the res cogitans as the
survivor of doubt in Meditation II. This evolution begins
and ends with what Descartes calls "generosity"--the willful
resolve to be guided solely by one's reason in all
matters--which is the cement binding the practical and
theoretical components of Cartesian philosophy. The
Meditations' concern with epistemology and metaphysics
must therefore be read as intermediary between the egoism
at the source of the Cartesian architectonic and the
technological mastery of nature as its fulfillment.

The Discourse is invaluable in deciding the question
of the theoretical supremacy of Descartes' physics or
theological metaphysics. In the order of presentation
the mathematical physics of Discourse V follows the
metaphysics of Discourse IV. That the order of presentation
is not the architectonic order has been suggested by the
following considerations. In the first place, contrary
to Descartes' claim in the Discourse, his study of
mathematics and physics was not in fact preceded by his
study of metaphysics (God and the soul). In the second
place, since the progression from doubt to metaphysics
in Discourse IV comes after the elaboration of the method

in _Discourse_ II, and since the _Discourse_ II summary of the _Regulae_ repeats the latter's identity between the foundations of method and science, this implies that physics precedes metaphysics in the order of discovery. The most telling evidence for the precedence of physics over metaphysics in the architectonic order is the way in which Descartes connects the two in _Discourse_ IV and V. He claims to have deduced his physics (the laws of nature) from the dual metaphysical roots of the tree of philosophy--God and the human soul. It is difficult to accept such a deduction as genuine given that the deduction in _Le Monde_, which _Discourse_ V summarizes, dispenses with the human soul and reduces the theological metaphysical foundations of science to one of God's attributes--immutability.

A tension between theology and rationalism is evident in the _Discourse_ account of the fabulous cosmogony. Since, Descartes claims, the laws of nature hold in all possible worlds, God's creativity would appear to be limited by an _a priori_ physics. Apart from this, to ground such changeless laws on God's immutability cannot account for the original content selection or creation. Arbitrary yet immutable laws are unacceptable to Cartesian rationality. When discussing the question of origins, Descartes contrasts the probability of the biblical genesis to the greater intelligibility of the materialistic genesis. To embrace the biblical genesis is therefore to violate the liberty of spontaneity which, ironically, is said to receive God's sanction.

In the _Meditations_ the question of God's goodness, the divine will, is at the heart of the theodicy. Apart from the definitional attempts at theodicy based on the concept of God as a perfect being, the theodicy assumes the form, or rather appears to, of traditional Christian moral psychology. God's goodness is not impugned, we are told, because error and sin are human misuses of God-given free will. However, such traditional moral psychology actually conveys an antitraditional doctrine. Contrary to appearances, Descartes' account of the soul is not one of a faculty psychology. Although the freedom of indifference suggests a faculty conception since the will acts independently of the intellect, what appears as traditional Christian voluntarism is in reality Cartesian rationalism since the will is compelled to accede to clear and distinct perception. To call the will's assent to clear and distinct perception freedom, in the absence of a real power to refuse, is to preserve only the name of freedom. This is the significance of the shift from freedom of indifference to freedom of spontaneity. The will is most free, i.e., forced to be free, when it is most rational. And since reason is a "universal instrument," the heretical implications of such a subordination of will to reason are unmistakable. We have seen the way in which the Letter to the Sorbonne announces that the _Meditations_ is a work of rationalist philosophy which as such threatens faith. Descartes wrote to [Mesland] of his desire to "avoid as far as possible all theological controversies,"[1] yet admits to Christian Huygens that "I am at war with the Jesuits."[2]

In _Meditation_ IV the elimination of teleology from physics is said to be deduced from God's inscrutable will.

In the name of piety we are to remain ignorant of God's plans. But if God's will is literally unintelligible to human reason a demonstration of God's beneficence can never be given. God is therefore culpable for creating a world showing no signs of the beneficence of its creator. To argue that God's will is good in the absence of clear and distinct proof (which Descartes does repeatedly in the Meditations) is once again to violate the freedom of spontaneity, the rational autonomy at the foundation of the Cartesian architectonic. The implication of the Cartesian categorical imperative of clear and distinct cognition is that reason and faith are mutually exclusive. Following Leibniz, we must conclude that Cartesian nature has become detheologized by means of a divine inscrutability as the personification of Cartesian mechanics.

The emancipation of reason from God is also evident in the doctrine of the divine creation of the eternal truths and the explanation of its absence from the Meditations. The unintelligibility of God's will means that His power cannot be known to be limited by His benevolence. The choice concerning the foundation of truth is therefore between God, who is recalcitrant to human reason, or unaided human reason. Descartes cannot ground the eternal truths on God's freedom of indifference since this merely reiterates the alogic of divine inscrutability. This, coupled with the failed theodicy, explains the absence of the divine creation of the eternal truths from the Meditations. Leibniz was correct when he labelled Descartes' theodicy a "philosophic feint."

The faculty account of the soul in Meditation IV, to repeat, assumed the guise of traditional Christian moral psychology as a cover for Cartesian rationalism. God's inscrutability serving as the personification of Cartesian nature, the issue of metaphysical foundations comes down to whether science or subjectivity is Descartes' first principle. We have seen that the res cogitans as the Archimedian point of certainty is dependent upon the Cartesian science of body as the first principle of being. This was shown by the way in which the structure of the res cogitans conforms to the epistemological requirements set by the nature of body as res extensa.

This conformity occurs as early as Meditation I. The methodological significance of the doubt argument was not so much the preparation for the establishment of the res cogitans, but rather the critique of the cognitive powers on the basis of a dogmatic intrusion of Cartesian science. There is developed an epistemic-ontic regression from sensation through imagination to intellect, whereby is explicated access to the nature of body in terms of the corporeal, the imaginative, and the conceptual. The dream assumption, whose purpose is to mediate the regression from the corporeal to the conceptual, is Descartes' method of abstracting images from their sensory origin. Imaginative limits are synonymous with the simple natures of Cartesian science. The transition from God to the finite evil genius suspends the doubt concerning mathematics. The exemption of mathematics from doubt is their presuppositionality throughout Meditation I and the cause of the circularity concerning Cartesian science whereby the simple natures

of physics are both the cause and resolution of the critique
of prescientific experience.

In _Meditation_ II the analyses of soul and body are
likewise determined by the conception of body (its doubtful
existence notwithstanding) according to Cartesian science.
Bodily doubt permits the explication of soul and body to
take place on the methodological level, but it is influenced
by the Cartesian ontology of body in the following ways.
The rejection of the Aristotelian soul as the unmoved mover
of the body in favor of the soul as _res cogitans_ was based
on a prior commitment to bodily automatism. Although this
dualistic presupposition is masked by presumptive bodily
doubt, the argument for _res cogitans_ is circular since
a dualistic premise is used to deduce a dualistic conclusion.
Bodily doubt permits the establishment of _res cogitans_
as an epistemic first principle whose relation to body
is left undetermined, thereby concealing the _aporia_ involved
in explaining the origin and nature of mind on the basis
of Cartesian materialism. Also left indeterminate at this
point is a judgment concerning the substantiality of _res
cogitans_.

The wax analysis accomplishes the rejection of
Aristotelian substantial form by reiterating the
ontic-epistemic regression of _Meditation_ I, which itself
had reiteratd the analysis of body in accord with the
cognitive order of _Regulae_ VIII. In every case the ground
of this cognitive order in the _Regulae_ and _Meditations_
is the Cartesian notion of body as _res extensa_. What appear
to be prescientific, phenomenological arguments establishing
the nature of body are in reality explications of _res extensa_
as an intellectual abstraction. What links the abstract
to the real is the bifurcation of the imagination into
an empirical and a pure employment, whose ground is the
correlation between the imageable, the possible, and the
real. Bodily doubt plus a working knowledge of the nature
of body, rather than the _res cogitans_ as a presuppositionless
first principle, is therefore responsible for the coordinate
accounts of body and soul in _Meditation_ II. This produces
the (mistaken) notion that the epistemic schema concluding
Meditation II--a methodological solipsism whereby the
encounter with objects is transformed into the perception
of ideas of objects--represents the true Cartesian epistemic
problem. Once the subject-object split is recognized to
originate in the very ontology it presumes to establish,
it is recognized that there is no such epistemic problem
for Descartes. The theory of the genesis of perception
given in _Meditation_ VI makes this clear.

The anthropology of _Meditation_ VI continues the
methodological dualism of _Meditation_ II; however, there
is implied in its characterization of mind as a
nonsubstantial unification of powers, rather than distinct
faculties, a resolution of the problem of embodiment in
the direction of epiphenomenalism. Mind or consciousness
is a one; its manyness is a manyness of applications.
Since mind is still _res cogitans_, i.e., not a substance
or a thing, to regard mind as the thinking capacity of
body is as plausible as regarding the diffusion of the
soul throughout the body as nothing more than the aliveness
of the body as automaton. The problem of embodiment is

not the problem of comprehending substantial dualism but rather of reconciling of Cartesian science and prescientific experience. The Cartesian problem is one of devising a conception of mind-body relation which does justice to the dependence on the body of mind as well as its experienced transcendence in the mode of will and intellect. Descartes' practical anthropology suffers from an inability to accommodate the heterogeneous accounts of value-free science and value-laden experience. Descartes' theoretical anthropology, the account of the mind as knower, abstracts from the aporia of materialism and is constituted on the plane of the intersection of methodology and epistemology. The cognitive relation between res cogitans and body is assured since the structure of body as res extensa dictates the cognitive structure of the soul. This is the significance of the epistemic-ontic correlation initiated in the Regulae, and which in the Meditations is consistent with the preservation of the metaphysical neutrality of res cogitans. The path from science to subjectivity in the Regulae and in the Meditations is discovered to be the same once the true metaphysical foundations of the Meditations--the epistemic-ontic correlation between res extensa and res cogitans--are accorded their rightful status. However, the aporia involved in their mediation by corporeal ideas is the price to be paid by such metaphysical foundations.

NOTES

PREFACE

1. Margaret Dauler Wilson, Descartes (London: Routledge
    & Kegan Paul, 1978), p. 3.
2. E. M. Curley, Descartes Against the Skeptics (Cambridge:
    Harvard University Press, 1978), p. 19.
3. Ibid.
4. Hiram Caton, The Origin of Subjectivity (New Haven:
    Yale University Press, 1973), p. 66.
5. Caton, "Tory History of Ideas," Independent Journal
    of Philosophy, 1985.
6. The Philosophical Works of Descartes, trans. E. S.
    Haldane and G. R. T. Ross (New York: Cambridge University
    Press, 1969), Vol. I, pp. 212-13. (Hereafter designated
    "HR"). Charles Adam and Paul Tannery, trans., Oeuvres
    de Descartes (Paris: Vrin, 1966), pp. 16-17. (Hereafter
    designated "AT").
7. Letter to the author, 28 March 1985.

CHAPTER 1: THE CARTESIAN ARCHITECTONIC

1. HR I, 81; AT VI, 1-2.
2. In Discourse VI he concludes that he "hardly ever
    . . . encountered any censor of my opinions who did
    not appear to me to be either less rigorous or less
    judicious than myself." HR I, 124; AT VI, 69.
3. HR I, 83; AT VI, 3.
4. HR I, 82; AT VI, 2-3.
5. HR I, 86; AT VI, 9-10.
6. Richard Kennington, "The 'Teaching of Nature' In
    Descartes' Soul Doctrine," The Review of Metaphysics
    26 (September 1972), p. 97.
7. HR I, 83; AT VI, 4.
8. HR I, 83; AT VI, 4.
9. HR I, 81; AT VI, 1.
10. HR I, 83; AT VI, 4.
11. HR I, 83-84; AT VI, 5.
12. HR I, 85; AT VI, 7.
13. HR I, 85; AT VI, 7.
14. HR I, 85; AT VI, 7-8.

15. Cf. <u>The Passions of the Soul</u>, Part First, Articles
    IV-VI, XLVII. HR I, 332-33, 352-54; AT XI, 329-31,
    364-66.
16. HR I, 85; AT VI, 8.
17. HR I, 87; AT VI, 10.
18. HR I, 86; AT VI, 8.
19. HR I, 85; AT VI, 7.
20. HR I, 86; AT VI, 9.
21. For an account of Descartes' critique of history,
    see David R. Lachterman, "Descartes And The Philosophy
    Of History," <u>Independent Journal of Philosophy</u>, Vol.
    IV, 1983.
22. Part Third, Article CLIII. HR I, 401-402; AT XI,
    445-46.
23. Part Third, Article CLI, HR I, 401; AT XI, 444-45.
24. HR I, 119; AT VI, 61.
25. Kennington, "Descartes," in <u>A History of Political</u>
    <u>Philosophy</u>, ed. L. Strauss and J. Cropsey (New York:
    Rand McNally, 1963), pp. 386-87.
26. HR I, 119; AT VI, 61-62.
27. On the relation between Descartes and Bacon, see
    Kennington, "Descartes And Mastery of Nature," in
    <u>Organism, Medicine, and Metaphysics</u>, ed. S. F. Spicker
    (Dordrecht: Reidel, 1978).
28. HR I, 87; AT VI, 11.
29. HR I, 87; AT VI, 11.
30. HR I, 88; AT VI, 12.
31. HR I, 88; AT VI, 12.
32. HR I, 88; AT VI, 13.
33. Part I, Principle LXXI. HR I, 250; AT VIII-1, 36.
34. <u>Discourse</u> II. HR I, 89-90; AT VI, 14-15.
35. <u>HR I, 90;</u> AT VI, 15.
36. HR I, 90; AT VI, 15.
37. <u>Passions</u>, Part Third, Article CLV. HR I, 402-403;
    AT XI, 447.
38. Joseph Cropsey, "On Descartes' <u>Discourse on Method</u>,"
    <u>Interpretation</u>, vol. 1/2, Winter 1970, pp. 142-43.
39. HR I, 120; AT VI, 62.
40. HR I, 120; AT VI, 62.
41. HR I, 120; AT VI, 62.
42. HR I, 92; AT VI, 19.
43. HR I, 92; AT VI, 18.
44. HR I, 35; AT X, 410.
45. HR I, 36; AT X, 412.
46. HR I, 37; AT X, 413.
47. HR I, 37; AT X, 413.
48. HR I, 37-38; AT X, 414.
49. HR I, 38; AT X, 415.
50. HR I, 38-39; AT X, 415-16.
51. HR I, 44; AT X, 423.
52. HR I, 40-41; AT X, 418.
53. This section is indebted to the excellent analysis
    by Jacob Klein in <u>Greek Mathematical Thought and</u>
    <u>the Origin of Algebra</u> (Cambridge: M.I.T. Press, 1968),
    pp. 197-210.
54. HR I, 54; AT X, 438.
55. HR I, 57; AT X, 442.
56. HR I, 56; AT X, 440-41.
57. HR I, 58; AT X, 443.
58. Letter to Clerselier, 12 January 1646. HR II, 131;
    AT VII, 212-13.

59. HR I, 116; AT VI, 57.
60. Letter to Queen Christina, 20 November 1647. A.
     Kenny, ed. and trans., Descartes' Philosophical Letters
     (London: Oxford University Press, 1970), p. 227.
     (Hereafter designated: Letters).
61. HR I, 95; AT VI, 22-23.
62. HR I, 95; AT VI, 23.
63. Cropsey, loc. cit., p. 136.
64. HR I, 95-96; AT VI, 23-24.
65. HR I, 96; AT VI, 24.
66. HR I, 96; AT VI, 25.
67. HR I, 96-97; AT VI, 25.
68. Hiram Caton, The Origin of Subjectivity (New Haven:
     Yale University Press, 1973), p. 57.
69. HR I, 97; AT VI, 26.
70. HR I, 98; AT VI, 28.
71. Part First, Article XL. HR I, 349-50; AT XI, 359.
72. HR I, 103; AT VI, 36.
73. See Jack R. Vrooman, Rene Descartes: A Biography
     (New York: Putnam, 1970), pp. 78-134.
74. HR I, 107; AT VI, 43.
75. HR I, 106; AT VI, 41.
76. HR I, 107; AT VI, 42.
77. HR I, 108; AT VI, 43.
78. HR I, 109; AT VI, 45.
79. HR I, 100; AT VI, 31.
80. HR I, 106; AT VI, 40.
81. HR I, 107; AT VI, 42.
82. HR I, 118; AT VI, 60.
83. HR I, 118; AT VI, 60.
84. HR I, 118; AT VI, 60.
85. HR I, 135; AT VII, 4.
86. HR I, 136; AT VII, 5.
87. HR I, 136; AT VII, 5.
88. HR I, 136; AT VII, 6.
89. HR I, 133; AT VII, 2.
90. HR I, 118; AT VI, 59.
91. HR I, 133; AT VII, 2.

CHAPTER 2: HYPERBOLIC DOUBT

1. HR I, 144; AT VII, 17.
2. See L. J. Beck, The Metaphysics of Descartes (London:
    Oxford University Press, 1965), pp. 72, 77; A. Kenny,
    Descartes: A Study of His Philosophy (New York:
    Random House, 1968), pp. 35-36; H. G. Frankfurt,
    Demons, Dreamers, and Madmen (Indianapolis:
    Bobbs-Merrill,1970), pp. 86, 92, 99; H. Caton, The
    Origin, pp. 118-21; Kenneth Dorter, "Science and
    Religion in Descartes' Meditations," The Thomist,
    XXXVII (1973), p. 323; F. Grayeff, Descartes (London:
    Philip Goodall, 1977), p. 11; L. Pearl, Descartes
    (Boston: G. K. Hall and Company, 1977), p. 106; M.
    Wilson, Descartes, p. 50; E. M. Curley, Descartes
    Against Skeptics, pp. 37, 42 (note); P. A. Schouls,
    The Imposition of Method (New York: Oxford University
    Press, 1980), pp. 93-94. The lack of omnipotence
    of the evil genius has been defended by Kennington,
    "The Finitude of Descartes' Evil Genius," Journal
    of the History of Ideas 32 (1971), pp. 441-46. See

also John Cottingham, "The Role of the Malignant
Demon," Studia Leibnitiana, vol. VIII (1976), pp.
257-64.
3. Kennington, "The Finitude of Descartes' Evil Genius,"
    p. 446.
4. Bernard Williams, Descartes: The Project of Pure
    Enquiry (New York: Penquin, 1978), pp. 62-63. But
    compare Descartes' apology for rehabilitating such
    "stale dishes" of ancient skepticism. Replies to
    Second Objections, HR II, 31; AT VII, 130.
5. Letter of August 1641. Letters, 119; AT III, 433.
6. Letters, 119; AT III, 434.
7. Regulae XII. HRI, 43; AT X, 421.
8. HR I, 314; AT X, 512.
9. HR II, 206; AT VII, 350.
10. Principles, Part I, Principle LXXI. HR I, 249; AT
    VIII-1, 35.
11. Kennington, "The 'Teaching of Nature' in Descartes'
    Soul Doctrine," p. 102; H. Caton, "Analytic History
    of Philosophy: The Case of Descartes," The Philosophical
    Forum, Vol. XII, No. 4 (Summer 1981), p. 279.
12. P. Schrecker, trans., Opuscles Philosophiques Choisis
    (Paris), p. 17.
13. Kennington, "The 'Teaching of Nature' in Descartes'
    Soul Doctrine," p. 101.
14. HR I, 145; AT VII, 19.
15. HR I, pp. 145-46; AT VII, 19.
16. Pearl, Descartes, 67, 70-71, 73.
17. HR I, 153; AT VII, 28.
18. HR I, 319; AT X, 518.
19. HR I, 319; AT X, 518.
20. Kenny, Descartes, p. 29.
21. Frankfurt, Demons, Dreamers, and Madmen, p. 40; See
    also Wilson, Descartes, p. 12.
22. HR I, 189; AT VII, 77.
23. HR I, 189; AT VII, 77.
24. HR I, 151; AT VII, 26.
25. Part Second, Article LXXIII. HR I, 364; AT XI, 83.
26. Passions, Part Second, Article CLXX. HR I, 409;
    AT XI, 459.
27. HR I, 146; AT VII, 19.
28. HR I, 146; AT VII, 19.
29. HR I, 152; AT VII, 28.
30. HR I, 146; AT VII, 20.
31. HR I, 146; AT VII, 20.
32. Pearl, Descartes, p. 69.
33. See J. Cottingham, "Mathematics in the First Meditation:
    A Reply to Professor O'Briant," Studia Leibnitiana,
    Vol. X (1978), p. 114.
34. HR I, 37; AT X, 413.
35. HR I, 147; AT VII, 20.
36. Frankfurt, "Descartes On The Consistency of Reason,"
    in Descartes: Critical and Interpretive Essays,
    ed. Michael Hooker (Baltimore: Johns Hopkins University
    Press, 1978), pp. 33-34.
37. HR I, 106; AT VI, 40.
38. Wilson, Descartes, pp. 28-31.
39. Kenny, Descartes, pp. 33-34.
40. HR I, 105-106; AT VI, 39.
41. HR I, 147; AT VII, 20.

42. HR I, 106; AT VI, 39.
43. HR I, 147; AT VII, 21.
44. HR I, 147; AT VII, 21.
45. According to Kennington, "Descartes' point is traditional:
    man is more likely to be imperfect and err if his
    cause is 'fate' or blind nature than if nature is
    ruled by intelligence." According to Caton, "Descartes'
    statement on nature as his author is a virtual paraphrase
    of Cicero's De divinatione I, 55, where the Stoic
    concept of natural necessity and determinism is advanced
    as the condition most favorable to the possibility
    of certainty." In H. Caton, "Kennington On Descartes'
    Evil Genius," Journal of the History of Ideas, XXXIV
    (October-December 1973), pp. 639-44. This article
    contains a response by Kennington and a rebuttal
    by Caton.
46. HR I, 147; AT VII,21.
47. Beck rightly distinguishes the three hypotheses of
    God, atheistic materialism, and the evil genius;
    however, he equates the epistemological function
    of the evil genius with that of God. He describes
    the evil genius as "Possibly the most daring metaphysical
    supposition a human mind can invent . . . a supernatural
    power, omnipotent . . . an epistemological Satan
    [which] . . . like the hypothesis of 'The Deceiving
    God' . . . strikes at the metaphysical bases of
    all our certainty. . . . even the manifest evidence
    of all the mathematical truths." The Metaphysics
    of Descartes, pp. 71, 72, 73. See above, note 2.
48. Kennington, "The 'Teaching of Nature' in Descartes'
    Soul Doctrine," p. 104.
49. HR I, 148; AT VII, 22. My translation of the Latin.
    Although there is no explicit correlation of power
    and deceit in the Latin ("eundemque summe potentem
    et callidum"), the French version, approved by Descartes,
    contains such a correlation. The evil genius is
    "non moins ruse et trompeur que puissant." AT IX,
    17.
50. HR I, 158-59; AT VII, 36.
51. Kennington, "The Finitude of Descartes' Evil Genius,"
    pp. 441-42.
52. The exemption of mathematics and logic from the evil
    genius phase of doubt is also pointed to by Kenny
    (Descartes, p. 36), yet he maintains that the evil
    genius is as powerful as God and that "the two hypotheses
    do not differ in any respect of epistemological importance.
    The hypothesis of the evil genius is substituted
    for that of the deceitful God simply because it is
    less offensive and less patently incoherent." Descartes,
    p. 35. On the present interpretation, the evil genius
    is used to question material existence while permitting
    reason and science to set the stage for the subsequent
    threat to them by the reintroduction of God in Meditation
    III.
53. Compare the view of Frankfurt concerning simple natures:
    Descartes "does not present his theory in the First
    Meditation as a doctrine to which he is committed
    or upon the truth of which the argument of the Meditations
    essentially depends. . . . It is a doctrine advanced

in behalf of common sense. Descartes does not assume
that he knows what stuff dreams are made of. He
is not developing his own position . . . he is explaining
the resources of common sense." Dreamers, Demons,
and Madmen, p. 57. According to Curley, who "want[s]
to consider how Descartes has continued to smuggle
the foundations of his physics into this treatise
on first philosophy. . . . In the First Meditation
nothing very much is done with the list of simple
and universal properties of things." Descartes Against
the Skeptics, pp. 207, 210.

54. HR I, 148; AT VII, 22.
55. Synopsis of Meditation VI. HR I, 142-43; AT VII, 15-16.
56. David Blumenfeld and Jean Beer Blumenfeld, "Can I Know That I Am Not Dreaming?" in Hooker, ed., p. 253.
57. George Nakhnikian, "Descartes' Dream Argument," in Hooker, ed., p. 279.
58. L. J. Beck, The Metaphysics of Descartes, pp. 66-67.
59. James D. Stuart, "The Role of Dreaming in Descartes' Meditations," The Southern Journal of Philosophy, Vol. XXI, No. 1, Spring 1983, p. 97.
60. Stuart, "The Role of Dreaming in Descartes' Meditations," p. 98.
61. HR I, p. 145.
62. Stuart, "The Role of Dreaming in Descartes' Meditations," pp. 103-104.
63. Bernard Williams, Descartes, p. 58.
64. Stuart, "The Role of Dreaming in Descartes' Meditations," p. 104.

CHAPTER 3: THE DUAL CRITIQUE OF ARISTOTLE

1. Letters, 94; AT III, 297-98.
2. Letters, 126-7; AT III, 491-92.
3. Letter of 14 November 1640. Letters, 84; AT III, 248.
4. Gerhardt Kruger, "Die Herkunft des philosophischen Selbstbewusstseins," Logos 22 (1933), p. 246. In Caton, The Origin, p. 125.
5. For a discussion of this issue, see the Kennington-Caton exchange referred to above (Chapter 2, note 45). This exchange contains an excellent gloss on the linguistic difficulty in pinning down the identity of Descartes' deceiver.
6. HR I, 150; AT VII, 25.
7. HR I, 150; AT VII, 25.
8. HR I, 150; AT VII, 25.
9. HR I, 151; AT VII, 26.
10. HR I, 153; AT VII, 28-29.
11. HR I, 158; AT VII, 36.
12. HR I, 150; AT VII, 25.
13. See, e.g., Kenny, Descartes, pp. 51-55; Frankfurt, Demons, Dreamers, and Madmen, pp. 91-112; Williams, Descartes, 72-101; Pearl, Descartes, pp. 77-87; Wilson, Descartes, pp. 51-71; Curley, Descartes Against the Skeptics, pp. 70-95. For a defense of intuition

see, e.g., Beck, The Metaphysics of Descartes, pp. 77-92; Caton, The Origin, pp. 140-43; Schouls, The Imposition of Method, pp. 104-27.

14. The Search After Truth. HRI, 319; AT X, 518.
15. HR II, 38; AT VII, 140.
16. Part One, Principle VII. HR I, 221; AT VIII-1, 7.
17. Part One, Principle X. HR I, 222; AT VIII-1, 8.
18. Part One, Principle XLIX. HR I, 239; AT VIII-1, 31.
19. This is also the view of Schouls, The Imposition of Method, pp. 104-27.
20. HR I, 7; AT X, 368.
21. Curley, Descartes Against the Skeptics, p. 72.
22. HR I, 150; AT VII, 25.
23. HR I, 151; AT VII, 26.
24. Curley (Descartes Against the Skeptics, p. 211) and Pearl see the aporia from the perspective of the natural attitude. Concerning the atomist account of the soul, Pearl writes, "This characterization of the soul was probably introduced by Descartes to indicate the ordinary man's allegiance to the senses; for, while the soul is not visible, he thinks that it must somehow resemble the things that are. Without explicitly criticizing the ordinary man's conception of the soul, Descartes implies that the ordinary man's state of mind is confused, for while he is convinced that bodies are incapable of initiating motion, he thinks that the soul is being composed of invisible rare and subtle bodies which, among other things, are supposed to explain self-movement." Descartes, p. 90. Compare the more penetrating appraisal of the relation between astonishment and dualism by Dorter: "From the dualist position, that body and thought are irreducibly distinct, one could never say that body has the ability to think, or the attribute of thought, but only that bodies are conjoined with minds that have this ability. But Descartes can scarcely be saying here that he once thought that no bodies were conjoined with minds and was astonished to discover otherwise; that would be incredible. In the light of his assertion that some bodies think, the argument for dualism cannot, then, be maintained. . . . Descartes, who supposedly throughout his life a devout Catholic, has been holding a materialistic view of the soul." "Science and Religion in Descartes' Meditations," pp. 332-33, 335.
25. As Caton has observed, "Descartes knows what to attribute to mind because of his prior knowledge of what to attribute to the powers of the human body." The Origin, p. 148.
26. HR I, 151, 153; AT VII, 27, 28.
27. Caton, The Origin, p. 90; AT XI, 201-202.
28. Caton rightly charges that "Descartes definitely commits the paralogism of inferring res cogitans from the dubiety of body." The Origin, p. 146.
29. In the Author's Letter to the French translation of the Principles Descartes explains that "Foreseeing the difficulty which would be felt by many in under-

standing the foundations of metaphysics, I tried
to explain the principal points in a book of Meditations.
. . . Then, finally, when it appeared to me that
these preceding treatises [including the Discourse,
etc.] had sufficiently prepared the mind of readers
to accept the Principles of Philosophy, I likewise
published them . . . the first part of which contains
the principles of knowledge, which is what may be
called the First Philosophy of Metaphysics. That
is why it is better to read beforehand the Meditations
which I have written on the same subject, in order
that it may be properly understood." HR I, 212;
AT IX-2, 16-17.

30. HR I, 222, AT VIII-1, 7.
31. Letter of June 1646. Letters, 197; AT IV, 444.
32. HR I, 152; AT VII, 27.
33. Letter of 24 December 1640. Letters, 87; AT III,
      264.
34. HR I, 152; AT VII, 27.
35. Part One, Principle LII. HR I, 240; AT VIII-1, 25.
36. Part One, Principle LIII. HR I, 240; AT VIII-1,
      25.
37. According to Kenny, "The terminology of essence is
      scholastic, and so, despite disclaimers elsewhere,
      is the whole method of procedure. . . . 'Thing' (res)
      is used by Descartes as a synonym for 'substance'
      (substantia). . . . Descartes took over the scholastic
      notion of substance. . . . Particular thoughts are
      variable properties of the substance that is mind.
      A mind must always be thinking, but it need not always
      be judging or willing or imagining. Thought is 'the
      principal property of (mental) substance which constitutes
      its nature and essence and on which all the others
      depend' (AT VIII-1, 25; HRI, 240)." Descartes, pp.
      65, 70. Grayeff claims that Descartes argues for
      mind as immaterial, that "as a pure mind he is a
      substance." Descartes, pp. 13, 30. Pearl states
      that, "The 'I' in 'I exist' refers . . . to a real
      subject, that is, substance." Descartes, p. 83.
      According to Wilson, "Descartes does clearly take
      the cogito reasoning to provide him . . . I am an
      existing thing (or res), and not merely with what
      Kant would call the bare 'I think' . . . . not merely
      that he thinks, but that thought pertains to his
      nature or essence". Descartes, pp. 73, 74. Most
      recently, Schouls concurs with the view that sum
      res cogitans "involves the concept 'thing', 'substance'
      res. For just as he holds that there cannot be
      'thinking-going-on' without there being ideas or
      thoughts, so he holds that there cannot be 'thinking-
      going-on' without there being 'a thing which thinks'.
      The latter relation as well is held to be one grasped
      through concepts which stand in an immediate and
      necessary relation; it is a relation of which one
      is aware through intuition." The Imposition of Method,
      pp. 122-23. I find it odd that Schouls supports
      this view by referring to the letter to Gibieuf (Letters,
      123-24; AT III, 474-76), in which Descartes says
      that substance is an abstraction. Schouls considers
      cogitatio rather than substantia as the abstraction,

stating that "In the <u>Meditations</u> one must come to
the recognition that to be aware of 'thinking-going-on'
is to be aware of an 'abstraction', and the task
in the <u>Meditations</u> is to come to notice the 'richer
idea' of which 'thinking-going-on' is an abstraction."
<u>The Imposition of Method</u>, 124.

38. HR I, 151-52; AT VII, 27.
39. HR I, 153; AT VII, 28.
40. Beck is correct in saying concerning the first passage
that "<u>Cogito ergo sum</u> would then appear to mean no
more than the existence in a problematical fashion
of a mind whose whole nature . . . is the instantaneous
awareness of a present conscious activity. We cannot
justifiably go even as far as Hume's 'congeries of
perceptions'." <u>The Metaphysics of Descartes</u>, p.
110. Concerning the second passage, Caton is correct
in saying, "After admitting that he does not know
that he is not a 'wind' or other subtle corporeal
substance, Descartes goes on to commit once more
the paralogism of inferring from doubt of the existence
of body that [res cogitans] is an incorporeal thinking
thing. The positive result is the specification
of thinking in relation to modes." <u>The Origin</u>, p.
151.
41. <u>Principles</u>, Part One, Principle LI. HR I, 239; AT
VIII-1, 24.
42. HR I, 154; AT VII, 30.
43. This lack of specificity has not been uniformly appreciated.
According to Grayeff, "Descartes carefully points
out that what he grasps by his act of the mind is
a single, individual object, <u>this</u> piece of wax and
not wax in general, i.e., not the class of pieces
of wax." <u>Descartes</u>, p. 15. Williams writes, similarly,
that "In the <u>Second Meditation</u> Descartes is emphatic
that he is not discussing matter in general, but
just the wax, . . . it is a thought-experiment.
Nor . . . is the argument even intended to demonstrate
what physical objects must be really like, if there
are any. It does in fact lay all the essential
foundations for that conclusion, but the conclusion
itself is drawn only in the <u>Fifth Meditation</u>." <u>Descartes</u>,
pp. 219, 227. Wilson (<u>Descartes</u>, pp. 81, 82, 92)
also separates the epistemology of <u>Meditation</u> II
from the ontology of <u>Meditation</u> V, though I find
it difficult to see the way in which <u>Meditation</u> V
is an advance over either <u>Meditations</u> I and II concerning
the nature of body. The "general particular" character
of the wax is pointed out by Pearl, who remarks that
"Descartes' claim that he is not dealing with 'bodies
in general' but one body in particular is . . . misleading.
For he is dealing with 'bodies in general', and the
fact that he is employing a particular piece of wax
. . . makes his study no less an inquiry into the
abstract nature of bodies." <u>Descartes</u>, pp. 100-101.
44. HR I, 154; AT VII, 30.
45. Such a theory of abstraction is implicit in <u>Principles</u>,
Part One, Principle LIII: "All else that may be
attributed to body presupposes extension. . . .
we cannot conceive figure but as an extended thing

. . . . on the other hand, we can conceive extension
without figure." HR I, 240; AT VIII-1, 25. Descartes
speaks of such "abstractions" as a "distinction of
reason" in Principles LVIII and LX. HR I, 242-43;
AT VIII-1, 27-28.
46. HR I, 154; AT VII, 30.
47. HR I, 154; AT VII, 31.
48. HR I, 155; AT VII, 31.
49. Dorter, "Science and Religion in Descartes' Meditations,"
    p. 323.
50. HR I, 141; AT VII, 14.
51. HR I, 155-56; AT VII, 32.
52. HR I, 156; AT VII, 33.
53. HR I, 157; AT VII, 33.
54. HR I, 27; AT X, 398-99.
55. Beck, The Method of Descartes (London: Oxford University
    Press, 1952), pp. 220-21.
56. HR II, 33; AT VII, 133.
57. HR I, 442; AT VIII-2, 357-58.
58. Grayeff writes, for example, that "mathematical ideas
    . . . are unique . . . constituted by the intellect
    prior to any sensuous experience of objects resembling
    them (such as a triangular, real object which resembles
    a pure geometrical triangle)." Descartes, p. 47.
    See also Beck, The Metaphysics of Descartes, p. 156.
59. Letter to Clerselier, June 1646. Letters, 197; AT
    IV, 444.
60. Norman Kemp-Smith, New Studies in the Philosophy
    of Descartes (London: Russell & Russell, 1966), p.
    147.
61. Caton, The Origin, p. 199.

CHAPTER 4: THEODICY

1. Beck, The Metaphysics of Descartes, pp. 136-37.
2. ibid., p. 161.
3. Curley, Descartes Against the Skeptics, pp. 37, 100,
   118, 170.
4. ibid., p. 98.
5. ibid., p. 198. Curley devotes scarcely half a page
   to this problem in Meditation IV. Concerning the
   relation between physics and divine inscrutability
   he writes, "It does not contribute a great deal to
   insinuating Descartes' physical theory, but it does
   lay the groundwork for one important negative result.
   . . . Here one of God's properties is made to yield,
   not a physical law, but the exclusion of a whole
   kind of explanation. . . . With the soundness of
   this exercise in theodicy I am not concerned. What
   does interest me is the amount of Cartesian science
   that is packed into it." Descartes Against the Skeptics,
   pp. 224, 233.
6. Williams, Descartes, p. 135.
7. ibid., p. 137.
8. ibid., p. 166.
9. ibid., pp. 209-10.
10. Grayeff, Descartes, pp. 18, 23.
11. Caton, "The Problem of Descartes' Sincerity," The
    Philosophical Forum 2 (1971), p. 366.

12. Caton, The Origin, p. 129.
13. Frankfurt, "Descartes on the Creation of the External
    Truths," The Philosophical Review, LXXXVI, 1 (January
    1977), pp. 36-57.
14. Frankfurt, "Descartes on the Consistency of Reason,"
    ed. Hooker, pp. 26-39.
15. HR II, 41; AT IX, 113-14.
16. Frankfurt, "Descartes on the Consistency of Reason,"
    ed. Hooker, p. 37.
17. HR I, 147; AT VII, 21.
18. HR I, 159; AT VII, 36.
19. Frankfurt, Demons, Dreamers, and Madmen, p. 49.
20. Frankfurt, "Descartes on the Consistency of Reason,"
    ed. Hooker, p. 34.
21. Letter of January 1641. Letters, p. 94; AT III,
    297-98.
22. See above, Chapter 2, the section on Intellect and
    Mathematics.
23. HR I, 158-59; AT VII, 36.
24. HR I, 185; AT VII, 71.
25. Dorter, "Science and Religion in Descartes' Meditations,"
    pp. 324-26.
26. Frankfurt, Demons, Dreamers, and Madmen, p. 175.
27. Ibid.
28. HR I, 172; AT VII, 53.
29. HR I, 172; AT VII, 54.
30. Williams, Descartes, pp. 163, 169.
31. HR I, 172; AT VII, 54.
32. HR I, 173; AT VII, 54-55.
33. HR I, 173; AT VII, 54-55.
34. HR I, 174; AT VII, 55.
35. HR I, 178; AT VII, 61.
36. HR I, 175; AT VII, 57.
37. HR I, 175; AT VII, 57.
38. HR I, 176; AT VII, 60.
39. HR I, 175; AT VII, 57.
40. HR I, 176; AT VII, 59.
41. HR I, 175-76; AT VII, 58.
42. HR I, 177; AT VII, 60.
43. HR I, 221; AT VIII-1, 6.
44. HR I, 233-34; AT VIII-1, 18-19.
45. Letters, p. 149. AT IV, 115-16.
46. Kenny, "Descartes on the Will," in Cartesian Studies,
    ed. R. J. Butler, (London: Oxford University Press,
    1972), p. 22.
47. Beck, The Metaphysics of Descartes, p. 204.
48. HR I, 175; AT VII, 58.
49. HR I, 175-76; AT VII, 58.
50. Letters, pp. 159-60. AT IV, 173.
51. Kenny, "Descartes on the Will," ed. Butler, pp. 29,
    31.
52. Letters, p. 160. AT IV, 174.
53. Letters, p. 161. AT IV, 175.
54. Such a consequence is drawn by Caton: "If error
    can be avoided by assenting only to clear and distinct
    ideas, and if, as Descartes says, the ideas of revealed
    religion are obscure because they exceed the limits
    of understanding, then it is sinful to be religious."
    "Will and Reason in Descartes' Theory of Error,"

The Journal of Philosophy, Volume LXXII, No. 4 (February
27, 1975), pp. 98-99.

55. Caton, "Will and Reason in Descartes' Theory of Error,"
     p. 90.
56. Kenny, "Descartes on the Will", ed. Butler, p. 9.
57. Ibid., pp. 4, 5.
58. Ibid.
59. Letters, pp. 102-103. AT III, 372.
60. HR I, 153; AT VII, 28.
61. Regulae XII. HR I, 42; AT X, 420.
62. HR I, 185; AT VII, 71-72.
63. HR I, 196; AT VII, 85-86.
64. Letter of May 1637. Letters, p. 32; AT I, 365.
65. Passions, Part First, XLVII. HR I, 353; AT XI, 364.
66. Letters, p. 15; AT I, 151.
67. Frankfurt, "Descartes on the Creation of the Eternal
     Truths," p. 41, note 7.
68. Letter of January 1641. Letters, p. 93; AT III,
     295.
69. HR I, 173; AT VII, 55.
70. Beck, The Metaphysics of Descartes, p. 175-76.
71. Grayeff, Descartes, p. 56.
72. Reply to Objections I. HR II, 18; AT VII, 113-14.
73. Principles, Part I, XXVIII. HR I, 231; AT VIII-1,
     16.
74. Frankfurt, Demons, Dreamers, and Madmen, pp. 184-85.
75. Letter of April 1634. Letters, p. 26; AT I, 284.
76. Frankfurt, "Descartes on the Creation of the Eternal
     Truths," pp. 50, 54, 55, 57.
77. Letter of 15 April 1630. Letters, p. 11; AT I, 145.
78. Meditation IV. HR I, 173; AT VII, 55.
79. Letter to Malebranche [?], June 1679. In A. Robinet,
     Malebranche and Leibniz (Paris, 1955), pp. 114-20.
80. Letter of 20 February 1639. Letters, pp. 63-64;
     AT II, 523.
81. Letter of August 1641. Letters, pp. 117-18; AT III,
     431-32.
82. Letter of 15 April 1630. Letters, p. 11; AT I, 145.
83. Ibid.; Letters, p. 12; AT I, 146.
84. Letter of 27 May 1630. Letters, p. 15; AT I, 152.
85. HR I, 185; AT VII, 71.
86. Letter of 2 May 1644. Letters, p. 151; AT IV, 118-19.
87. Ibid.
88. HR II, 248; AT VII, 431-32.
89. Frankfurt, "Descartes on the Creation of the Eternal
     Truths," p. 50.
90. Discourse on Metaphysics, para. 11.
91. Theodicy, para. 186.
92. According to Caton, "If God can create contradictory
     states of affairs, and if his actual creation is
     not governed by goodness or truth, which themselves
     are determined by the fiat of the creating will,
     then any attempt to prove that God guarantees a correspondence
     between our ideas and the world must shatter upon
     the rock of God's 'incomprehensibility'." The Origin,
     p. 127. Such failure is not to be taken as driving
     a wedge between epistemology (science) and metaphysics,
     between certainty and truth, because Cartesian science
     is a science of what is, not what merely appears.

93. HR I, 439; AT VIII-2, 353-54.

94. HR I, 183; AT VII, 68.

95. Cf. the compatibilist position of Wilson, who states,
     "I have been assuming that the unlimited creative
     power of God, the dependence of all being on his
     will, was a genuine primitive intuition or basic
     premiss of Descartes'--just as he seems to present
     it. But it is also natural to suppose that this
     doctrine must have seemed in some way convenient
     to Descartes--more congenial to other aspects of
     his system than the entrenched alternative position
     that necessity and possibility depend only on God's
     understanding. It is certain, I think, that Descartes
     intends to mark off the comprehensibility of the
     world to us, from the incomprehensibility of God.
     That the eternal truths are God's creatures, his
     effects, means that we do not have to understand
     His nature in order to understand them". Descartes,
     p. 136. Wilson substantially follows Frankfurt in
     combining the intelligibility (for us) of truth with
     the unintellibility of its source. But given such
     an origin, what do we really understand by such truth?
     It is not the truth of such truths that we understand,
     but rather their indifferent selection by God. So
     long as the possibility remains that God's creation
     is not constrained by the law of contradiction and
     that God's will is ever mysterious, it is conceivable,
     on this account, that God may have decreed a mathematics
     (and thus physics) impenetrable to human reason.
     Then not even certainty would remain.

96. Schouls, who accepts Descartes' theodicy, takes intuition
     of simple natures to be free from theological doubt
     from the start. For him the issue of the validation
     of reason is the threat to composition and deduction
     posed by the evil genius, about which he states:
     "But the hypothesis which states the existence of
     the evil genius is self-contradictory. There is,
     therefore, no reason for doubting the efficacy of
     composition, or of doubting the validity of deduction.
     The imposition of the general method is completely
     justified. To hold otherwise would, for Descartes,
     be inexcusable." The Imposition of Method, p. 140.
     I agree with Schouls' conclusion, but because the
     method is self-certifying from start to finish.

97. Charles Larmore, "Descartes' Psychologistic Theory
     of Assent," History of Philosophy Quarterly, Vol.
     1, No. 1 (January 1984), pp. 61-74.

98. HR II, 41; AT IX, 113-14.

99. Frankfurt, "Descartes On the Consistency of Reason,"
     ed. Hooker, p. 37.

100. Larmore, "Descartes' Psychologistic Theory of Assent",
     p. 63.

101. Ibid., pp. 70-71.

102. Ibid., p. 71.

103. Caton, The Origin, p. 129.

104. Hiram Caton, "Tory History of Ideas," The Independent
     Journal of Philosophy, VI, 1985.

105. Caton, The Origin, pp. 198-99.

106. Bernard Williams, <u>Descartes</u>, pp. 228-77, gives a
      helpful analysis of the problem of Cartesian physics
      in terms of the tension between the abstract and
      the concrete. In one sense Cartesian science is
      too abstract:
           Descartes' conception of physical science, and
           of the material world as understood by it, is
           inadequate, particularly because of his too drastic
           assimilation of the concepts of physics to those
           of mathematics. (p. 239)
      Yet in another sense it is not sufficiently abstract:
           Having thought away <u>in general</u> everything but
           what he took to be the minimal basis of a mathematical
           physical system, he was left with no way in which
           he could think away the particular conditions
           of a particular physical transaction and be left
           with anything coherent at all. (p. 255)
      As Williams explains, Cartesian science, a physics
      of body qua mathematical, posits the "conceptual
      equivalence of physics and geometry," with the consequence
      that physics becomes nothing but applied mathematics.
      And such an applied mathematics is incapable of grasping
      the precise physical mechanisms producing the phenomena
      of bodies in motion. While not an operationalist,
      Descartes does therefore acknowledge the need for
      experimentation to close the abstract-concrete gap.
      The actual mechanisms and laws of physics cannot
      be deduced by <u>a priori</u> mathematical deduction. Nonetheless,
      claimed Descartes, the most basic principles can
      be intuited <u>a priori</u>.
107. Caton, <u>The Origin</u>, p. 198.
108. Ibid., p. 201.
109. Ibid.
110. Ibid., p. 202.
111. The following is based in part on Stanley Rosen,
      <u>The Limits of Analysis</u> (New York: Basic Books, 1980),
      pp. 217-46.
112. Ibid., p. 223.
113. See Jacob Klein, "On the nature of Nature," <u>Independent
      Journal of Philosophy</u>, Vol. 3 (1979), pp. 101-109.
114. Rosen, <u>The Limits of Analysis</u>, p. 239.
115. Kennington, "Strauss's Natural Right and History,"
      <u>Review of Metaphysics</u> 35 (September 1981), p. 85.

CHAPTER 5: MIND AND BODY

 1. HR I, 109; AT VI, 45.
 2. HR I, 118; AT VI, 59.
 3. HR I, 116; AT VI, 56-57.
 4. HR I, 116; AT VI, 57.
 5. Letter of 23 November 1646. <u>Letters</u>, p. 206; AT
     IV, 574.
 6. Letter of 23 November 1646. <u>Letters</u>, p. 208; AT
     IV, 576.
 7. Letter of 23 November 1646. <u>Letters</u>, pp. 207-208;
     AT IV, 576.
 8. HR I, 116; AT VI, 57.
 9. HR I, 117; AT VI, 58.
10. Letter of 2 May 1644. <u>Letters</u>, p. 146; AT IV, 110.

11. HR I, 117-18; AT VI, 59-60.
12. Kenny, Descartes, pp. 222-23.
13. HR I, 185; AT VII, 71-72.
14. HR I, 186; AT VII, 72-73.
15. Wilson, Descartes, pp. 178-79.
16. HR I, 38-39; AT X, 415.
17. Wilson, Descartes, p. 181.
18. Ibid., pp. 182-83. Betty Powell argued similarly
     that the dualism arises from science in the sense
     that Decartes introduces an incorporeal soul in order
     to escape from a futile epistemological regress in
     the thoroughgoing automatism he may have in fact
     tried to maintain. "Descartes' Machines," Aristotelian
     Society 71 (1970-71), pp. 209-22.
19. HR I, 186; AT VII, 73.
20. Wilson, Descartes, p. 185.
21. HR I, 186; AT VII, 73.
22. HR I, 190; AT VII, 78.
23. Caton, The Origin, p. 162.
24. HR I, 196; AT VII, 86.
25. HR I, 190; AT VII, 78.
26. Williams, Descartes, p. 113.
27. Ibid., pp. 112-13.
28. Ibid., p. 114.
29. Ibid., p. 124.
30. Ibid., p. 193.
31. Ibid., p. 197.
32. Ibid., p. 196.
33. Ibid., p. 198.
34. HR I, 190; AT VII, 78.
35. Letter of 24 December 1640. Letters, p. 87; AT III,
     264.
36. Letter of 21 May 1643. Letters, p. 137; AT III,
     666-67.
37. HR I, 141; AT VII, 13.
38. AT XI, 326.
39. Caton, The Origin, p. 180, note.
40. Letters, pp. 140-1; AT III, 691-92.
41. Letters, p. 142; AT III, 693.
42. Wilson, Descartes, pp. 206, 207.
43. Letters, p. 141; AT IV, 692.
44. HR I, 185; AT VII, 72.
45. HR I, 186; AT VII, 72.
46. Wilson, Descartes, p. 201.
47. HR I, 191; AT VII, 79.
48. HR I, 191; AT VII, 79.
49. Kennington, "'The Teaching of Nature' in Descartes'
     Soul Doctrine," p. 103.
50. Ibid., pp. 113-17.
51. HR I, 193; AT 82-83.
52. Wilson, Descartes, p. 209.
53. HR I, 345; AT XI, 351.
54. Wilson, Descartes, p. 206.
55. Ibid. Compare the similar objection by Williams:
     "When he said that the soul is 'joined to all parts
     of the body', but that 'it exercises its functions
     more particularly' in the gland (Passions of the
     Soul i 30-31), his statement is in fact very confused.
     There is no one sense in which the soul is joined

to every part of the body, but particularly connected
with the gland. In the phenomenological sense in
which it is joined to the whole body, it is not particularly joined to the gland." Descartes, p. 289.
Mattern also finds Descartes' position inconsistent
in claiming in the Meditations that mind and body
are both distinct and united. Concerning the statements
to Elizabeth, she finds the notion of mind coextensive
with body "surprising, given the view of mind-body
relation that he suggests elsewhere. . . . The
Meditations . . . certainly conveys the impression
that mind is not really spread throughout the body
but is located at a single point in the brain."
Concerning the consistency of Descartes' views in
the Meditations, Correspondence, and Principles she
writes: "His views appear to vacillate in a peculiar
way, since the letters to Elizabeth followed the
Meditations but preceded the Principles. Though
the motives for such a vacillation are not obvious,
we can construct an explanation of it which has some
plausibility. Descartes may have felt impelled to
develop an interpretation of mind-body union which
allows for the genuine 'intermingling' of mind and
body, in order to do justice to the substantial union
of these two things." Ruth Mattern, "Descartes'
Correspondence with Elizabeth: Conceiving Both the
Union and Distinction of Mind and Body," In Descartes:
Critical and Interpretive Essays. ed. Hooker
(Baltimore: Johns Hopkins University Press, 1978),
pp. 217, 218.

56. HR I, 192; AT VII, 81.
57. Williams, Descartes, pp. 278, 280, 289.
58. Passions, Part First, Article XL. HR I, 349-50;
    AT XI, 359.
59. HR I, 188; AT VII, 76.
60. HR I, 196; AT VII, 86.
61. HR I, 196; AT VII, 86.
62. Caton, The Origin, p. 90; AT XI, 202.
63. Mattern, "Descartes' Correspondence with Elizabeth,"
    ed. Hooker, pp. 217-18.
64. HR I, 38; AT X, 415.
65. HR I, 38-39; AT X, 415-16.
66. HR I, 195-96; AT XII, 85.
67. Beck, The Metaphysics of Descartes, pp. 260-61.
68. HR I, 199; AT VII, 90.
69. Williams, Descartes, pp. 251-52.

CONCLUSION

1. Letters, p. 150; AT IV, 117.
2. AT III, 752.

BIBLIOGRAPHY

Adam, Charles and Tannery, Paul, trans. Oeuvres de
    Descartes. Paris: Vrin, 1965-75.
Beck, L. J. The Method of Descartes. London: Oxford
    University Press, 1952.
Beck, L. J. The Metaphysics of Descartes. London: Oxford
    University Press, 1965.
Blumenfeld, David and Blumenfeld, Jean Beer. "Can I Know
    That I Am Not Dreaming?" In Descartes: Critical
    and Interpretive Essays. Edited by Michael Hooker.
    Baltimore: Johns Hopkins University Press, 1978.
Caton, Hiram. "The Problem of Descartes' Sincerity." The
    Philosophical Forum 2 (1971).
Caton, Hiram. The Origin of Subjectivity. New Haven:
    Yale University Press, 1973.
Caton, Hiram. "Kennington On Descartes' Evil Genius."
    Journal of the History of Ideas XXXIV, (October-December
    1973).
Caton, Hiram. "Will and Reason in Descartes' Theory of
    Error." The Journal of Philosophy LXII, 4 (February
    1975).
Caton, Hiram. "Analytic History of Philosophy: The Case
    of Descartes." The Philosophical Forum XII, 4 (Summer
    1981).
Caton, Hiram. "Tory History of Ideas." Independent Journal
    of Philosophy VI (1985).
Cottingham, John. "The Role of the Malignant Demon." Studia
    Leibnitiana VIII (1976).
Cottingham, John. "Mathematics in the First Meditation:
    A Reply to Professor O'Briant." Studia Leibnitiana
    X (1978).
Cropsey, Joseph. "On Descartes' Discourse on Method."
    Interpretation 1/2 (Winter 1970).
Curley, E. M. Descartes Against the Skeptics. Cambridge:
    Harvard University Press, 1978.
Dorter, Kenneth. "Science and Religion in Descartes' Medita-
    tions." The Thomist XXXVII (1973).
Frankfurt, Harry G. Demons, Dreamers, and Madmen. Indianapolis:
    Bobbs Merrill, 1970.
Frankfurt, Harry G. "Descartes on the Creation of the
    Eternal Truths." The Philosophical Review LXXXVI
    (January 1877).

Frankfurt, Harry G. "Descartes on the Consistency of
    Reason." In Descartes: Critical and Interpretive
    Essays. Edited by Michael Hooker. Baltimore: Johno
    Hopkins University Press, 1978.
Grayeff, Felix. Descartes. London: Philip Goodall, 1977.
Haldane, E. S. and Ross, G. R. T., trans. The Philosophical
    Works of Descartes. New York: Cambridge University
    Press, 1969.
Kennington, Richard. "Descartes." A History of Political
    Philosophy. Edited by Cropsey, J. and Strauss, L.
    New York: Rand McNally, 1963.
Kennington, Richard. "The Finitude of Descartes' Evil
    Genius." Journal of the History of Ideas 32 (1971).
Kennington, Richard. "The 'Teaching of Nature' in Descartes'
    Soul Doctrine." The Review of Metaphysics 26 (September
    1972).
Kennington, Richard. "Descartes and Mastery of Nature."
    In Organism, Medicine, and Metaphysics. Edited by
    Stuart Spicker. Dordrecht: Reidel, 1978.
Kennington, Richard. "Strauss's Natural Right and History."
    Review of Metaphysics 35 (September 1981).
Kenny, Anthony. Descartes: A Study of His Philosophy.
    New York: Random House, 1968.
Kenny, Anthony, ed. and trans. Descartes' Philosophical
    Letters. London: Oxford University Press, 1970.
Kenny, Anthony. "Descartes on the Will." In Cartesian
    Studies. Edited by R. J. Butler. London: Oxford
    University Press, 1972.
Klein, Jacob. Greek Mathematical Thought and the Origin
    of Algebra. Cambridge: M.I.T. Press, 1968.
Klein, Jacob. "On the nature of Nature." Independent
    Journal of Philosophy 3 (1979).
Lachterman, David R. "Descartes and the Philosophy of
    History." Independent Journal of Philosophy IV (1983).
Larmore, Charles. "Descartes' Psychologistic Theory of
    Assent." History of Philosophy Quarterly, Vol. 1,
    No. 1 (January 1984).
Mattern, Ruth. "Descartes' Correspondence with Elizabeth:
    Concerning Both the Union and Distinction of Mind
    and Body." In Descartes: Critical and Interpretive
    Essays. Edited by Michael Hooker. Baltimore: Johns
    Hopkins University Press, 1978.
Nakhnikian, George. "Descartes' Dream Argument." In Descartes:
    Critical and Interpretive Essays. Edited by Michael
    Hooker. Baltimore: Johns Hopkins University Press,
    1978.
Pearl, Leon. Descartes. Boston: G. K. Hall & Company,
    1977.
Powell, Betty. "Descartes' Machines." Aristotelian Society
    71 (1970-71).
Ree, Jonathan. Descartes. London: Allen Lane, 1974.
Rosen, Stanley. The Limits of Analysis. New York: Basic
    Books, 1980.
Schouls, Peter A. The Imposition of Method. New York:
    Oxford University Press, 1980.
Smith, Norman Kemp. New Studies in the Philosophy of Descartes.
    London: Russell & Russell, 1966.

Soffer, Walter. "The Methodological Achievement of Cartesian
     Doubt." The Southern Journal of Philosophy XVI, 1
     (1978).
Soffer, Walter. "Descartes, Rationality, and God." The
     Thomist 42 4 (1978).
Soffer, Walter. "Descartes' Rejection of the Aristotelian
     Soul." International Studies in Philosophy XVI, 1
     (1984).
Soffer, Walter. "Dreaming, Dogmatism, and Hyperbole".
     Idealistic Studies (forthcoming).
Stuart, James D. "The Role of Dreaming in Descartes' Medita-
     tions." The Southern Journal of Philosophy XXI, 1
     (Spring 1983).
Vrooman, Jack R. Rene Descartes: A Biography. New York:
     Putnam, 1970.
Williams, Bernard. Descartes: The Project of Pure Enquiry.
     New York: Penguin, 1978.
Wilson, Margaret Dauler. Descartes. London: Routledge
     & Kegan Paul, 1978.

INDEX

Anthropology, of error,
86-89.
Architectonic, the Cartesian,
1-24; and the genesis
of philosophical reason,
1-14; and the moral component, 14-17; and the hermeneutic problem of the
Meditations, 17-24.
Aristotle: and the critique
of the Aristotelian soul,
50, 57-61; the dual cri-
tique of, 49-76; and ego
sum, ego existo, 50-57;
and his metaphysics, 83;
and imagination, 69-72;
and intellect, 72-76;
and intuition versus inference, 54-57; and ontolog-
ical indifference, 65-67;
and res cogitans as the
first principle, 64-65;
and res extensa, 67-76;
and sensation, 69; and
sum res cogitans, 61-67.
Atheistic materialism, 40,
42.
Automatism: and res extensa,
75-76; and sum res cogitans,
60, 61-67.

Beck, L. J.: on Descartes'
theology, 77-78; on the
freedom of spontaneity,
91-92; on methodological
skepticism, 43-44; on

the relation between mind
and body, 150; on res extensa,
75; on theology and rationalism,
100-102.
Blumenfeld, David and Jean
Beer, 43.
Body: and imagination and
sensation, 140; and res
cogitans, 139-42; and res
extensa, 142; the distinction
between mind and, 127-39;
existence of, 139-42.
See also Mind, and body.

Cartesian science: and the
dream argument, 36, 37;
and hyperbolic doubt, 25,
26, 28; and res extensa,
67; and theodicy, 82; and
theology, 77, 80; Bernard
Williams on, 115 n.106.
Caterus, Johannes, 101-2.
Caton, Hiram: on atheistic
materialism, 40; on the
Cartesian circle, 76; on
Descartes' theology, 80;
on the divine creation
of the eternal truths,
110 n.92, 113; on ego sum,
ego existo, 52, 53; on
the freedom of spontaneity,
94; on metaphysics and
science, 113-19; on sum
res cogitans, 62.
Clerselier, Claude, 64.

About the Author

WALTER SOFFER is Associate Professor of Philosophy at the State University of New York at Geneseo. His earlier work includes co-editing *The Crisis of Liberal Democracy: A Straussian Perspective* and numerous articles in journals such as *The Southern Journal of Philosophy, The Thomist* and *International Studies in Philosophy.*